John Galliano

Pierre Cardin

Yves Saint Laurent

Ralph Lauren

Oscar de la Renta

Paco Rabanne

Bill Blass

Coco Chanel

Mary Quant

Vivienne Westwood

Charles Frederick Worth

• (1825–1895) - FRANCE
COSTUME HISTORY, LUXURIOUS MATERIALS, ART, THE "GRAND STYLE"...
THE WORTH PERFUMES, JE REVIENS, MISS WORTH...

A corsage being draped at Worth's Paris, 1907.

Opposite:
The Countess Greffulhe wearing a Worth dress, photographed by Nadar, circa 1900. Considered to be one of the most beautiful women in high society, Greffulhe is said to have been the model upon which Marcel Proust based the character of the Duchess of Guermantes.

The concept of Parisian haute couture was the shrewd brainchild of an Englishman, Charles Frederick Worth. His powerful sense of style elevated him from a common dressmaker to become the first known couturier, an arbiter of fashion.

After serving as a high-class draper's assistant in London, Worth went to Paris to work for the well-known firm Gagelin, which sold textiles, among other items. While employed there, he opened a dress-making department, using Gagelin fabrics. Customers no longer needed to separately purchase fabric and bring it to a dressmaker. Worth provided the fabric and the inspiration. Henceforth, as the journalist Marcelin remarked in *La Vie Parisienne*, grand ladies would be seen at his premises, "awaiting their turn with all the stoicism of a valet in his antechamber." Princess Pauline de Metternich was one of the first to wear Worth's creations. She introduced him to the Empress Eugénie, who brought him to the forefront of the fashion world. Napoleon III was also impressed, realizing that Worth's extravagant styles could do no harm to the French silk-manufacturing industry.

Worth developed an unprecedented understanding of the importance of publicity. He showed his dresses on live models, who passed among his clients as they sipped tea and nibbled petits fours. Most importantly, he put in place an enterprising manufacturing system that ensured that even the largest orders could be delivered in record time: ladies were known to order an outfit one day for an occasion the next, and this system meant his clients were never disappointed.

Worth was also a highly sought-after authority on taste in an increasingly egalitarian society where the nouveaux riches sometimes found themselves at a loss when it came to social graces. Worth launched the vogue for an opulent style, which emphasized rich

fabrics, lavish trims, and embroidery on ball gowns and court dresses. Under his influence, the crinoline disappeared and was replaced by the bustle. A tireless innovator, in 1864 Worth introduced the princess gown, a dress with no horizontal seaming at the waist.

Upon Worth's death in 1895, his sons inherited a business that had dressed the royal courts and wealthy families of Europe, as well as rich Americans. But the principle of haute couture had already attracted competitors, and Worth's sons faced serious rivalry from firms such as Poiret and Chanel. The House of Worth survived for another generation before being bought by Paquin in 1954; the company closed its doors in 1956.

?

Where was the House of Worth located?

Artists as Agents of Reform

- FROM THE FRENCH REVOLUTION ONWARDS
- ARTS & CRAFTS, BAUHAUS, RUSSIAN CONSTRUCTIVISTS, ITALIAN FUTURISTS, FRENCH REVOLUTION, RUSSIAN REVOLUTION...

One of Varvara Stepanova's proposed sports outfits drawn from a series of drawings reproduced in 1923 in the journal *Lef*. Stepanova's *prozodezda* (or production clothes) were based on functionality: "A sports outfit is characterized by its simplicity required by freedom of movement (...) neither buttons nor openings should hinder movement" (*Lef* no. 2, 1923).

! At 7 rue de la Paix in Paris. By choosing this address in 1858, Worth displaced the center of gravity in the fashion world from Palais Royal to west Paris, a stylish neighborhood for new fortunes.

Artists sometimes seek to impose their own particular vision of fashion upon society. When pressed into the service of a revolution or included in the construction of a new art form, artists and designers often propose fundamental changes to the way the public should dress. The French Revolution, for instance, popularized the notion of abandoning aristocratic knee breeches in favor of the form of dress adopted by the radical sans-culottes. Though made famous through illustrations of the Jacobin artist Sergent-Marceau, in the end, only street demonstrators and prominent members of the Paris Commune adopted this new style of dress. More than a century after this failed attempt at dress reform in France, the Russian revolutionaries embarked on a quest for a form of dress appropriate to their ideals. In 1919, at the suggestion of the People's Commissariat for Public Instruction, the renowned Russian couturier Nadezhda Lamanova launched a concept of modern, rational female clothing, in which the form of garments was dictated by their use. Alongside this development, Russian Constructivist artists developed an interest in fashion as a form of art that was both useful and productive; Alexander Rodchenko, for example, experimented with wool-and-leather overalls that gave him the aura of a factory worker.

Throughout Europe, artists enthusiastically responded to the idea that a brave new world should be dressed in correspondingly brave new fashions. The system invented by the industrial era, governed by the dictatorship of the great couture houses and the imperious demands of each passing season, now seemed irrelevant to "the people." Inspired by the Arts and Crafts movement founded in England by William Morris, among others, the

idea grew that fashion should form part of the creative arts in general. In 1903 the architect Josef Hoffmann, a central figure of the Wiener Werkstätte (Vienna Workshops), formed by architects and designers of the Vienna Secession, further refined this idea. Hoffman and his collective conceived of a cross section of workshops that aimed to create the same harmonious aesthetic in which furniture, decorative objects, clothes, and accessories joined together to embody an ideal union of art and life. Also at this time, the Italian Futurists declared that clothes should favor man's evolution in the modern urban environment and be an aid to communication. The Italian artist Giacomo Balla sported—to the astonishment of those he encountered—clothes of many colors and celluloid cravats intended to convey the concepts of line/speed and shape/sound found in his paintings. In 1914 he published a manifesto for a playful, dynamic approach to clothes, in opposition to the artificiality of fashion. After World War I, Ernesto Michahelles, known as Thayaht, an Italian artist who would go on to work with Madeleine Vionnet, created the *tuta*—a single garment for all occasions. Overalls were also the preferred clothing of the Hungarian artist and photographer László Moholy-Nagy of the Bauhaus in Weimar, Germany, in the 1920s.
Later he would make the first experiments in the realm of standardized garment production with the firm Polytextil. Meanwhile, the Ukrainian-French artist Sonia Delaunay created her "simultaneous" dresses and jackets in Paris beginning in 1912; in 1918 she opened a fabric workshop, Casa Sonia, in Madrid; and in 1925 she opened her Boutique Simultanée in Paris.
Although many of these artistic experiments had only a limited immediate impact, they reflected a desire for change that would continue to resurface. In the 1960s, the development of prêt-à-porter collections and style agencies helped to further democratize the fashion industry, making stylish clothes accessible to a larger market.

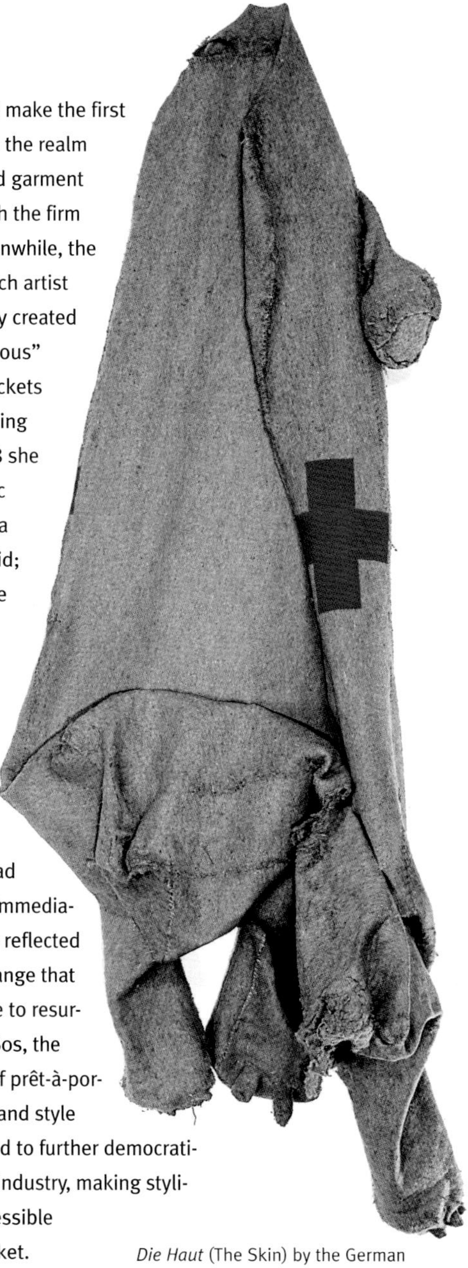

Die Haut (The Skin) by the German artist Joseph Beuys, 1984.
Felt and leather, Musée national d'art moderne, Centre Georges Pompidou, Paris.

Paul Poiret

- (1879–1944) - FRANCE
- COUNTRIES OF THE EAST AND NORTH AFRICA; THE FUTURE, THE DIRECTOIRE, AND THE FIRST EMPIRE; ANCIENT AND CONTEMPORARY ART...
- PARFUMS DE ROSINE: TOUTE LA FORÊT, CHEZ POIRET, LA ROSE DE ROSINE, FAN FAN LA TULIPE, LE MINARET, NUIT DE CHINE, BORGIA, LE FRUIT DÉFENDU, SAKYA MOUNI, LE MOUCHOIR DE ROSINE, MEA CULPA...

Poiret "the Magnificent" (shown here examining fabric) put himself on display even in the intimacy of his office.

Below:
The dresses of Paul Poiret as interpreted by Paul Iribe. Etchings by Paul Iribe, 1908.

Opposite:
Couturier Paul Poiret hosts the Catherinettes celebration. Coats inspired from traditional Eastern dress exemplify the innovation of the flat cut.

Acknowledged as the inventor of contemporary fashion, Poiret "the Magnificent" nevertheless died in poverty in 1944. Over the course of his meteoric career from 1903 to 1929, however, he laid the foundation for today's luxury industries and developed the concept of spin-off products. As a trainee with Jacques Doucet and later the House of Worth, Poiret caused a scandal in 1901 with a Chinese coat dubbed Confucius, which consisted of a single woolen panel. When the coat was presented to the Russian princess Bariatinska, she recoiled in horror, shrieking that it reminded her of the bags into which her country's executioners tossed the decapitated heads of their victims. Yet, just two years after this event, Poiret founded his own house and breathed new life into Western clothing through his studies of Eastern fashion, caftans, and kimonos. His skills in draping and cutting "on the flat" freed women from the restrictive corsets then in fashion. His prototype chemise dress of 1911, cut in a simple rectangle, would be adopted as the de facto uniform of liberated flappers. Indeed, the year 1911 was a memorable

one for Poiret: he launched his perfume and cosmetics house, Les Parfums de Rosine, the first of its kind in haute couture, and the powerful François Coty offered to buy the business.

The man who in 1906 had designed the first dress to be worn without a corset would become a major creative force in the world. As a patron of the arts, Poiret had many artist friends who participated in his ventures. With Paul Iribe and later Georges Lepape, he launched the first couture catalogs in 1907, although these books, filled with paintings of gowns with no indication of price, were more effective at communicating the designer's vision than making sales.

Poiret's costume parties were legendary and everyone who was anyone in Paris society would attend. Like the new style of dress he launched in 1907, Poiret drew upon the East for these flamboyant evenings. In 1911 he threw a now-infamous theme party, the Thousand and Second Night, with guests dressed as characters from the Arabian tales and received by the Sultan—Poiret himself.

Poiret's extravagant confidence inverted the traditional relationship between couturiers and their clients, raising the couturiers' importance. He was also the first to organize promotional tours, taking models around Europe to show his collections at gala evenings. The taste for freedom that Poiret's corset-free stylings had granted women would ultimately bloom into a desire for more wearable, practical garments such as those offered by his contemporary Coco Chanel, and the economic slump caused by World War II drove Poiret to bankruptcy.

What was Paul Poiret's inspiration for creating two companies, "Les Ateliers de Martine" and "Les Parfums de Rosine" in 1911?

Madeleine Vionnet

• (1876–1975) - FRANCE
GRECO-ROMAN ANTIQUITY, DRAPING, BIAS CUT, GEOMETRY, SCULPTURE, THE BODY IN MOTION...
PERFUMES "A," "B," "C," AND "D," MADELEINE VIONNET GREEN

! They were named after his daughters, Martine and Rosine.

This magical name evokes the holy grail of couture, the chimera of the perfect gown. Madeleine Vionnet is an inspiration for any student or designer who wants to make a contribution that counts to the history of haute couture. As Christian Dior wrote in his 1956 autobiography *Dior by Dior*, "She used fabric with genius, and invented the bias cut that would cling so softly to the female figure between the wars. Henceforth, gowns could dispense with turn-of-the-century trimmings and decorative motifs *à la* Poiret. The cut was all that mattered; all the rest was superfluous." Establishing a perfect harmony between the intrinsic qualities of the fabric, the cut of the garment and the way it lay against the body—this was the quest of Madeleine Vionnet.

Beginning in 1912, in the era when Paul Poiret banished the corset, Vionnet sought a way to clothe the body without relying on this former cornerstone of the traditional wardrobe. Her solution became her most spectacular invention: the bias cut. Before her, this method of cutting across the grain of the fabric had been reserved only for decorative details such as flounces. She was the first to apply it to the whole garment. Cut on the bias, fabrics swirl and float without constraining the body. This cut transformed geometrical shapes—squares, rectangles, and triangles—into filmy gowns that rippled sensuously over the skin. Fascinated by classical Greek and Roman dress, Vionnet sought to reinvent the freedom of their draperies by reducing seams and openings: three fasteners were all she needed to keep her Greek goddess gowns in place. When her clients came to slip into their evening gowns, however, they were frequently confronted with the true complexities of this mystery and had to send out frantic appeals for Vionnet's seamstresses to come to

their aid. And all for an end result of such apparent purity and simplicity, as though the gown had barely been touched by human hands.

In the 1920s and '30s, it was goddess gowns in Rosalba crepe (developed by Vionnet in association with the Lyon silk manufacturer Bianchini-Férier) that made the reputation of the House of Vionnet. But its suits and coats benefited equally from the skills of Vionnet, who worked on articulated wooden dolls to take into account the shape of the body.

Vionnet was also a conspicuously benevolent employer, who provided for the welfare of her employees at 50 Avenue Montaigne with light and airy ateliers, chairs with backs, free medical and dental consultations, a cafeteria, and sewing courses.

In 1952, Vionnet donated her archives to what is today the Musée de la Mode et du Textile in Paris. With 120 gowns, 750 toiles, 75 albums of photographs and original drawings, plus account books and personal documents, the archives represent a treasure of inestimable value. In 1988, the House of Vionnet was bought by the de Lummen family, which has since made a number of attempts to relaunch it.

Furred dress worn by the Russian Sonia, Vionnet's star model. Beneath it, a black tulle skirt embroidered with roses. The rose motif and its growing dimensions toward the hemline (which increases the length of the body) are fundamental themes for Vionnet.

Opposite: Evening gown in Moroccan ivory crepe, winter 1935–6. With its complicated construction, the barely-sewn "Vionnet drape" only takes its shape when placed on the body.

Fashion illustrators
Who drew what?

Answer

1. CARL ERIC ERICSON (known as **ERIC**), illustration for *Vogue*, 1936. **2. ROMAIN DE TIRTOFF-ERTÉ**
3. CHRISTIAN BÉRARD, illustration for *Vogue*, 1936. **4. GEORGES LEPAPE**, illustration for *Vogue*, 1924.

1

2

CHRISTIAN BÉRARD

•

ERIC

•

GEORGES LEPAPE

•

ERTÉ

3

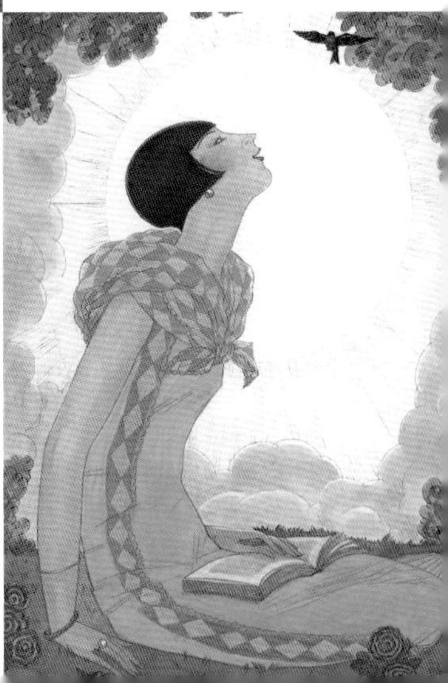

4

Show for a group of buyers at Bergdorf Goodman in New York at the end of the 1940s.

Department Stores

- LES TROIS QUARTIERS (1829), THE MARBLE PALACE (1848)
- LE BON MARCHÉ, LE PRINTEMPS, LA SAMARITAINE, LES GALERIES LAFAYETTE, LORD & TAYLOR HOLT RENFREW, MARSHALL FIELD'S, BLOOMINGDALE'S, SELFRIDGES, HARROD'S, NEIMAN MARCUS, WOOLWORTH, LANE CRAWFORD, SAKS 5TH AVENUE, MACY'S, BERGDORF GOODMAN...

With their great range of merchandise for sale under one roof and—crucially—freedom of entrance and prominently displayed prices, department stores have played an active part in the democratization of fashion. When department stores first opened in the mid-nineteenth century, customers loved the large selection of products divided into separate areas and the ready-made garments offered for sale. The origins of department stores lie on the grounds of the Palais Royal in Paris. Built by the Duc d'Orléans at the cusp of the nineteenth century, these wooden galleries sold a series of ready-made garments at fixed prices, an initiative that was taken up by many other shops. About fifty years later, La Belle Jardinière and Les Trois Quartiers opened, in 1824 and 1829, respectively, and served as a model for stores to come. Le Bon Marché, a small draper's shop founded in 1838 on the left bank of the Seine, expanded into what today we would recognize as a department store—arguably the world's first—in 1852, under the management of Aristide Boucicaut. A shrewd businessman, Boucicaut offered fixed prices, guarantees, and exchanges, and famously declared, "Here we take anything that has gone out of favor." He also gave rise to a rash of emulators in Paris: Jules Jaluzot with Printemps in 1865; Ernest Cognacq and his wife, Marie-Louise Jay, with La Samaritaine in 1869; and Alphonse Kahn and Théophile Bader with Galeries Lafayette in 1895. During this same period, Bloomingdale's opened in New York (1872), Marshall Field's in Chicago (1881), and Marks & Spencer and Harrod's in London (1884 and 1901, respectively).

Other New York innovators included Alexander Turney Stewart, who built his "Marble Palace" in 1846 in order to sell imported European goods at fixed prices. Upstairs he staged the first fashion shows. Not far away, Rowland Hussey Macy opened his department store in 1858. The original logo of this emporium, for many years considered the largest store on Earth, was a cockerel, until Macy had the inspired idea of replacing it with a red star like the one tattooed on his hand—in gratitude to the guiding star that once saved his life when he was lost at sea.

Clearly, the early pioneers of department stores were not afraid of risk,

?

Why did the German authorities force Madame Grès to close her house in 1942?

Department Stores

Bloomingdale's store in New York, 1997.

nor of thinking big. With their majestic iron-and-glass structures inspired by the prodigious Crystal Palace erected in London for the Great Exhibition of 1851, these stores were indeed temples of commerce. As respectable places for decorous distraction and gentle strolling, department stores offered a perfect pretext for nineteenth-century ladies to get out and about. In some respects, they may have contributed to women's entrance into public life.

The great economic depression of the 1930s led to the development of self-service dime stores selling goods at a single price, such as Woolworth's and King Kullen in the United States. In France, Les Nouvelles Galeries launched Uniprix in 1928, Le Printemps opened Prisunic in 1931, and Galeries Lafayette started Monoprix in 1932. Stores such as these would be a great help to millions of women as they took their first steps toward financial independence.

The postwar years saw the rise of out-of-town shopping centers following the example of the Southdale Mall in Minnesota, built in 1956 by Victor Gruen, an Austrian immigrant who wanted to create a place for social meetings and activities. Ten years later, Parly II in France remained faithful to Gruen's vision of a retail center as a mini-town. But by the 1960s, an anti-consumerist backlash and the growing strength of feminism had combined to erode the positive image of these celebrations of unashamed materialism. In the 1970s, department stores sought to distance themselves from the shopping mall experience by concentrating on a more selective, luxury image. Taking their example from the upmarket Bergdorf Goodman in New York, they now offered exclusive designer ranges in their fashion and beauty departments, and so reinvented themselves as purveyors of luxury goods.

! Madame Grès refused to dress the wives of German officers. As a sign of her unabashed patriotism, she had her models walk the runway in dresses the colors of the French flag—blue, white, and red.

An example (to use the French writer Emile Zola's expression) of the "cathedral of luxury": the hall and the majestic display windows of Galeries Lafayette in Paris, completed in 1912 by the architect Ferdinand Chaput.

Chanel n°5

Arrange the bottles in chronological order.

Answer

3. BOTTLE FROM 1921. 2. BOTTLE FROM 1924. 5. BOTTLE FROM 1950. 4. BOTTLE FROM 1970. 1. BOTTLE FROM 1986.

EAU
DE PARFUM
N°5
CHANEL
PARIS

1

N°5
CHANEL
PARIS

2

CHANEL

3

PARFUM
N°5
CHANEL
PARIS

4

N°5
CHANEL
PARIS

5

Jeanne Lanvin

• (1867–1946) - FRANCE
NATURE, ROMANTICISM, MODERNITY, COLOR, DECORATION...
MON PÉCHÉ-MY SIN, ARPÈGE, CHYPRE, LAJEA, PRODIGE, SCANDAL...

A gouache on canson paper in the French *raisin* format, announcing the 1928 exposition in Athens. The House of Lanvin has retained all of the watercolors of the designs from Jeanne Lanvin's time in its archives.

Opposite: Jeanne Lanvin and her daughter before attending a costume ball in 1907. This photo became the basis for the house logo, attributed to Paul Iribe (from his drawing "Woman and Child").

The House of Lanvin is an archivist's dream, possessing one of the finest archive collections in haute couture. Sheaves of original drawings and hundreds of dresses dating from the era of its founder, Jeanne Lanvin, document a doyenne of the Paris haute couture houses.

Lanvin started out as a milliner working for Madame Félix in Paris. Like Coco Chanel twenty years later, Jeanne Lanvin started her own millinery shop in 1885 with modest funds in small and sparsely furnished premises. In 1897 she gave birth to a daughter, Marguerite (later known as opera singer Marie-Blanche), who grew into a pretty little girl whom her mother dressed as a princess—and who became her mother's major inspiration. Lanvin's millinery clients increasingly asked her to make clothes for their daughters as well, and she opened a children's department in 1903. As Marguerite grew up, the House of Lanvin grew with her. Lanvin opened girls' and women's departments, thus graduating from millinery to dressmaking. The Lanvin logo, designed by Paul Iribe from one of Lanvin's drawings, shows a mother and daughter holding hands; this image encapsulates the fairy–tale ideal behind the company's origin.

In developing her couture house, Jeanne Lanvin took her example from her friend Paul Poiret and integrated many activities within it: a dye factory at Nanterre; a home decoration department headed by the talented designer Armand Albert Rateau; Lanvin Sport; and one of the first menswear departments. Lanvin also enjoyed tremendous success with her perfumes, beginning with Arpège, created with André Fraysse in 1927. The Lanvin style, whether for girls, mature women, or actresses, was the epitome of femininity. Jeanne Lanvin dressed numerous celebrity performers, including the Dolly Sisters and

Arletty (who wore Lanvin creations in Marcel Carné's film *Children of Paradise* in 1945). She also combined historical references in her designs, often drawing from her rich library of fashion books. Her famous *robes de style*, for instance, offered a romantic alternative to the geometrical Art Deco look for young girls going to their first ball.

After Jeanne Lanvin's death, a string of talents succeeded her as artistic director, including Antonio Canovas del Castillo, Jules-François Crahay, Maryll Lanvin, and Claude Montana.

?

Madeleine Vionnet got her start with which couturiers?

Haute couture

From its beginnings to the 1930s

Haute couture was a French invention inspired by the work of an Englishman, Charles Frederick Worth (1826–1895). Before the advent of haute couture, there were milliners on the one hand and dressmakers on the other. Milliners embellished gowns with ornaments and created hats and other head coverings. At a time when the French guild system limited craftsmen to a specific type of work, only these *marchands de mode* were authorized to create the styles of the day in the elaboration of gowns and headdresses. Because of their ability to influence the direction of fashion, *marchands de mode* are considered to be the ancestors of today's great couturiers. Still, the great milliners Sieur Beaulard, Madame Eloffe, and Rose Bertin remained suppliers and retailers, subservient to the whims of their clientele. For the coronation of Napoleon I in 1804, for instance, Louis-Hippolyte Leroy, *marchand de mode* to Empress Josephine, merely executed the costumes that had been designed by the painter Jean-Baptiste Isabey.

With the abolition of the guilds in 1791, dressmakers gained authority. Madame Roger was the first to take the bold step of selling fabric in addition to making gowns, and she described her store as "the only firm in Paris selling ready-made gowns of all types for women and children." Worth's innovation was to claim for himself the right to invent new patterns, which he showed on live models in his Paris shop, allowing clients to select from among them. In shifting creative power from the client to the dressmaker, Worth elevated fashion design to a professional status.

For many years, there was nothing in the nineteenth-century fashion vocabulary to distinguish the major couturiers from the multitude of minor ones and the growing number of clothes manufacturers (Paris in 1872

! Kate Reily in London, the Callot sisters, then Jacques Doucet in Paris.

counted 684 of the former and 307 of the latter). In 1868 the various businesses were brought together under the same professional umbrella, the Chambre Syndicale de la Confection et de la Couture pour Dames et Fillettes. In 1875, Jacques Doucet added a haute couture department of "ready-made costumes for ladies" to his lingerie company. Charles Poynter soon opened the Redfern house in Paris on the model of his London premises, and won fame by designing, in 1885, the first ladies' suit "tailor-made" for Alexandra, princess of Wales. In 1900, Worth's son Gaston listed ten great couture houses; ten of very good quality; and twenty that he deemed respectable.

In 1910 the couturiers left the manufacturers in order to found their own Chambre Syndicale de la Couture, which henceforward would be distinguished by its costly and creative designs. The great couturiers of the early twentieth century included Paul Poiret, Jeanne Lanvin, Madeleine Vionnet, and Jean Patou. In 1905, Lady Duff Gordon introduced the idea of a fashion parade set to music at her fashion house, Lucile, and by the early 1930s such shows had become so successful that the Chambre Syndicale was obliged to draw up a calendar for them. Appearing on this calendar, in turn, was an indication of a fashion house's standing in the ranks of haute couture alongside such illustrious names as Lucien Lelong, Edward Molyneux, Nina Ricci, Elsa Schiaparelli, and Maggy Rouff.

The studio of the House of Dior in the 1950s.

Opposite: Dresses by Charles James, including the balloon dress, a drape supported by exquisite engineering that mixed references to various epochs, photographed by Cecil Beaton in 1948.

Detail

Who was the designer?

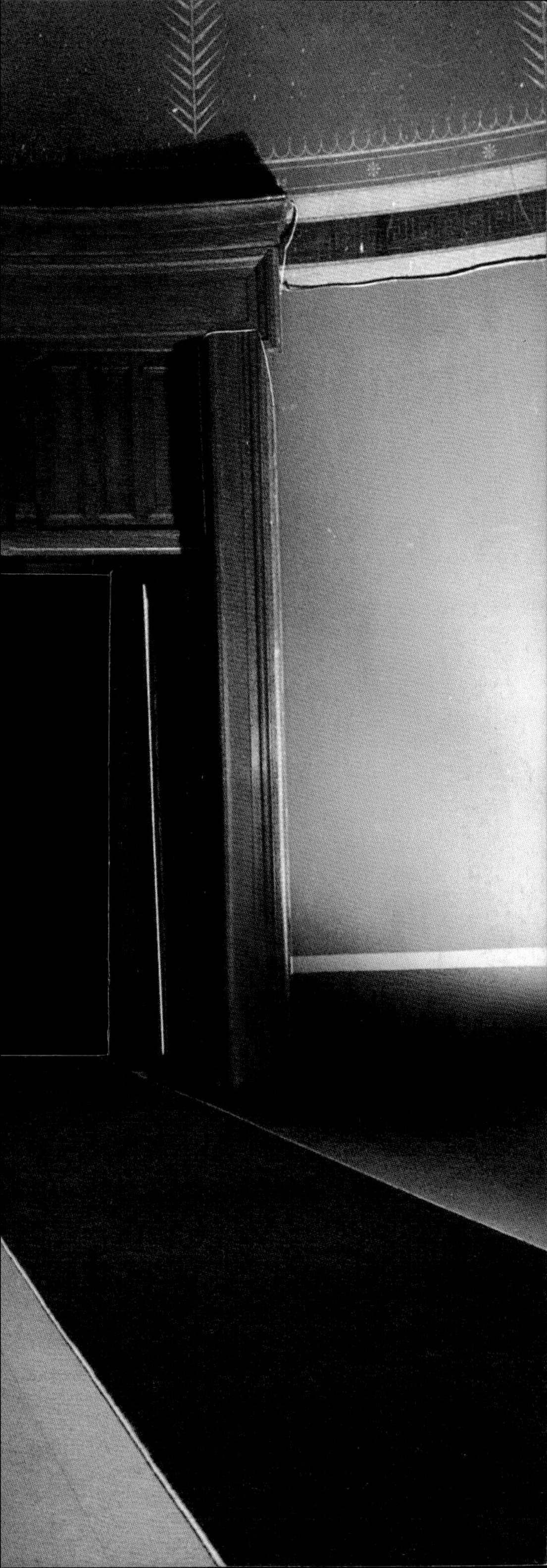

MARIA

This sheath c

in a pleated silk ponge

of Greek statues. I

of rolling his c

so that the p

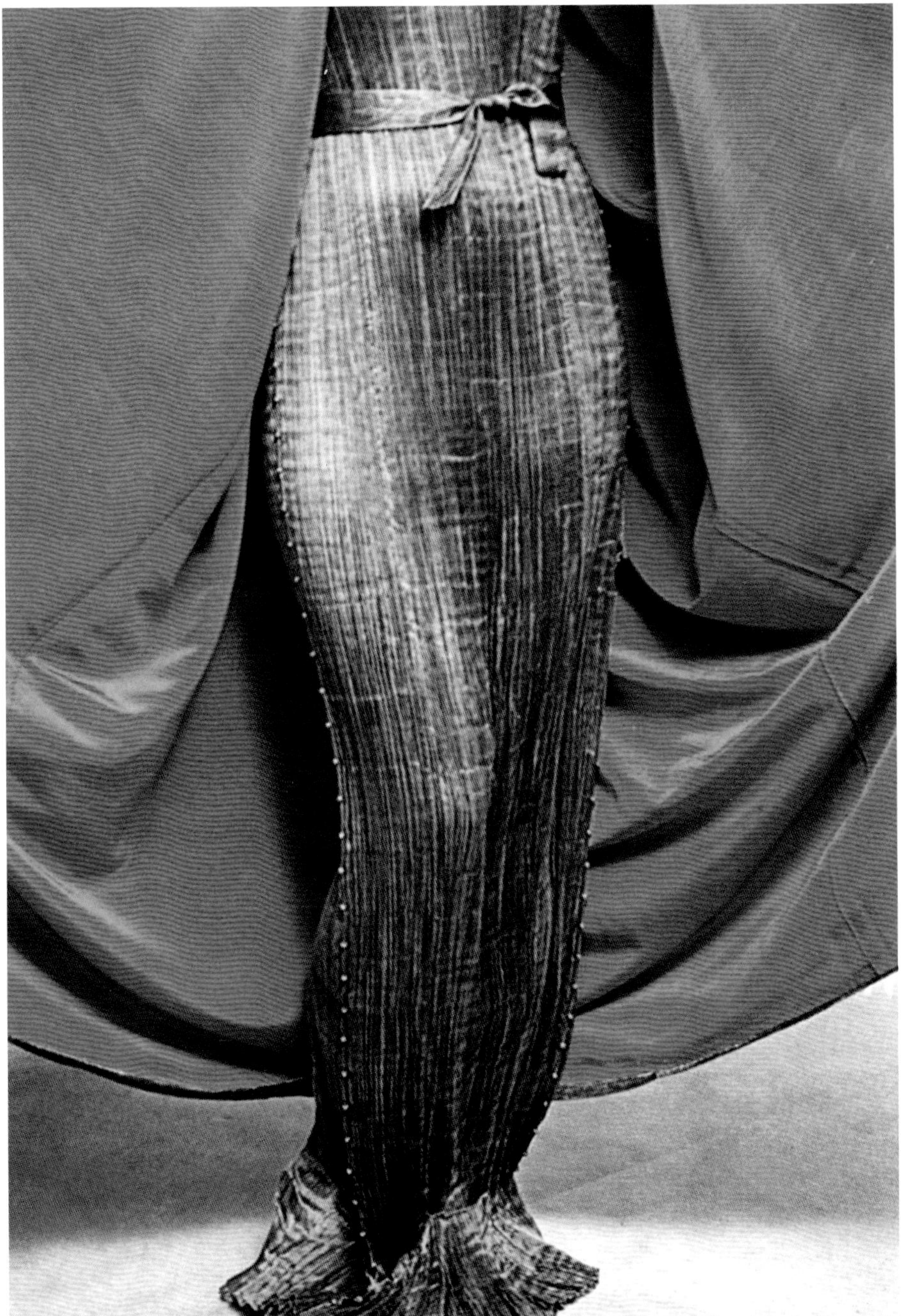

Jean Patou

• (1880–1936) - FRANCE
MODERNITY, SPORTING ELEGANCE, EXOTICISM, MODERN TEXTILES, CELEBRITIES...
AMOUR AMOUR, QUE SAIS-JE, ADIEU SAGESSE, JOY, NORMANDIE, VACANCES, COLONY, L'HEURE ATTENDUE, CÂLINE, MONSIEUR NET, 1000, EAU DE PATOU, MA LIBERTÉ, SUBLIME...

Evening gown in silk velour and black muslin with strass embroidery (front view). Circa 1927–29.

Opposite:
Models pose wearing Jean Patou in front of a mosque. A pleated skirt and a long sailor's jacket with contrasting colors embodies the quintessence of the sport-couture style.

Often credited as the inventor of haute couture sportswear, Jean Patou designed a revolutionary outfit consisting of a calf-length pleated skirt—scandalously short for the time—and a sleeveless sweater for the tennis legend Suzanne Lenglen in the 1920s. Lenglen, in turn, was an adviser for Patou's boutique, called Le Coin des Sports. A huge success, it offered a sport-city crossover, with designs for urban wear based on tennis or beachwear—then much more than a niche market. In this modern, dynamic version of couture, Patou soon emerged as the chief rival to Chanel.

Even more original than his daring sportswear was Patou's determination to introduce a new canon of feminine beauty based on the slender, lithe, and toned physique of American models. The six models whom he brought to France in 1924 to show his new collection attracted a great deal of attention in the press. On these lovely young American girls, Jean Patou's simple, uncluttered styles created a sensation. The athletic and liberated clientele for whom Patou designed were soon wearing his jersey dresses and accessorizing them with "little trifles" from his Coin des Riens.

But this modern outlook did not prevent Patou from excelling in the design of dazzling evening gowns, such as the embroidered and beaded creations worn by Louise Brooks and Josephine Baker. Alert to the dangers of unauthorized knockoffs (so damaging to the Paris couture houses), he was the first, in 1924, to use his initials, J. P., as a label on some of his clothing. This monogram-logo, framed by a lozenge, did not merely authenticate the garment but, as time went on, became a style feature in its own right.

But beyond his successful clothing lines, it was his perfumes that made Patou a fashion legend. Joy, launched in 1930 as "the world's most expensive perfume," was conceived as an antidote to the doleful years of the Depression, and was marketed in the famous Baccarat crystal bottle designed by the architect and

interior designer Louis Süe.
Upon Patou's death in 1936, his brother-in-law, Raymond Barbas, took over the management of the business, administering it with rigorous efficiency. Numerous prominent figures succeeded one another on the creative side, meanwhile, including the costume designer Rosine Delamare, Marc Bohan, Angelo Tarlazzi, and Jean Paul Gaultier. In 1980, Jean Patou's great-nephew Jean de Moüy took over the reins and appointed Christian Lacroix as artistic director, ushering in a return to haute couture, marked elsewhere by Karl Lagerfeld's arrival at Chanel in 1983.

?

Who founded the Small Hats League in 1905?

Hats

From the nineteenth-century heyday to the 1940s

ROSE BERTIN, CAROLINE REBOUX, MADAME AGNÈS...
POUF, BOWLER, BONNET, HOODS, BIBI, CLOCHE, TURBAN, FUR HAT...

!

Countess Elisabeth Greffulhe created the league so that ladies in the theater would not disturb spectators with their immense hats. French actress Sarah Bernhardt put the following notice on tickets to her theater: “Women in hats are not allowed in the orchestra.”

As Oliver Wendell Holmes once noted, “The hat is the ultimum moriens of respectability,” and indeed, in the relatively short time since hats ceased to be indispensable, we have forgotten that this accessory was for centuries the incontrovertible symbol of its wearer’s place in society.

Historically, the simple head coverings required by religious practice rapidly became—in western Christendom at least—symbols of secular pride. By the fifteenth century church authorities had been moved to denounce tall headdresses as the work of the devil. By that time these headdresses had reached heights of as much as three feet (eighty centimeters)! Several hundred years later, the fascination with elaborate headpieces remained undiminished, and the lofty wigs of the late eighteenth century reached their apogee, in the creations worn by Marie-Antoinette, embellished with flowers, jewels, birds, and ships in full sail. These precursors to the modern hat were unambiguous statements of superiority by the ruling classes.

But it wasn’t until the latter half of the nineteenth century that we find a truly golden age for the great milliners. Caroline Reboux, milliner to Empress Eugénie, adorned elegant society ladies of the Second Empire with bonnets and broad-brimmed hats. Esther Mayer and Suzanne Talbot embellished Belle Epoque beauties with immense cartwheel hats and tiny toques. In the 1920s, Madame Agnès and Madeleine Panizon created cloche hats that were pure Art Deco in style. Until World War II, only the most impoverished women would flout convention and risk public opprobrium by venturing out of doors hatless.

And even during the German Occupation of France in World War II, the milliner Gerard Albouy proposed tiny newspaper creations that could be copied by any woman keen to keep up appearances, no matter how reduced her circumstances.

Others opted for the trusty turban, dressed for the fortunate few by Rose Descat, the Legroux sisters, or Rose Valois.

Fashion during wartime: woman with a felt hat, circa 1942. Photograph by John Rawlings.

Opposite:
Cover of *Vogue*, October 1935.

Hats

Match names with shapes.

Answer

1. STETSON. 2. BORSALINO. 3. BERET. 4. BOWLER. 5. TOP HAT. 6. PANAMA.

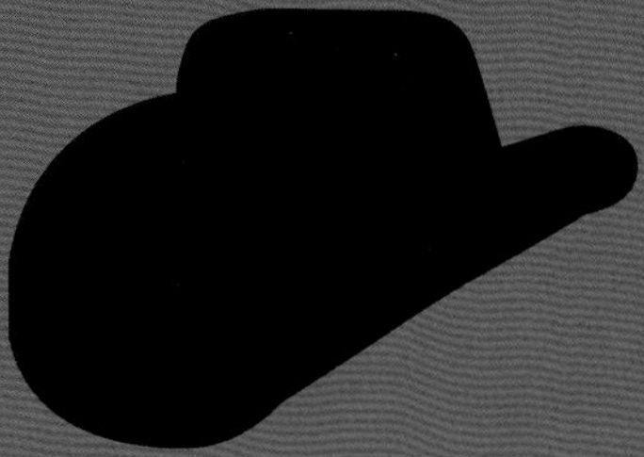

1

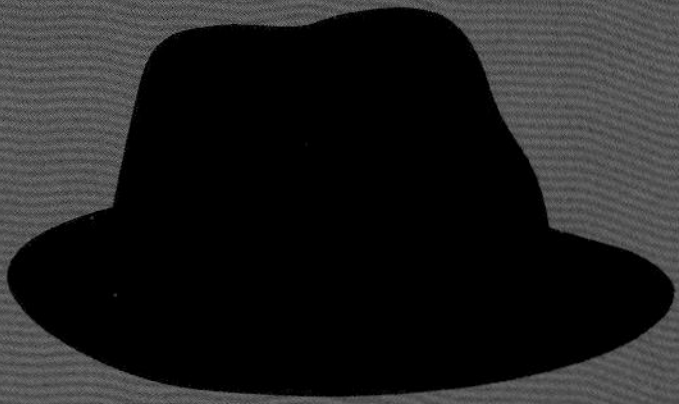

2

PANAMA
•
BOWLER
•
STETSON
•
TOP HAT
•
BERET
•
BORSALINO

3

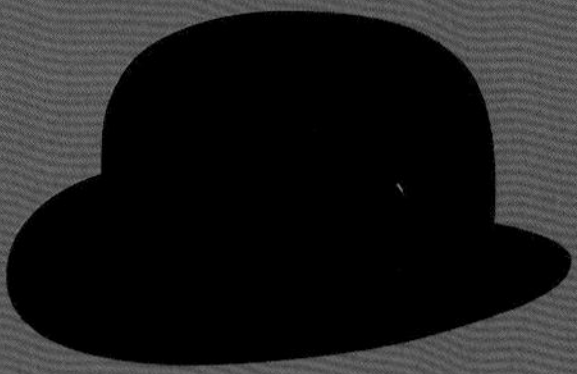

4

5

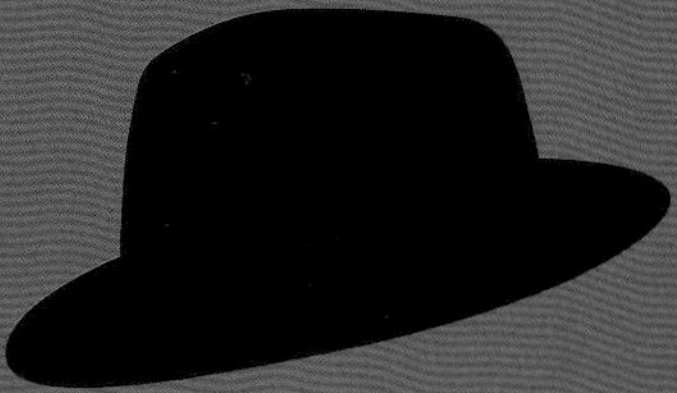

6

Fashion Icons

From the nineteenth to the early twentieth century

Luisa Amman, the future Casati, and Bice Amman, her cousin, around 1898. With this masculine style suit, the future marquise showed a penchant for eccentricity even at the age of seventeen.

The theater has always been a powerful engine for the creation and promotion of fashion, a phenomenon that goes back to the seventeenth and eighteenth centuries. The early eighteenth-century French actress Mimi Dancourt, playing the character of Glycérie as she rose from childbirth, was credited with launching a vogue for flounced dresses à la Watteau. The fashionable ladies of the court duly followed suit, heedless of the fact that the voluminous gown was designed to conceal the actress's own pregnancy.

During the nineteenth century and into the twentieth, audiences would flock to the theater in order to see in person the latest styles illustrated on fashion plates. Fashionable magazines, in turn, would relate every detail of what the actresses wore, with due acknowledgement to their appointed couturiers. Partly in order to dress actresses, Lady Duff Gordon opened her couture house, Lucile, in London in 1890. Among her clients was the great Sarah Bernhardt, consummate icon of her time, who was also dressed by Charles Frederick Worth. She and her rival at the Comédie Française, Réjane, vied with each other for the limelight in the vaporous, sinuous, and lace-ruffled creations of Jacques Doucet, who reserved this special style for them. In the glamorous and slightly louche world of the Folies Bergère, demimondaines such as La Belle Otéro and Liane de Pougy provided invaluable publicity for the couturiers, as they

were only too happy to sport their most risqué creations; living on the fringes of high society, these dancers were free to flout the conventional rules governing female modesty.

Ironically, while the theater was an important venue for the debut of trends as well as artists, one the biggest stars of the Jazz Age caused a fashion frenzy by wearing nothing at all. When Josephine Baker appeared naked in La Revue Nègre in 1925, her exotic charms and lacquered hair, arranged by the hairstylist Antonio Magagnini, made a lasting impression.

Above:
Sarah Bernhardt at the start of her career and her glory, photographed by Nadar. She was one of the first stars to use photography and the media as tools for personal promotion. Her unusual and decadent beauty, with her thin body and red hair, contributed greatly to her celebrity.

The beautiful Cléo de Mérode. A perfect and traditional beauty highlighted by a banded hairstyle with a part down the middle.

?

Which designer released the first perfume for men?

Elsa Schiaparelli

• (1890–1973) - ITALY
SURREALISM, ITALIAN ART, AVANT-GARDE TEXTILES, COLOR, DAILY LIFE, THE STREET...
SHOCKING, SALUT, SOUCI, SCHIAP, SLEEPING, SNUFF, LE ROI SOLEIL, SUCCÈS FOU, SI, "S"...

Art and imagination entered the world of haute couture in the most extravagant, eccentric fashion in the work of this surrealist couturier. Her signature color, shocking pink, set the tone for a shocking life (as she entitled her autobiography). Born into Roman high society, Schiaparelli would probably never have followed this career path had it not been for a reversal in fortunes that obliged her to earn her own living. Having studied philosophy in Rome, she married early and went to live in New York. In 1922, finding herself alone with a small child, she arrived in Paris and started to design knitwear. Self-taught and fearless, she was nevertheless astonished when one of her early designs—a black sweater with a trompe l'oeil white bow at the neck—was featured in *Vogue*. In 1927 she started having her designs manufactured by Armenian knitters who used a method that produced an effect similar to intarsia; this proved so successful that in the same year she opened the first ready-to-wear boutique in Paris, on the hugely fashionable Rue de la Paix. Few, however, were bold enough to wear creations such as her hat featuring an upturned court shoe, designed with Salvador Dalí in 1937, or another embellished with a bloody cutlet. Every Schiaparelli collection told a story, with clothes and accessories making the chapters; a principle revived by numerous contemporary designers, including Jean Paul Gaultier, Alexander McQueen and John Galliano. In 1938 P. T. Barnum's circus inspired a realm of animals, jugglers, prancing clowns, and shimmering embroideries. Artists—futurists, cubists, surrealists, and Dadaists—influenced her work, and Dalí and Cocteau contributed buttons shaped like lips. Schiaparelli played with

! Elsa Schiaparelli.

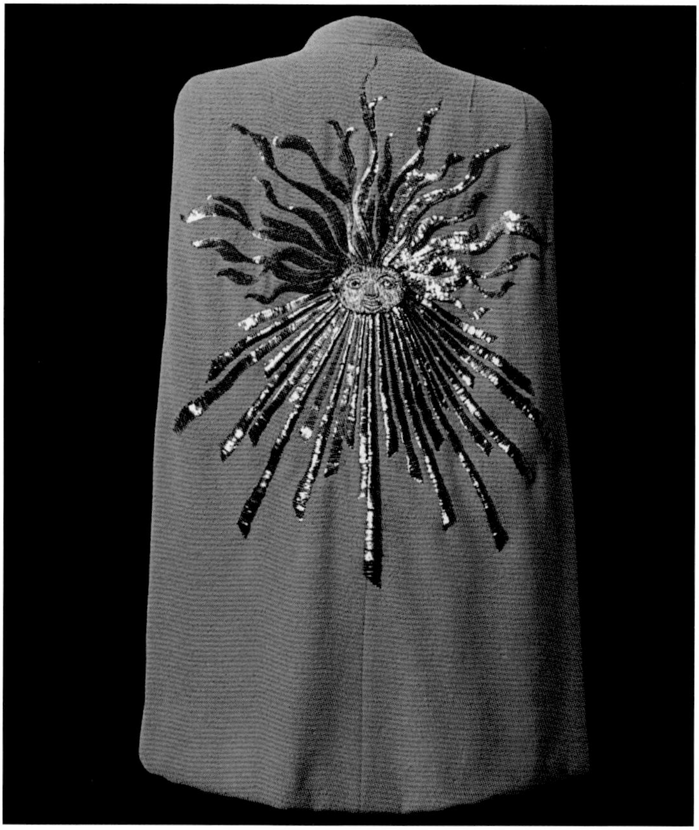

The Phoebus cape from the winter 1938 Cosmic collection. "Shocking" pink, the fetish color of the creator, illuminated by embroidered rays (by Lesage) with golden splinters and shards, an allusion to the Sun King.

Below:
Schiaparelli presented black-and-white suede gloves with red snakeskin fingertips resembling human hands in her 1936–7 winter collection. The gloves were worn with a surrealist suit that had pockets resembling desk drawers. The ensemble was designed in collaboration with Salvador Dalí.

Opposite:
Portrait of Elsa Schiaparelli.

these artists' ideas, for example in one gown referencing the sexual weight that Dalí gave to lobsters in his work. Schiaparelli's lobster crawls along the thigh of an evening gown offered to Wallis Simpson for her wedding to the Duke of Windsor—an offer rejected by the future duchess on the eve of the ceremony because of the dress's, ahem, impropriety.

But in addition to all this wild excess, Schiaparelli was a great innovator in her use of new synthetic fabrics and in the beauty of her cuts ("Never fit a dress to the body," she declared, "but train the body to fit the dress."). But everyday life also offered inspirations. Schiaparelli trumpeted culottes and designed a cozy teddy for keeping warm in air-raid shelters during the German occupation, as well as a traveling coat with capacious pockets. Her Phoebus cape, embroidered with a giant sun, earned her a reputation in Hollywood that would rarely be matched by another Paris couturier. Indeed, Schiaparelli was never to be outdone by the sheer glamour and spectacle of her designs. She once observed wryly, "Women dress alike all over the world: they dress to be annoying to other women."

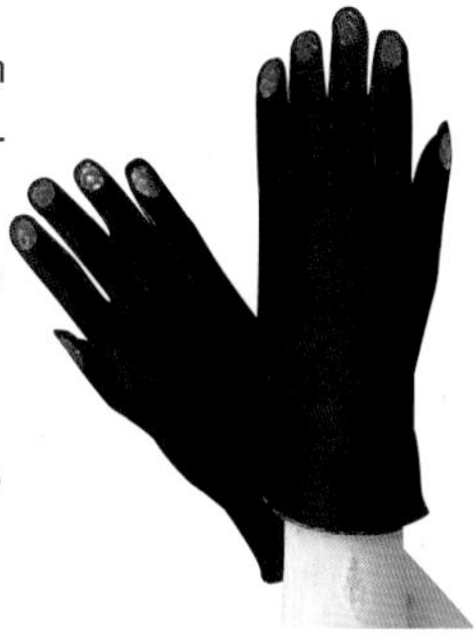

Fashion and surrealism

Who made what?

Answer

1. MANNEQUIN BY MARCEL DUCHAMP, photographed by Man Ray. 2. MANNEQUIN BY MAN RAY, photographed by Man Ray. 3. MANNEQUIN BY ANDRÉ MASSON, photographed by Man Ray. 4. MANNEQUIN BY JOAN MIRÓ, photographed by Man Ray.

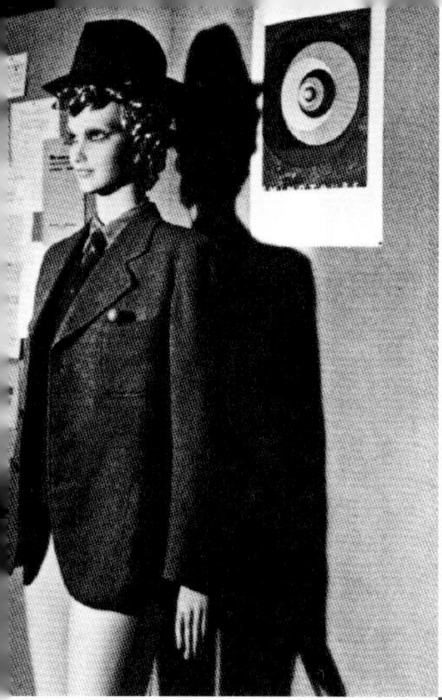

1

2

ANDRÉ MASSON

•

MAN RAY

•

JOAN MIRÓ

•

MARCEL DUCHAMP

3

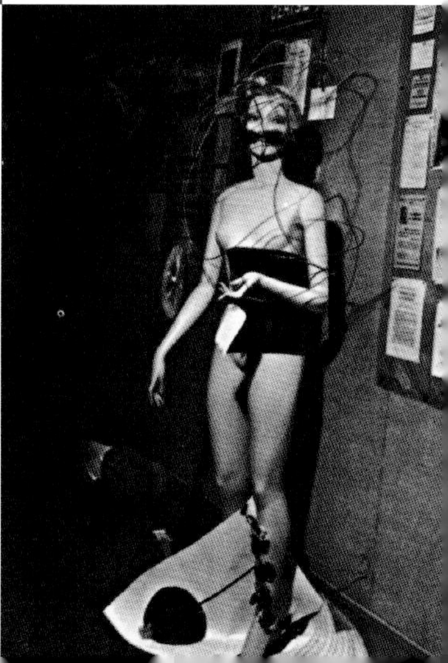

4

Fashion Icons

From the 1920s to the 1960s

Marlene Dietrich in the men's suit that she wore on-screen as well as in her daily life.

Below:
Real beauty from the roaring years.
Louise Brooks with a pageboy haircut and makeup as distinctly stylized as the Art Deco furniture, circa 1930.

In the early 1920s, cinema took over from theater as the vehicle as the vehicle for propagating the current feminine ideal, and Hollywood studios created the potent model of the femme fatale oozing glamour. The first star to inspire a generation was Louise Brooks, an icon of gamine sophistication dressed by Jean Patou, with her trademark sleek bob created by the hairdresser Antoine.

But Hollywood's first true femme fatale was Marlene Dietrich, who rose to stardom with her smoldering performance in *The Blue Angel* in 1930. Her costumes, created by the Italian tailor Arturo Cifonelli, had a masculine style ahead of its time. For *Shanghai Express* (1932), Dietrich plucked her eyebrows entirely, redrawing them in dramatic arcs in order to emphasize the strangeness of her character, Shanghai Lil. Millions of women followed suit. Dietrich's sole rival in beauty and elegance was Greta Garbo; the fierce competition between their respective studios, Paramount and MGM, was mirrored by that between their costumers, Travis Banton and Gilbert Adrian.

In the 1950s and '60s, movie stars abandoned their studio-based costumers for the big names of couture and ready-to-wear. The famous white halter-neck dress with the flyaway sunray-pleated skirt that Marilyn Monroe wore in *The Seven Year Itch* (1955), for example, came from a department store. Now and for several decades to come, it was the turn of couturiers to create the dreams that the public craved. The sublime outfits designed by Hubert de Givenchy for Audrey Hepburn, for instance, fixed for eternity an ideal of Parisian elegance. And the elegant Yves Saint Laurent designs worn by Catherine Deneuve in *Belle de Jour* (1967) attained a mythical status.

Above:
Sportswear was among the genres for such glamorous actresses as Greta Garbo, which allowed her to make a statement beyond the world of elegance.

How many designs were presented for the Miniature Fashion Theater show in 1945?

Silver Screen Style

TRAVIS BANTON, GILBERT ADRIAN, JEAN LOUIS, EDITH HEAD...
RITA HAYWORTH'S BLACK SHEATH DRESS IN *GILDA*...

! 237 dolls, dressed by all of the major French designers, appeared in sets created by Christian Bérard, Jean Cocteau, Boris Kochno, Louis Touchagues, etc.

In the early days of cinema, the couturiers of Hollywood cut adrift from the dictatorship of the great Paris couturiers—and in so doing helped to shape the tastes of millions of women.
In the 1920s, Hollywood's great showman, Cecil B. DeMille, hammered home his credo that the success of any film depended on three things: sex, sets, and costumes. It is thought that the first person chosen to design costumes specifically for a film was Paul Iribe, during the making of DeMille's *Male and Female* (1919). The film made a star of Gloria Swanson, who insisted on playing each scene in a different costume by Clare West, thus establishing the reputation for excess, luxury, and fantasy that was to define Hollywood films for so many years to come.
Many producers of the 1930s came to the movies from the world of fashion: Samuel Goldwyn had been a glove maker and Harry Warner a shoemaker. Doubtless their background gave them the idea of marketing copies of gowns worn by their stars. The dresses, produced by the Modern Merchandising Bureau, were promoted in *Harper's Bazaar*, *Modern Screen Magazine*, and *Vogue*, and sold for $15 to $35 each.
Fame at this time depended on celebrated partnerships between actresses and couturiers, such as that arranged by Paramount between Marlene Dietrich and the costumer Travis Banton, their answer to George Cukor's success with Greta Garbo and the designer Gilbert Adrian in *Camille* (1936). Film producers also appropriate the power of fashion. In 1930, Chanel was offered a fortune by Samuel Goldwyn, but failed to impress the actresses in his studio with her "deluxe poor look." Elsa Schiaparelli found more success with her eccentric style, and the famous Jean Louis Berthauldt designed the legendary strapless gown and black fur worn by Rita Hayworth in Charles Vidor's *Gilda* in 1946.
But the constraints of cinema spelled complications for couturiers and designers, who were required to imply unfettered luxury while observing the notoriously prudish strictures of the Hays Code, introduced in 1930, which forbade any form of nudity. The absurdities that resulted included the banning for three years, beginning in 1943, of Howard Hughes' film *The Outlaw* because of Jane Russell's eye-catching cantilevered silhouette in the bra Hughes designed for her.

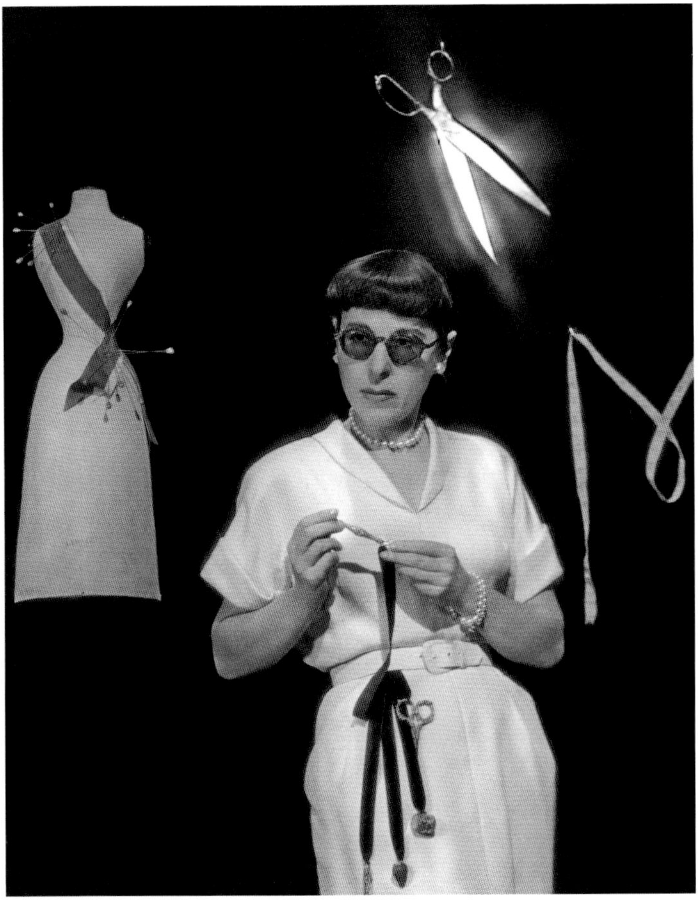

Edith Head was much in demand as
a costume designer by studios competing with her mainstay, Paramount, and was close to many stars with whom she consulted. She was made famous by her Sarong dress, created for Dorothy Lamour in *The Jungle Princess* (1936).

Wartime restrictions obliged the Hollywood studios to economize on sets and to dress their stars in ready-to-wear costumes rather than haute couture. The grandes dames of the studios, with their elegant wardrobes, were replaced by actresses such as Marilyn Monroe, able to fill the screen with their talents alone. Studio shoppers now took the place of couturiers, who left Hollywood to open up their own couture houses. Some American designers, such as Edith Head, nevertheless forged successful careers in the film industry. French couturiers, meanwhile, continued to uphold the principle of strong costume design, and in so doing created legends of elegance for generations to come, including Audrey Hepburn dressed by Hubert de Givenchy, and Diane Keaton by Jean-Charles de Castelbajac in *Annie Hall* (Woody Allen, 1977).

Models
Who's who?

Answer

1. BETTINA, cape and hat, Jacques Fath, 1951. **2. LISA FONSSAGRIVES**, 1949.
3. CARMEN, photographed by Gleb Derujinsky, 1958. **4. SUZY PARKER**, photographed by Sharland, 1951.

1

2

SUZY PARKER

•

LISA FONSSAGRIVES

•

BETTINA

•

CARMEN

3

4

Jewelry Design

- FROM THE 1920S TO THE PRESENT
- FRANCIS WINTER, ROGER JEAN-PIERRE, ROGER SCÉMAMA, ROBERT GOOSSENS, JEAN SCHLUMBERGER, JEAN CLÉMENT, MAX BOINET...
- CHANEL'S NEST EARRING, DIOR'S SPRIG OF LILY OF THE VALLEY...

Victoire de Castellane rattled the world of jewelry with her eccentric, naturalist, baroque, and decadent jeweled creations. Shown here is her sizeable Diorette ring made of yellow gold, diamond, citrine, amethyst, tsavorite, pink sapphire, mandarin garnet, and lacquer.

Opposite: Making jewelry less dramatic by placing it on a simple T-shirt: Christy Turlington, photographed by Gilles Bensimon, wears the Étoile brooch from Chanel made of platinum and diamonds for American *Elle* in 1994.

Briefly banished by the minimalism of the 1990s, jewelry has since staged a spectacular comeback, reclaiming its place of prominence bequeathed by legendary designers of the twentieth century. Its position of favor has been marked by the abolition of the traditional distinction between fine jewelry and costume jewelry. As early as the 1910s, couturiers were giving their seal of approval to costume jewelry. Previously, fake or imitation jewelry, requiring tremendous skill if the illusion was to be convincing, had been dismissed contemptuously as "cheap."

In 1912, Paul Poiret and Madeleine Vionnet first experimented with the idea of creating jewelry to go with their gowns. But it was Coco Chanel in the 1920s who lent immortality to the concept with a revolutionary insight: an elegant woman does not need real diamonds in order to shine. Boldly mixing artificial pearls with real stones, she employed a team of jewelers to create a new range for each season. In 1961 these craftsmen and women formed the Chambre Syndicale des Paruriers (Federation of Costume Jewelers), so claiming recognition for their creative contribution to the haute couture collections. Distinguished names in the field include Desrues, Robert Goossens, Gripoix, Roger Jean Pierre, Roger Scémama, and Francis Winter. Today small but innovative ateliers such as Lumen, Charlotte Parmentier, and Stefano Poletti have joined their ranks.

In adding jewelry to their range of activities, the great couturiers have achieved several goals at once, introducing the inspiration of fashion to the world of jewelry, breathing creativity into a field hitherto devoted to slavish imitation, accessorizing their collections with jewelry in their own style, and increasing their sales of spin-offs from their couture. Beginning in 1993, Chanel, later followed by Dior, with its department of *haute joaillerie* entrusted to Victoire de Castellane, led the field.

?

For which couturier did Roger Vivier create the square-heeled shoe and square metal buckle?

Shoes

From bespoke cobblers to designers

- BETWEEN 1860 AND 1960
- FRANÇOIS PINET, ANDRÉ PÉRUGIA, SALVATORE FERRAGAMO, ROGER VIVIER…
- PÉRUGIA'S HEEL WITH RIVETS, FERRAGAMO'S "INVISIBLE" SHOE, VIVIER'S COMMA HEEL…

In 1858 the American Lyman R. Blake invented a machine to sew the soles of shoes to the upper, and six years later an improved version of this machine enabled a single worker to assemble shoes at a rate of three dozen pairs per hour. Americans soon flooded the European market with low-priced shoes. Britain alone imported a million pairs in 1901. And so traditional makers of bespoke shoes turned to the more lucrative market of women's shoes. The most celebrated house of these master craftsmen remains that of Frenchman François Pinet, who established his business in 1863 on Rue de Paradis in Paris and was famous for the slenderness of his heels.

! For Yves Saint Laurent in 1965. This design would go on to sell in the thousands, and it remains to this day part of the brand's collections.

The shorter skirts that came into vogue around 1915 revealed the work of these early shoe designers. The first true shoe designer, with all the artistry and vision the term now implies, was André Perugia. The son of an Italian shoemaker, this elegant young ladies' man exhibited his earliest creations in the windows of the exclusive Hôtel Negresco in his hometown of Nice. His rapid success depended on three factors: exorbitant prices; ostentatious publicity; and breathtaking inventiveness and wit. Soon Paul Poiret commissioned him to create court shoes, or "pumps," in colors to match his gowns. In 1920, Perugia opened his own Paris salon on Faubourg Saint-Honoré. Two or three wildly creative models would cement his reputation each year, such as the shoe with the screw heel of 1925 and the fish pump of 1931. Of course, more realistic, conservative designs ensured his financial success.

Perugia's sole rival was the Italian Salvatore Ferragamo. Born into impoverished circumstances in southern Italy, Ferragamo emigrated to America in 1914, when he was sixteen, and settled in Hollywood; within a few years, he became known as "the shoemaker

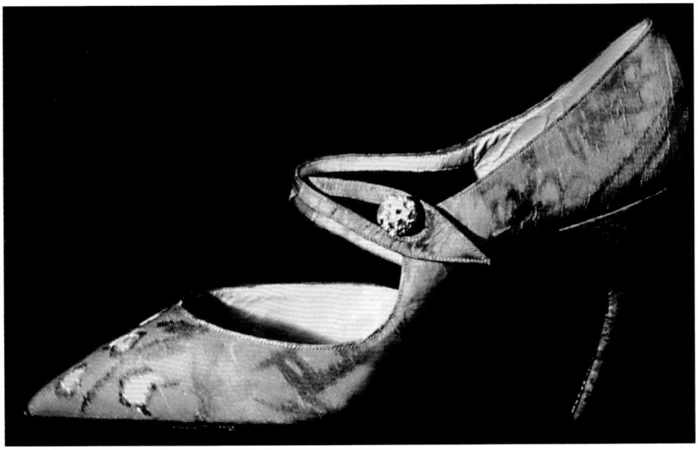

The comma heel by Roger Vivier, 1959, with crisscrossed straps made of Abraham's china green taffeta. An inventive heel made by the master shoemaker, who spent his entire life seeking to free feet from Earth's gravity.

Below:
Chanel shoe, 1958.

Opposite:
Ferragamo sandal, black velour and silver goatskin, with an open heel and a wood sole, 1938–9. This is an extravagant version of the prototype of the platform shoe worn by women during the Occupation.

to the stars." When women complained that his shoes hurt their feet, he studied anatomy in order to alleviate the problem.

Ferragamo returned to Italy in 1927 and set up shop. Though his venture met with bankruptcy, his business recovered and he launched his own label in 1935. The following year, in response to a government embargo on the use of steel (which was requisitioned for Italy's war in Abyssinia), Ferragamo created his first platform heels using cork. An alternative to the traditional steel arch support, the cork sole became an icon of wartime design. Consistently inventive, Ferragamo also carried out bold experiments with cellophane, fish scales, straw, plaited paper, and nylon thread, which he used to create his "invisible" shoes. Stars of the famous Cinecittà film studios flocked to his door, and on one occasion Greta Garbo placed a single order for no fewer than seventy pairs. The successor to these designers was a former sculpture student at the École des Beaux-Arts in Paris, Roger Vivier, who ushered in the reign of the stiletto and a vogue for jeweled creations that earned him the epithet "the Fabergé of footwear." Vivier was also the virtuoso of innovative heel shapes, such as his inwardly curved heel of 1959 and his famous comma heel of 1961. His career began in 1937, when he opened a boutique on rue Royale in Paris, where he created designs for great shoemakers such as Delman, Miller, and Pinet. But an encounter with Christian Dior proved to be the turning point in his career. Recognizing Vivier's rare imagination and extraordinary talent for designing shoes that appeared to defy the laws of gravity, Dior invited him to work within his couture house, and from 1953 to 1963, Vivier enjoyed the then-unique privilege of signing his creations alongside those of the great couturier.

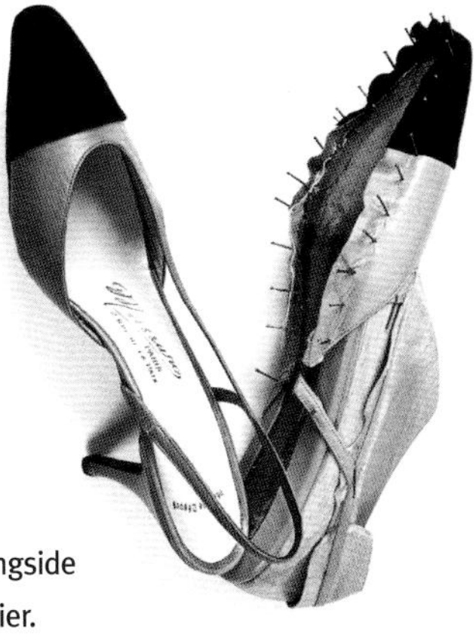

THE FASHION GAZETTE

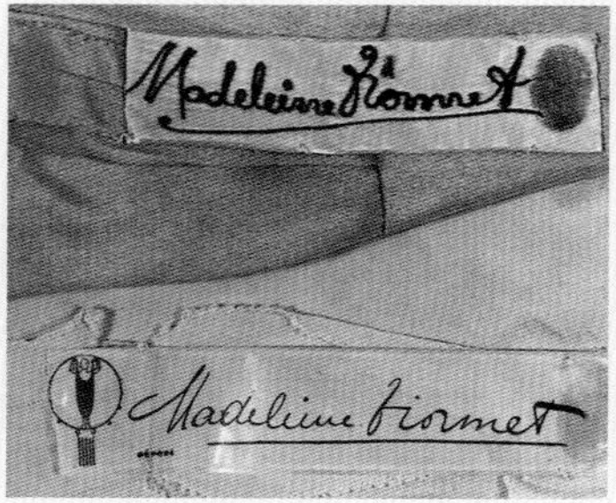

CURRENT AFFAIRS AND NEWS

• December 30, 1921: Fashion is art!

The House of Madeleine Vionnet, supported by the entire profession, was victorious in its infringement suit brought against Madame Boudreau and the Miller sisters. The court based its verdict on the law of July 19–24, 1793, which was heretofore reserved for artistic creations.

• Scandal at the Longchamp races
Three young women appeared at the races "almost nude," according to shocked witnesses, some of whom remarked on their "outrageous bosoms." Our investigation revealed that these were models for Paul Poiret, who has, since last season, sought to bring the high waist back into fashion, with a more daring taste than the dowdy A-line skirts floating around. (1908)

FEMINA'S QUIZ GAME
An excerpt from a 1905 issue of French fashion magazine *Femina*: "Here are nine pictures of beautiful women, each with different nationalities. Are the characteristic features of the models' races sufficiently pronounced on their faces for you to determine each one's homeland with certainty?"

• The Great Designers' Tour For several years, small foreign couture houses have been shamelessly imitating and copying great Parisian designers; the result has been an unscrupulous traffic in designs. As a result, Parisian designers have decided to cross the seas to show the genuine original articles. Therefore, Madame Jeanne Paquin, under the direction of her sister-in-law, Madame Henri Joire, has organized one of these expeditions of elegance. A small troop of models has landed in America to win over the United States with a marvelous collection of the most recent creations." (*Femina*, 1905)

• Pockets in fashion
Is the trend of tailored pockets permanent or perhaps just a fleeting fantasy by couturiers facing a dearth of new ideas? We would of course love to see pockets reappear, but give us useful pockets! (1905)

RUMORS AND SCANDALS

Countess Greffulhe founds the "Small Hats League"
with the quite laudable goal of banishing from the theaters hats which are too voluminous and which prevent the audience from seeing the show as it should. We must applaud, for who among us has never decried the hatted hussy sitting just in front? (1904)

"They are a bit disappointing in evening dress and as for their shoes and their coiffures, alas ! They are execrable."

BOUTET DE MONVEL (*New York Times,* 1915)

The celebrated fashion chronicler Boutet de Monvel dubbed American women "magnificent" but decried their appearance in a quote in the *New York Times*, 1915.

Venice supplants Paris?
Venice has become the new cradle of fashion ever since the Delphos dress, created using dozens of subtle tones by Mariano Fortuny in his Venetian studio, was seen worn by Countess Casati, Isadora Duncan, Eleonora Duse, and Cléo de Mérode… (1907)

Paul Poiret dumps Baroness Henri de Rothschild!
"Madame, I no longer consider myself your supplier!" he said, throwing her out of his studio's daily show. The Baroness had affronted him by summoning him for a private show at her home during which she and her guests mocked his most beautiful dresses and his most beautiful models. (1910)

• Paul Poiret strikes again by putting "bloomers" on the ladies, with pants inspired by those worn in the harem! The world of fashion follows suit and transforms flirts into odalisques. (1911)

Alix Grès

• (1903–1993) - FRANCE
GRECO-ROMAN ANTIQUITY, THE EAST, INDIA...
CABOCHARD, CABOTINE, CABARET, CÂLINE...

Madame Grès occupies a unique position in the pantheon of great couturiers who were bravura creators in the art of cut. The depth and breadth of her knowledge of couture, combined with her uncompromisingly high aesthetic standards, earned her many comparisons with Madeleine Vionnet. Early in their careers, these two designers did indeed share a passion for free-flowing classical drapes. However, Madame Grès created her own personal style, evoking the "wet" folds of the drapery in Greek statuary. Using a gossamer-fine silk jersey that she commissioned from Rodier from 1935, she created gowns with the fine twisted pleats that were to become her signature style. A virtuoso technician, Grès manipulated fabric into twists and spirals, directing its flow and changing its rhythm to create a complex surface interplay. But Grès was not only an innovator of technique, she was also an innovator of materials, devising novel uses for fabrics such as cellophane, nylon crin, mohair, ciré satin, and knitted hemp, and from the 1950s on she exploited the intrinsic qualities of silk taffeta in shapes that were both geometric and draped.

Crêpe dress made of two-tone pleated silk, with a high cross on the bodice, 1975.

Opposite: A perfect example of fine pleats, the signature of the Grès style, appeared in *Le Figaro Illustré*, September 1937.

Above all, Madame Grès was an individualist of stubborn integrity and a rebel. Born Germaine Krebs in 1903, as a young woman Madame Grès trained in design and worked as a milliner for the Bon Marché department store before becoming a designer at the couture house of Premet. In 1934, she launched the couture house Alix Barton (which shortly became known as Alix) with her friend Juliette Barton. In 1942, she managed to open a couture house in occupied Paris, a courageous move for a couturier of Jewish origins. The name she chose,

Grès, was a pseudo-anagram of the first name of her husband, the Russian painter Serge Cezrefkov. When she refused to dress the wives of German officers, the German authorities closed down her couture house.

Clearly, Madame Grès was a woman of strong convictions, and she was opposed throughout her life to snobbery, though she was nonetheless courted by prominent society figures such as Princess de Polignac, the Aga Khan, Princess Grace of Monaco, Marella Agnelli, and Marie-Hélène de Rothschild. Yet despite her skills and renown, Madame Grès died in obscurity in 1933, bankrupt and neglected; when her death was made public months later, the French fashion industry responded with shock and shame. In New York, the Metropolitan Museum mounted a major retrospective of her work in 1994.

?

What artistic profession would Madame Grès have wished to exercise?

The Little Black Dress

- FROM 1926 TO THE PRESENT
- CHANEL ORIGINALLY AND ALL COUTURIERS AFTERWARD
- EDITH PIAF'S STAGE DRESS

Sketch of "Chanel's Ford," an earnest attempt for a democratic look, appearing in *Vogue*, 1926.

Opposite: Drawing by Grau for the cover of *L'International-Textile* in 1955.

When French *Vogue* published a sketch of a plain black dress by Coco Chanel in 1926, it described it as "Chanel's Ford," anticipating both the concept's popularity and its availability. And so the little black dress was born. All the essential characteristics are there in this early sketch, summed up in one word: simplicity. Devoid of decorative detail, this was a dress designed to be adaptable to all functions and occasions—for day, cocktail parties, or evening—according to the way it was accessorized. Most importantly, this discreet little dress was neutral enough to be worn more than once without giving the impression that the owner had nothing else to wear. This highly democratic invention would eventually serve as an essential element in every woman's wardrobe. The little black dress (LBD, in fashion parlance) swiftly became a feature of couture collections. Two articles of faith of the fashion world—that true elegance resides in simplicity, and that black sets off female beauty to perfection—ensured its success. Each era invested the little black dress with its own particular nuance: in the 1930s, it was the uniform of the femme fatale; in the 1950s it was the epitome of sexy glamour; and in the 1980s it said "rock and roll." Guy Laroche made it a specialty and created the famous backless LBD worn by Mireille Darc in the 1972 Yves Robert film *Le grand blond avec une chaussure noire*. But perhaps the most iconic little black dress in American cinema was worn by Audrey Hepburn in *Breakfast at Tiffany's* (1961). Hubert de Givenchy's take on the classic style effortlessly conveyed elegance and charm.

In the 1980s, Azzedine Alaïa created an astonishing series of little black dresses, most famously his sheath

! A sculptress. She would often say, "I wanted to be a sculptor. For me, working with fabric or stone is the same thing."

dress, which practically begged to be unpeeled with its spiral zipper. In 1996 the concept was relaunched by the vintage haute couture specialist Didier Ludot, who produced a series of exhibitions and publications devoted to the glories of the little black dress.

The Little Black Dress
Who made what?

Answer

1. CHANEL, silk muslin, Didier Ludot collection, Paris. **2. PIERRE CARDIN**, jersey, 1969, Didier Ludot collection, Paris. **3. CHRISTIAN LACROIX**, silk gazar, 1993, Didier Ludot collection, Paris. **4. THIERRY MUGLER**, vinyl, 1985, Didier Ludot collection, Paris.

1

2

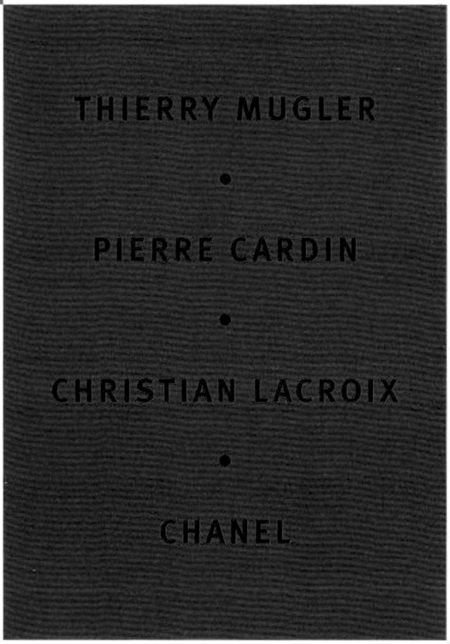

3

4

Coco Chanel

- (1883–1971) - FRANCE
- MODERNITY, MINIMALISM, THE POOR LOOK, SPORTS ALLURE, THE WOMAN OF ACTION, ANCIENT CIVILIZATIONS...
- N°5, N°22, CUIR DE RUSSIE, BOIS DES ÎLES, N°19...

Miss Chanel and her model Odile de Croÿ in the apartment at 31 Rue Cambon.

Opposite: Marie-Hélène Arnaud, Chanel's favorite model, photographed at Rue Cambon by Sante Forlano for French *Vogue*, 1958.

Chanel's concept of the "deluxe poor look" (*misérabilisme de luxe*) has been pondered over by generations of designers fascinated by the enduring success of the Chanel brand. When the young Coco Chanel set up business on Rue Cambon in 1910, she was a slender, flat-chested *garçonne* with a boyish haircut and new ideas about styles of dress. Chanel's ideal woman, freed from the shackles of patriarchy and boldly forging her own destiny, required a new wardrobe, and she would be the couturier to supply it. Taking her inspiration from sportswear, she created clothes for a woman of action, and in the process, repudiated all the frills and furbelows of the Belle Epoque.

In 1916, Chanel used jersey fabric, until then reserved for men's undergarments, to create ensembles of skirts and loose-fitting tops. It was a daring move that subverted jersey's humble origins and drab colors to ensure its entrée into the exclusive world of couture. For women who had worked in factories and on production lines during World War I, these easy-to-wear outfits were perfectly suited to their new, active lives.

In the 1920s, the Chanel style stood in opposition to the prevailing taste for nouveau riche excess. By now her lover was the duke of Westminster, and the "tweedy" clothes of the British aristocracy inspired her to design comfortable tweed suits, accessorized with simple costume jewelry. Her message was clear: A woman's personality counted more than her finery, and all the diamonds in the world could not lend class to a woman who had none.

In 1926, she invented the little black dress, a concept that revolutionized women's formal wear and made it much more democratic and accessible. Chanel's No. 5 perfume, launched in

1924, was one of the first perfumes to mingle natural and artificial essences. Chanel closed her business in 1939. After she reopened in 1954, the "Chanel look" was greeted with delight as the liberating counterpoint to the tightly corseted Dior look. All the components that would define her look were in place—tweed or jersey suits; gilt chains; buttons with the double "C" of her initials or with lions; camellia brooches; ponytails; quilted bags; boaters; and two-tone shoes, tan with black toes, to make feet look neat and small. But of all these icons, perhaps the most celebrated is the Chanel suit. With the outstanding quality of the cut, the free movement it gave to the arms and back, the specially weighted lining that ensured a perfect hang, it all added up to a garment that remains an absolute must-have.

? Why are Chanel shoes two-toned?

Charles James

• (1906–1978) - UNITED STATES
GLAMOUR, SECOND EMPIRE, ARCHITECTURE, SCULPTURE, SPLENDOR...

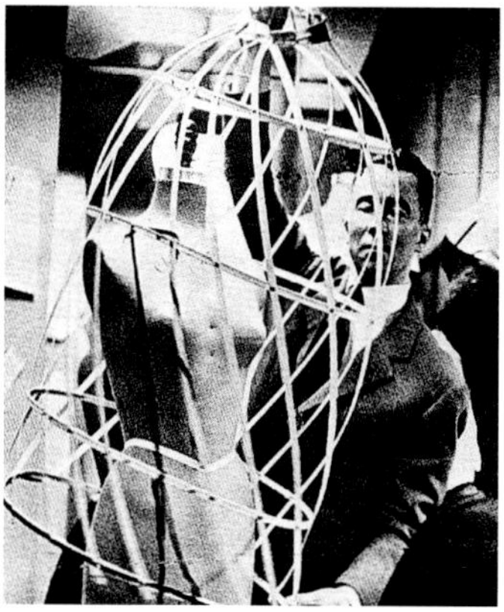

Charles James was the Christian Dior of American fashion. Born in England the year after Dior, in 1906, he was nevertheless the first American couturier to gain admiration among his European contemporaries. Combining a made-to-measure business with sales of his designs to the big stores, he successfully adapted the Parisian haute couture system to the American market. With his virtuosic creations, he launched himself as a clear competitor to his French rivals. Like Dior, James understood women's longing for fantasy. As Austine Hearst, the wife of William Randolph Hearst and James's favorite client, recalled, "I shall always remember the magic in wearing one of those ravishing Charles James gowns for romantic balls and in being transformed by him from a Cinderella into a radiant princess."

James excelled at the creation of magnificent and unique ball gowns, recognizable by the tension between the grace of their design and the (apparent) sculptural weight of the finished garment. In order to turn his designs into reality, he had recourse to a complex architecture of bustiers, pronounced hips, and crinolines, which he used as the substructure for his draping. When finished, these marvels of construction would stand up unaided. Clients might present James with any number of physical flaws, yet his gowns would conceal them all to reveal a perfect woman. Gowns such as the Lampshade, the Balloon, the Empire, the Four-Leafed Clover, the Petal, and the Swan imposed beauty on even the most unpromising figures. But James also worked in a light, airy style, as seen in his 1930s evening gowns and in the day dresses and hats he designed under the name of Charles Boucheron, beginning in 1926. His coats were masterpieces of abstraction, variations on the concept of the cocoon or the cone. One could easily see his

! To make the foot appear smaller by associating beige (the color of the skin) with black (cutting across the foot).

Taxi gown of 1929–30, bias cut and spiral draped, disappearing into the back of said cab, while his Siren gown, constructed of soft stitched pleats flanking a central column, recalled the technical virtuosity of Madame Grès.

James tended to stand apart from the fashion world. He antagonized his enemies and alienated patrons and clients alike with his exorbitantly and unjustifiably high prices.

Contemptuous of the commercial side of the fashion business, James lived his final years as a ruined man, ill and alone. Posterity would not forget him, however. The 1970s rediscovered his bias-cut gowns, and the 1980s, his crinolines. Halston took up the flame of the master's grand style, notably in the skillful coils of his famous down jacket. And indeed it was the collaboration between these two men—together they created new variations on bias cutting—that would ensure the immortality of the French designer's work.

Opposite:
Charles James as a creator, sculptor, and architect, building one of his complex evening gown structures. Photo published in *Look* in 1952.

Balloon dress from 1955. A concentration of references to fashions past that resulted in a modern reading: With a high Empire waist and a skirt in the spirit of the crinolines from the second Napoleonic empire, this dress was draped in the manner of the pouf dresses from the turn of the eighteenth century.

Designer Perfumes
Who made what?

Answer

1. ROCHAS, Femme. **2. LANVIN,** Arpège. **3. ISSEY MIYAKE,** L'Eau d'Issey. **4. THIERRY MUGLER,** Angel. **5. JEAN PATOU,** Joy. **6. CALVIN KLEIN,** CK One. **7. DIOR,** J'adore. **8. LOLITA LEMPICKA,** Lolita Lempicka.

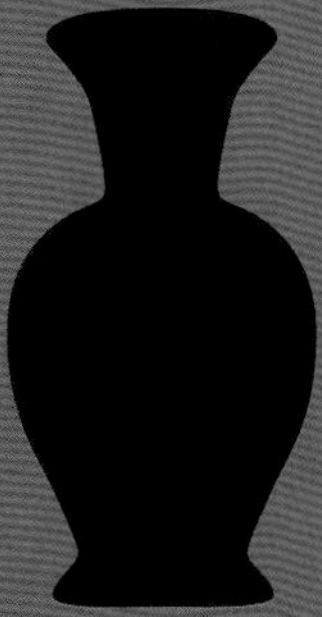

1

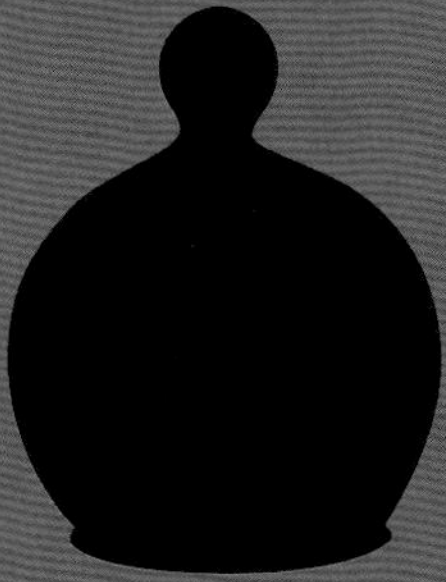

2

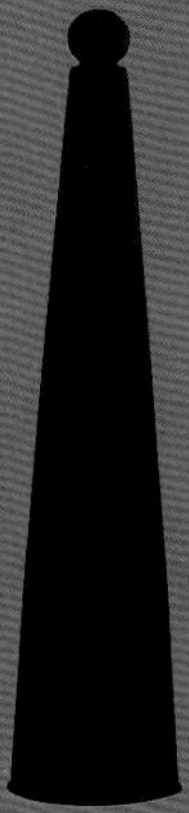

3

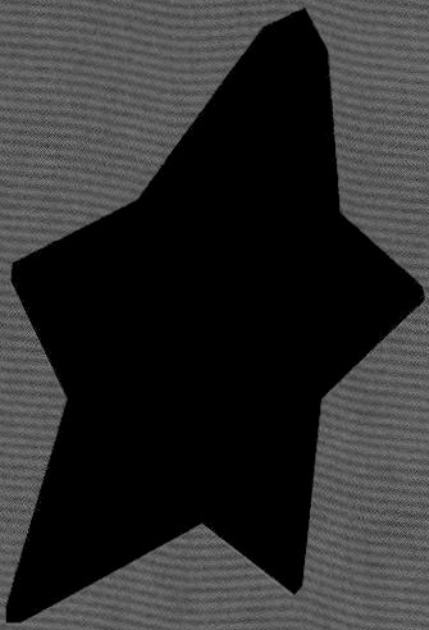

4

LANVIN

CALVIN KLEIN

THIERRY MUGLER

ISSEY MIYAKE

DIOR

JEAN PATOU

ROCHAS

LOLITA LEMPICKA

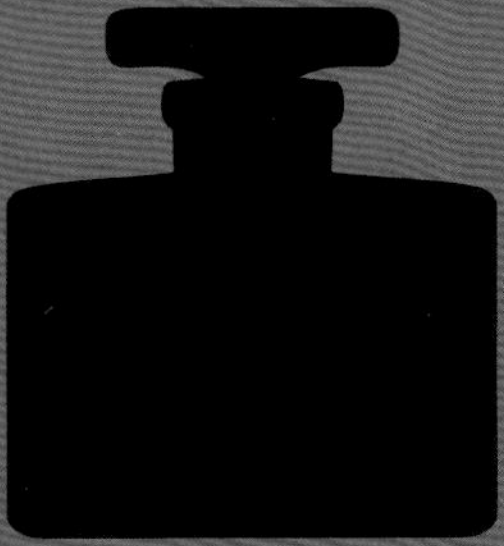

5

6

7

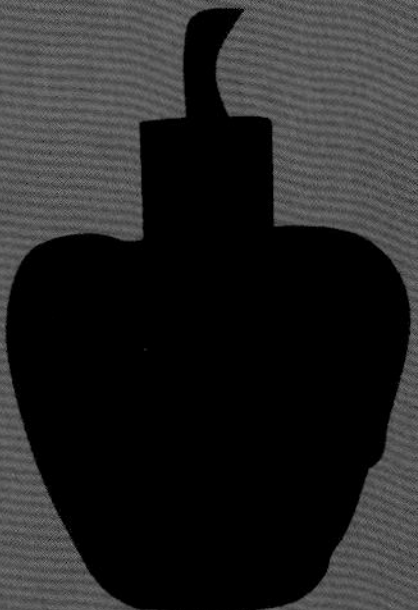

8

The American School

• BEGINNING IN THE 1940S
CLAIRE MCCARDELL, OLEG CASSINI, HATTIE CARNEGIE, NORMAN NORELL, BILL BLASS, OSCAR DE LA RENTA, BETSEY JOHNSON, RALPH LAUREN, DONNA KARAN, CALVIN KLEIN, PERRY ELLIS, MARC JACOBS, ZAC POSEN...

Opposite:
Halston and his models dressed in Halston, 1974.

Claire McCardell's models in 1946.

Lights, drama, suspense, and excitement—New York Fashion Week is one of the unmissable showcases of the fashion calendar. While some critics accuse it of monotony, others are fascinated by the possibility for spotting new and emerging talents. In recent years, New York has shown an alternative side of the industry that has succeeded in piquing the curiosity of buyers and the fashion press alike, and that can truly be termed an "American school."

The origins of the American school go back to the Second World War. However, as early as the 1910s, the magazine *American Dressmaker* testified to a desire within the American fashion industry to assert its independence from its European counterparts, and in the 1920s the couturiers of Hollywood developed their own distinctive, glamorous style. By 1932 the Fifth Avenue department store Lord & Taylor was promoting its dresses in the "American style," and the New York Couture Group was founded in 1947. The Wall Street crash of 1929 and the Depression of the 1930s, as well as the development of mass distribution and discount chains, confirmed this growing independence in fashion, but it was the country's isolation from France during World War II that finally made the break, freeing American designers from their thralldom to the Paris couturiers.

Of course, then as today, the heart of American fashion lay in New York. Dressmakers, couturiers, and designers on Seventh Avenue specialized in women's suits, coats, and dresses. But the influence of Californian sportswear was on the rise, and the

widespread use of rayon, or artificial silk, posed a threat to the traditional expertise of New York garment manufacturers. At the same time, the arbiters of style gradually removed the distinction between indoor and outdoor clothing, further simplifying the way American women dressed.

As postwar America evolved, consumers drifted away from the European model of doing things and began to embrace a truly American way of life. Suburban living, the embodiment of the American dream, brought with it new dress codes founded less on formal entertaining and more on the practicalities of an active lifestyle. The expansion in the number of students

?

Who was the official dressmaker for Jacqueline Kennedy?

The American School

Naomi Campbell wearing Isaac Mizrahi's totem-pole dress on the cover of *Time*, September 1991.

Opposite: Diane von Furstenberg, photographed by Ara Gallant, around 1983. After a spectacular start in the 1970s, the popularity of Diane von Furstenberg's brand waned. However, the brand has made a remarkable comeback over the last two decades.

! The Russian aristocrat Oleg Cassini.

attending college on university campuses, with their emphasis on sports, encouraged the younger generation to look for comfort and practicality in their clothes. By 1974, Claudia Kidwell and Margaret Christman observed in their book *Suiting Everyone* that the overriding characteristic of American dress was that it had erased all ethnic origins and scrambled social distinctions. All three of these factors—the creation of suburbia, university life, and the democratization of fashion—made America the land of sportswear.
The pioneer in this distinctively American field was Claire McCardell, who brought a subtle haute-couture sophistication to sportswear during the 1940s and '50s. In the following decades the press latched on to the reinvented glamour of Bill Blass, Hattie Carnegie, the Hollywood designer Oleg Cassini, Norman Norell, and Oscar de la Renta; the elegant sportswear of Anne Klein and Pauline Trigère; the professional polish of Liz Claiborne; the "hippie chic" of Giorgio di Sant'Angelo; and the youthful exuberance of Betsey Johnson. This galaxy of talent succeeded in banishing America's inferiority complex in matters of design and good taste. In the 1980s, American fashion gained international recognition with the growing reputations of Perry Ellis, with his clean-cut classics; Carolina Herrera, with her jet-set style; Donna Karan, with her streamlined separates; Calvin Klein, with his minimalist elegance; Ralph Lauren, with his preppy chic; and Todd Oldham and Isaac Mizrahi, with their fresh takes on sportswear.
Today designers such as Zac Posen, Lazaro Hernandez and Jack McCullough of Proenza Schouler, L'Wren Scott, and Isabel Toledo occupy a delicate position in a time when designs are judged by rather doctrinaire tastes. The success stories of such high-profile designers as Alber Elbaz, Tom Ford, Michael Kors, and Marc Jacobs are also reflected in the interest shown by European apparel companies. The American school of design has come full circle.

Designers and muses
Who inspired whom?

Answer

1. Naomi Campbell and Azzedine Alaïa.
2. Bettina and Jacques Fath.
3. Hiroko Koshino and Pierre Cardin.
4. Denise Poiret and Paul Poiret.
5. Sofia Coppola and Marc Jacobs.
6. Audrey Hepburn and Hubert de Givenchy.
7. Marie Seznec and Christian Lacroix.
8. Inès de la Fressange and Karl Lagerfeld.
9. Anne Rohart and Sonia Rykiel.
10. Victoire Doutreleau and Yves Saint Laurent.

1  

2  

3  

4  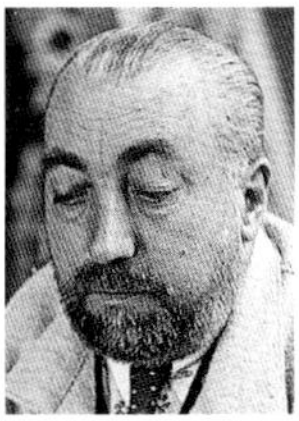

5  

6  

7  

8  

9  

10  

Atout Coeur ball gown, made of royal red faille with draped demi-cut scoop neck, revealing the shoulders, spring-summer 1955 collection. Photograph by Laziz Hamani.

Opposite: Portrait of Christian Dior by Ellis Marcus.

Christian Dior

• (1905–1957) - FRANCE
ROMANTICISM, SPLENDOR, THEATRICALITY, GLAMOUR, HYPER-FEMININITY...
MISS DIOR, DIORISSIMO...

The name of Christian Dior—now synonymous with haute couture—erupted into the fashion world like a bolt from the blue. On February 12, 1947, this unknown designer held his first show at 50 Avenue Montaigne. The New Look (as his Corolle line was soon to be dubbed by the press) instantly made the wartime silhouette of the period look old-fashioned. Gowns by Dior were a backlash against the austerity and privations of war. "We were emerging from a time of war, of uniforms, of women soldiers with the shoulders of boxers. I drew flower-women (*femmes-fleurs*), soft shoulders, rounded busts, waists as slender as reeds, and skirts as full as corollas," he remembered in his autobiography, *Dior by Dior*. Bowing to the pressure of public opinion, foreign buyers returned to Paris. Every woman, rich or poor, longed for this new retro-romantic style, epitomized by the star turn of that first show, the iconic Bar suit, with its overtones of the Second Empire and the Belle Epoque. Accorded the prestigious Neiman Marcus Award for Distinguished Service in Fashion, Christian Dior set off on a triumphant tour of the United States.

The following year he signed the first licensing agreements in the history of fashion.

Dior was the first to make the connection between design and communication, accompanying each fashion show with a booklet explaining the collection for the benefit of journalists. Each collection was defined by a particular line, such as the H-line of winter 1954 or A-line of summer 1955, and each redefined the latest trends, making it indispensable for the fashion-conscious woman to renew her wardrobe every season. When Christian Dior died suddenly in 1957, it was his twenty-one-year-old assistant, Yves Saint Laurent, who took over as artistic director.

? Who baptized Christian Dior's first collection?

House of Dior

- HOUSE FOUNDED IN 1947
- CHRISTIAN DIOR (1947), YVES SAINT LAURENT (1957), MARC BOHAN (1960), GIANFRANCO FERRÉ (1989), JOHN GALLIANO (1997)
  DIOR HOMME: HEDI SLIMANE (2000), KRIS VAN AASCHE (2007)
- DIORELLA, POISON, DUNE, FAHRENHEIT, DOLCE VITA, REMEMBER ME, ADDICT, J'ADORE...

> ! Carmel Snow. At the finale of Dior's first couture show in 1947, the then-editor of *Harper's Bazaar* exclaimed: "It's quite a revelation, dear Christian. Your dresses have such a new look!"

Yves Saint Laurent made his debut as Dior's successor with the Trapeze line of summer 1958 and was given a rapturous reception. The *Daily Mirror* proclaimed, "Yves, Idol of Paris." The collection heralded a new, contemporary vision for the 1960s. But Saint Laurent's triumph was cut short by his military service, and in 1960 Marc Bohan took his place. Bohan's slim look of summer 1961 continued the tradition of a specific line for a specific season, and his precision tailoring was popular with clients such as Elizabeth Taylor. But over his long career, the panache and spirit associated with the house of Dior gradually waned, though the fur department founded by Frédéric Castet in 1968 continued to distinguish itself with its sumptuous creations well into the 1980s.

Much had changed in the more than twenty-five years since Christian Dior's death, and in 1985 Bernard Arnault, the new chief executive of Dior, decided that it was time to return the legendary couture house to its former luster. In 1989 Gianfranco Ferré took over as artistic director, bringing with him the aura of a *condottiere*, or mercenary, of Italian fashion. In 1996, an homage to the New Look created by a young and iconoclastic designer on the British fashion scene caught Arnault's attention. Thus John Galliano arrived at Avenue Montaigne, bringing with him a punk-rock spirit and a British eccentricity that shocked devotees of classic French couture. His public was fascinated by his outrageous makeup (inspired by the performance artist Leigh Bowery), the extravagant Japanese-influenced proportions of his designs, and the wildly original outfits he wore on the catwalk when he took his bow. As Galliano succeeded in imposing his own New Look,

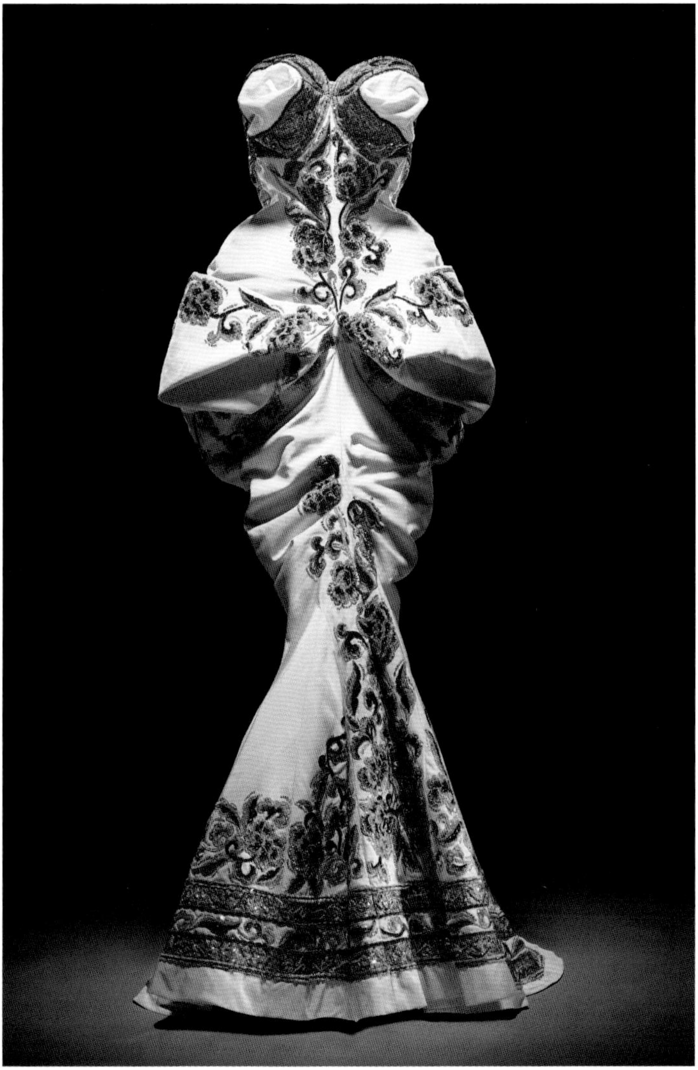

Long corset dress made of white moiré with coral embroidery, fall-winter 2004–5 collection. Photograph by Laziz Hamani.

Opposite:
Portrait of John Galliano by Peter Lindbergh.

Hedi Slimane took over Dior menswear in 2000, revolutionizing the male wardrobe with designs inspired by the underbelly of Berlin and London society. Slimane combined a louche romanticism—hat, narrow jacket, tie, and jeans—with the lanky silhouette of a slim fit. At the height of Slimane's glory, his former right-hand man, Kris Van Assche, took over the menswear throne, and the story of the house of Dior thus continues to unfold in a thrilling sequence of revolutions in styles and silhouettes. One constant, however, always remains—excellence in haute couture.

Dior Dresses

Name the designer.

Answer

1. YVES SAINT LAURENT, short silk dress, Armide, fall-winter 1959–60 collection. Silver-sequined white tulle. **2. CHRISTIAN DIOR,** Curaçao dress, fall-winter 1954–5 collection, H. Robe line in ivory faille, scoop neck with wide, gathered shoulder straps. **3. JOHN GALLIANO,** embroidered jacket with gray tennis lines, worn over a silk and skirt with blue and fuchsia polka dots, fall-winter 2003–4 collection. **4. MARC BOHAN,** cocktail dress, fall-winter 1967–8 collection, yellow satin by Abraham, fuchsia and gold embroidery by Mesrine.
5. GIANFRANCO FERRÉ, Koh-I-Noor dress, fall-winter 1996–7 collection, Indian Passion line. Pleated tulle dress with peach lace, embroidered with arabesques and paste jewels, stones, and gold beads.

1

2

3

4

5

Jacques Fath

• (1912–1954) - FRANCE
FRIVOLITY, FANTASY, MASCULINE ELEGANCE, YOUTH...
CHASUBLE, IRIS GRIS, CANASTA WATER, YANG, FATH BY FATH...

Two models—including Bettina, the star model discovered by Jacques Fath—wearing one of the designer's faille dresses (around 1950).

Jacques Fath was the enfant terrible of the fashion world in the 1940s and '50s—striking and unorthodox, young and elegant. His charming, lighthearted nature seemed out of place in the respectable, slightly stuffy world of haute couture at this time. Could he have been responsible for inventing the cult of the celebrity couturier? Given the plethora of photographs of Fath in the full fever of creation, it seems likely. In his time, he was the couturier in vogue, in the way that Lagerfeld, Galliano, and Lacroix were after him. His clients adored his youthful spirit, the freshness of his inspiration, and the touches of whimsy and imagination that spiced up his haute couture. His temperament was reflected in designs such as his reworked fur-lined jacket, turned inside out and transformed into a cocktail outfit, cut from satin, lace, and organza. He presented his shows as theatrical events sometimes with a comical theme, and had his models' hair cut in the latest styles by Georgel. The model Bettina, whom he personally discovered, was featured in numerous magazines sporting an urchinlike haircut—a Fath and Georgel collaboration. Other famous women assured Fath's reputation. The actress Rita Hayworth was a faithful client, and each of her visits to his couture house in Paris attracted attention in the fashion press. When Hayworth married Prince Aly Khan, Fath designed her sky-blue wedding gown.

Fath's unique personality extended to every part of the couture house he founded in 1937. Indeed, the house

became particularly renowned for the chic elegance of its hats—all of them initially modeled by the master himself. Unbridled and eccentric creativity reigned chez Fath, whether in the Calabrian brigand hat, the "jewel casket" hat (complete with lid), or the hat that featured fresh walnut shells—the contents of which had just been consumed by the couturier. His taste for party clothes and his instinct for publicity encouraged him to host balls at his country estate, Corbeville, just after the autumn collections; this meant he could receive American buyers in surroundings of suitable splendor and forge solid transatlantic bonds. Thus he orchestrated one of the earliest experiments in exporting ready-to-wear lines, bearing the label "designed in America by Jacques Fath for Joseph Halpert." For Americans who demanded the best goods at the best price, he created toiles and cuts that would inspire mass-manufactured models for his ready-to-wear line, Jacques Fath Université, launched in 1953. Sadly, Jacques Fath died at the height of his fame and his powers, struck down by leukemia at the age of forty-two.

Above:
Evening gowns by Fath (spring-summer 1951), with ample tops and skirts that recall the crinolines of the Second Empire.

What patent did Jacques Fath file in July 1945?

Pierre Balmain

- (1914–1982) - FRANCE
- PARISIANS, GOOD TASTE, PRETTY AND ESTABLISHED WOMEN...
- VENT VERT, BALMAIN, IVOIRE, MISS BALMAIN, MONSIEUR BALMAIN, JOLIE MADAME, EAU D'AMAZONIE, BALMYA, BALMAN...

Pierre Balmain, fully engaged in sculpting fabric, was a favorite subject of the press in the 1950s.

Pierre Balmain represented the quintessence of haute couture, of beautiful clothes for beautiful women. He was the declared enemy of superfluous decoration. "If a dress doesn't work during a fitting, you might as well destroy it. No amount of frills, accessories, or embellishments will ever save it; this is my credo," he said. His training as an architect revealed itself in this uncompromising approach, softened occasionally with touches of fantasy. Alongside his classic, impeccably cut suits and his dazzling ball gowns, a slightly longer silhouette emerged. Bold strokes, such as his coolie jacket for fall-winter 1945, showed off the full range of his imagination, as did the evening skirts decked in ermine or decorated with fish swimming beneath waves. Leopard-skin trousers even found their place in his fall-winter 1952 collection.

In the postwar period, Balmain offered women a return to opulence and charm. Gertrude Stein and Alice B. Toklas, who encouraged him to open his couture house, described his work as "the new French style." Or perhaps it was a Parisian style, more specifically, as when Balmain launched his series of Jolie Madame collections, featuring gowns with bustles and short cocktail dresses. An avid traveler, Balmain was also a self-appointed ambassador for French fashion in Asia, Australia, and South America. In 1953 he showed collections in Morocco and Algeria, in 1962 in South Africa, in 1970 in Lebanon and Afghanistan, and in 1971 in Iran.

After Balmain's death in 1982, the talented Erik Mortensen took his place. He was followed as artistic

! The "corbeille bra," which accentuates the bust. Fath believed that a beautiful bust was more important than the wasp waists obtained with a corset.

director by a succession of designers: Hervé Pierre, Oscar de la Renta, Christophe Lebourg, Laurent Mercier, and most recently, Christophe Decarnin.

Model wearing a dress of printed organdy on a taffeta skirt, drawing by Vertes and photograph by Horst P. Horst, circa 1953.

Cristóbal Balenciaga

• (1895–1972) - SPAIN
ANATOMY, AUSTERITY, SCULPTURE, SPANISH PAINTING, SPANISH COSTUME...
LE DIX, LA FUITE DES HEURES...

Portrait of Cristóbal Balenciaga circa 1952. All of the gentlemanly elegance of the Grand Master of Couture.

Opposite: Draped dress by Balenciaga.

Balenciaga was the master of creating the dress-as-sculpture to adorn the female body. He devoted his life to exalting the female physique by adjusting its proportions and thereby investing women's gestures and attitudes with grace. He favored sleek, distinguished looks over ostentatious glamour. A woman did not need to be a great beauty to be dressed by Balenciaga; his gowns would make her beautiful. A Balenciaga gown is recognizable by its lightness and ease of wear. Unlike his rivals, Balenciaga never needed to pad his shapes with tulle or squeeze them in with whalebone corsets. In 1958, Balenciaga joined forces with the Swiss textile manufacturer Abraham to make silk gazar fabric, diaphanous but stiff, which enabled him to build voluminous shapes without the aid of internal support.

Balenciaga started young. He worked with his mother, a dressmaker in Getaria, in the Spanish Basque country, and was encouraged by the Marquesa de Casa Torres. After serving his apprenticeship as a tailor, he opened his own couture house in San Sebastián. He would buy gowns from couturiers in Paris, take them apart, and put them back together again in his own way. With the start of the Spanish Civil War, Balenciaga was forced to leave Spain; he set up his Parisian couture house on Avenue Georges V in 1937. Buyers lost no time in showering the gifted young talent with praise, even if his relations with the fashion press were more strained, as he was deeply suspicious of anything that might lay his work open to copying. To protect his designs, he held his shows a month apart from the other Paris shows.

Spanish style imbued Balenciaga's work. He drew upon toreador boleros, duenna gowns, peasant headdresses, and fishermen's nets for inspiration. Paintings from the Spanish old masters inspired a palette of blacks and browns and brilliant shades against

somber backgrounds. He emulated the pure, almost abstract shapes of Velázquez's infantas, the skillfully hung pleats of Zurbarán, and the black lace of Goya. But the overwhelming preoccupation of the ascetic Balenciaga, who always worked in enigmatic silence, was with cut. His innumerable inventions in this field included his balloon dresses of the 1950s, semifitted looks, raised hemlines that dropped sharply at the back, baby-doll dresses, peacock's-tail gowns, sack dresses, kimono sleeves, and garments sewn without darts. The early 1960s marked the apotheosis of Balenciaga's success. But by 1965, the success of his former colleague, André Courrèges, convinced the once visionary designer that his time was past. In 1968 he abruptly closed his couture house, leaving the newspaper headlines to lament, "Balenciaga retires and fashion will never be the same again."

What was one special physical characteristic of Cristóbal Balenciaga?

House of Balenciaga

- HOUSE FOUNDED IN 1937 - SPAIN
- CRISTÓBAL BALENCIAGA (1937), MICHEL GOMA (1986), JOSEPHUS MELCHIOR THIMISTER (1992), NICOLAS GHESQUIÈRE (1997)
- QUADRILLE, HO HANG, PRÉLUDE, RUMBA, BALENCIAGA POUR HOMME, BALENCIAGA TALISMAN, CRISTOBAL...

Opposite:
A design from the Ghesquière collection as an homage to Cristóbal Balenciaga (fall 2006). The incline of the dress's cut emphasized the exaggerated gathers of the skirt.

Below:
Finale of the spring-summer 2007 show with a futuristic style, including robotic silhouettes inspired by Fritz Lang's film *Metropolis*.

After the retirement of its founder in 1968, the House of Balenciaga passed through several decades in obscurity before being purchased by the Gucci group in 2001, thanks to the growing fame of the house's young artistic director, Nicolas Ghesquière. His position as a leader of his generation had been felt since his start at Balenciaga in 1995, and having shown his ability to honor the line's heritage, Ghesquière proves, to this day, his capacity to call forth a unique vision. Even if each of his collections surprises, Ghesquière remains faithful to certain themes and references, including futurism and the movie *Star Wars*. Between cybernetic robots and classical beauties, the women of Ghesquière's imagination cultivate a detached elegance that seems to come from another world. His homage collection to Cristóbal Balenciaga in 2006—which focused on the relationship between the body and clothing, so dear to the grand master—was a brilliant interpretation and won him numerous magazine covers throughout the world. That year Ghesquière was named one of the 100 most influential people in the world by *Time* magazine; in 2008, he was named the world's top designer by the *Journal du Textile*. Ghesquière sees every collection as an occasion to test new subjects and materials, like neoprene sandwiched between two layers of refined silks inspired by those contained in the house's archives. The material is stiff yet malleable—a modern take on the silk gazar of the house's founder.

! His ambidexterity. He could cut or sew with either hand.

How much does it cost?

The Jacques Fath archives

Answer

$3,500,000 (around €2,550,000).
Sold in 2007, Neiman Marcus, United States.
This collection included 26 volumes of sketchbooks filled between 1948 and 1956
with more than 3,400 sketches of haute couture designs.
The collection also included haute couture dresses.

PRINTEMPS 1954

Nina Ricci

• (1883–1970) - ITALY
ELEGANCE FOR ITS OWN SAKE, ROMANTICISM, SPORT-CHIC, COLOR, CONTEMPORARY ART...
CŒUR JOIE, L'AIR DU TEMPS, FILLE D'ÈVE, CAPRICCI, FAROUCHE, SIGORICCI, PHILEAS, NINA, RICCI CLUB...

The timeless perfume L'Air du Temps, by Nina Ricci.

Below: Portrait of Madame Ricci.

Opposite: An Olivier Theyskens design for Nina Ricci, fall-winter 2007–8 collection.

In 1932, Nina Ricci was preparing to retire after a successful career in couture at Raffin, when her son, Robert, persuaded her to found her own couture house. He took care of the management of the family firm, leaving the creative side to his mother. Nina Ricci offered great technical expertise, elegant and understated designs, and no publicity: nothing but haute couture, always favoring stylish femininity over the latest fashion trends for a wealthy clientele seeking discreet good taste. The perfume l'Air du Temps, launched by Robert Ricci in 1948 with its celebrated bottle designed by Marc Lalique, would make the name Nina Ricci famous throughout the world, and became one of the greatest successes in the history of perfumery.

Madame Ricci looked to younger designers as well, and Robert Ricci recruited Jules-François Crahay to give the firm a boost in 1959. Crahay rediscovered a harmony between garments and the body, far removed from the geometric trends then fashionable. The collection was a triumph, and John Fairchild, then editor of the highly respected *Women's Wear Daily*, rushed to telegraph his approval to the editorial desk. The Crocus suit, with its slightly fitted jacket, met with universal approval and was sold a hundred times over.
Gerald Pipart proved a brilliant successor to Crahay in 1964.
A young man in tune with the latest trends, he brought with him a dual training in haute couture (at Balmain, Fath, Givenchy, and Patou) and ready-to-wear (at Chloé). Pipart set about reinventing the classics, bringing a sporty touch to couture, notably with his flounced jersey capes. He excelled in the romantic style: organdy, chiffon, gazar, and

pastel prints became his signature fabrics. In 1971, Robert Ricci commissioned a young English photographer to create a new publicity campaign for l'Air du Temps. David Hamilton, yet to find fame with his book *Dreams of a Young Girl*, interpreted the perfume so perfectly in his photographs that Robert Ricci offered him an exclusive contract, free of all artistic constraints. The images he produced, featuring the ballerina Suzanne Farrell, represent the perfection of perfume, dreams in their purest state. Several decades later, in 2006, the young designer Olivier Theyskens returned to these images when he was appointed artistic director by the Puig group, which bought Nina Ricci in 1998.

What is the standard design of the robe-chemise from the '20s?

Emilio Pucci

• (1914–1992) - ITALY
SPORT CHIC, CAPRI, FLORENTINE ARCHITECTURE, COLOR, OP ART, PSYCHEDELIC ART...
VIVARA, ZADIG...

! The ivory satin Lavallière dress designed by Paul Poiret in 1911.

Emilio Pucci, the Prince of Prints, was the master of a glamourous style that evoked the image of a life spent jet-setting between Gstaad and Capri. Born the Marchese Emilio Pucci di Barsento, scion of a venerable Florentine family, he grew up surrounded by the works of Botticelli, da Vinci, and Raphael. His strikingly good looks exuded a debonair man-about-town allure that captivated the American press, and, to cap it off, he was an athlete of distinction and a member of the Italian Olympic ski team in 1932. In the 1930s, he attended the University of Milan (and received a doctorate in political science from the University of Florence) as well as the University of Georgia before finally enrolling at Reed College, in Portland, Oregon, for a master's degree in social science. There he designed the college skiing team's uniform and so made his first improvised venture into couture. When *Harper's Bazaar* editor Diana Vreeland saw photographs by Toni Frissell showing Pucci on the slopes in an outfit of his own design, she contacted him with an offer to create some ski clothes for a 1948 issue. She also introduced him to the department store Lord & Taylor, which sold Pucci's first collection in the spring and summer of that year. So successful was this venture that two years later he launched his own boutique, La Canzone del Mare, on the island of Capri.
During his time as a student in the United States, Pucci noticed that American sportswear lacked the elegance and innovative flair found in French couture. And so he opened up a third, Italian, sensibility that straddled the line between sportswear and townwear. Pucci combined Italian

craftsmanship with industrial production techniques and French prestige with American pragmatism. His groundbreaking designs did away with the petticoats, linings, and padding that were so dear to Dior and instead used vibrant colors and exclusive prints to create his signature style. His bold, brightly colored prints recalled stained-glass windows, on the one hand, and anticipated psychedelic art on the other. The black, white, pink, and green marble marquetry of the facade of the Duomo in Florence—a stone's throw from the Palazzo Pucci, where he set up his ready-to-wear house—was also a constant source of inspiration. Other prints were inspired by Taormina, Agrigento, Sicily, and Bali. But above all, Capri would become the major source of his style. Pucci's trademark Capri look, an Italian counterpart to the Saint-Tropez style in France, was built around a summer wardrobe of swimsuits in nylon and Helanca synthetic silk, white cotton piqué skirts, shorts, Capri pants, straw hats, and suntanned bare feet—a look rapidly adopted on Mediterranean beaches by icons such as Marilyn Monroe, Grace Kelly, and Jacqueline Kennedy. In 2000 the company's leadership shifted to his daughter, Laudomia, who became image director of the brand when it was bought by LVMH.

Emilio Pucci surrounded by his models for the release of his perfume Vivara. Acapulco, February 1966.

Opposite:
A design painted on Veruschka, star model of Emilio Pucci, as photographed by Franco Rubartelli in 1966. Veruschka created her own makeup, coiffures, and styles for most of the photographs taken by her then-companion Rubartelli.

The Italian School

• FROM 1951 TO THE PRESENT
THE SISTERS FONTANA, VALENTINO, ROBERTO CAPUCCI, PRINCESS GALITZINE, MILA SCHÖN, ROBERTA DI CAMERINO, FIORUCCI, ARMANI, CERRUTI, VERSACE, ROBERTO CAVALLI, BOTTEGA VENETA, FENDI, PRADA, GUCCI, DOLCE & GABBANA, COSTUME NATIONAL, MARNI...

It is indicative of the deep roots and glorious history of Italian fashion that Mario Boselli, director of the country's trade association, is descended from a line of silk merchants stretching back to the sixteenth century. Long a hub of international commerce, Italy was the source of Florentine velvets and fine textiles from Sicily and Venice, which were

Missoni. Spring-summer 1996 collection. Photograph by Mario Testino.

considered the height of Renaissance luxury. During the following centuries, however, the fragmentation of the country into rival city-states weakened Italy's sway over international fashion. Finally, after World War II, Italy reemerged as one of the world's style capitals, and Italian fashion found a warm welcome in America.

Indeed, Italian and American styles had much in common. The major film studio Cinecittà, like Hollywood, encouraged a popular taste for elegance. The heroines of Italian cinema, such as Anna Magnani, Monica Vitti, and Sophia Loren, satisfied their audience's desire for the spectacular and the sexy while retaining an earthy realism. The Italians' highly developed artistic sensibility was tempered by a certain nonchalance and hedonism. And above all, the Italians were wedded to the notion of *fare bella figura*, literally, "make a beautiful figure," resulting in a heady stylistic mixture of pleasure and seductiveness. The quality of the supply chain guaranteed the success of the emerging Italian fashion industry, defined by a sense of decorum and luxurious fabrics—the essence of modern sportswear.

In February 1951, a show staged in Florence by Giovanni Battista Giorgini marked Italy's arrival among the movers and shakers of the international fashion world, with the participation of couture houses in Rome, such as Carosa, Alberto Fabiani, the Sisters Fontana, and Germana Marucelli, and ready-to-wear labels from Florence, including Bertoli, Gallotti, and Emilio Pucci.

From left to right: Gianfranco Ferré, Luciano Soprani, Aldo Ferrante, Giorgio Armani, and Walter Albini, with Mariuccia Mandelli of Krizia.

? Who was Valentina?

The Italian School

Below:
Roberto Cavalli, fall-winter 1997–8 collection.

Opposite :
Marni by the designer Consuelo Castiglioni in June 2002.

Eight American buyers were present, and the trade newspaper *Women's Wear Daily* trumpeted, "Italian Styles Gain Approval of U.S. Buyers." A second event in July brought together the designers of Florence, Milan, Rome, and Turin in front of 200 buyers. On this occasion, the French press expressed unease about the new rival on the fashion scene.

Italian designers continued to exploit the seductive image of la dolce vita until the 1960s. Simonetta designed the costumes for the Federico Fellini film of that name; the Sisters Fontana dressed numerous stars, including Ava Gardner and Elizabeth Taylor; Valentino designed Jacqueline Kennedy's wedding gown for her marriage to Aristotle Onassis; and Princess Irene Galitzine became known for her famous palazzo pajamas. In Milan reputations were made by Mila Schön, for her immaculate tailoring in double-faced wool; Roberta di Camerino, for her trompe l'oeil effects; Tai and Rosita Missoni, for their artistic fabrics and knits; and Elio Fiorucci, for his psychedelic style.

One of the keys to the success of Italian fashion lies in the country's textile manufacturers' willingness to invest financially in new talent. In the 1970s, the first generation of Italian designers was joined by Giorgio Armani, Nino Cerruti, and Gianni Versace, who gained international reknown. Leather, fur, and accessories ensured the success of many labels through the '80s and '90s, including Roberto Cavalli, Fendi, Gucci, Marni, Prada, and Bottega Veneta. Dolce & Gabbana, the latest success story (founded in 1985), meanwhile, has focused on updating the link between Italian fashion and cinema. The company's designers, Domenico Dolce and Stefano Gabbana, have declared that they set out "to make stars look like stars."

! Valentina Nicholaevna Sanina Schlee (1899–1989) was a Russian designer who fled the 1917 revolution. Her fashion house, with shops in New York and Paris, dressed Greta Garbo, Katharine Hepburn, Paulette Godard, and Gloria Swanson.

Writers' words

Who said what?

Voltaire

Alexander Pope

Oscar Wilde

Victor Hugo

Jean Cocteau

Françoise Sagan

Francis Bacon, Sr.

George Bernard Shaw

Mark Twain

Jean Cocteau

Hubert de Givenchy

• (1927–) - FRANCE
BALENCIAGA, AUDREY HEPBURN, PAINTING, SPORTS, CONTEMPORARY ART...
LE DÉ, L'INTERDIT, MONSIEUR DE GIVENCHY, VÉTIVER, GENTLEMAN, INSENSÉ, AMARIGE...

Opposite:
Audrey Hepburn with Hubert de Givenchy, a duo who inspired a legend of beauty and elegance.

Bettina wearing her famous namesake blouse.

The perfect lines of Hubert de Givenchy remain the unassailable benchmark throughout the world for the ineffable superiority of elegance *à la française*. And of course, no one embodied his designs quite so gloriously as the British-born Hollywood icon Audrey Hepburn. In Givenchy's designs for the films *Breakfast at Tiffany's* and *Funny Face*, the tradition of haute couture met the postwar spirit of youth to devastating effect.

Born into an aristocratic, artistic family, Givenchy served his apprenticeship with the couturiers Jacques Fath, Robert Piguet, and Lucien Lelong and spent some years running Elsa Schiaparelli's boutique. These years would prove influential when Givenchy struck out on his own. In 1952 he opened his couture house, and the following year friends and models supported the launch of his first collection. The star of that first show was the model Bettina, who also gave her name to a blouse in raw cotton and broderie anglaise. She shared the spotlight with his separates, skirts and tops to mix and match, which attracted attention and propelled the collection to immediate success. In 1954 Givenchy launched Givenchy Université, one of the first luxury ready-to-wear lines, with the manufacturer Jean Prouvost.

Inspired both by the grace of Audrey Hepburn, his muse for forty years, and by the influence of his spiritual mentor, Cristóbal Balenciaga, Givenchy created lines

of purity and restraint, architectural and sublimely sophisticated. The great Spanish designer's influence was particularly evident in Givenchy's pencil-slim lines and geometric approach. Upon his former mentor's retirement in 1968, Givenchy inherited Balenciaga's clientele, including the Duchess of Windsor, Greta Garbo, Marlene Dietrich, Elizabeth Taylor, Lauren Bacall, Princess Grace of Monaco, Mrs. Henry Ford, and Diana Ross. From Schiaparelli, meanwhile, he retained the notion of using whimsical details, such as decorative buttons and pockets, to highlight the perfection of the cut. Hubert de Givenchy's own natural elegance laid the foundations for his men's ready-to-wear line, launched in 1973, and the label continued to diversify into accessories, home decoration, and automobiles.

?

For whom was the perfume L'Interdit by Givenchy created?

House of Givenchy

- HOUSE FOUNDED IN 1951
- HUBERT DE GIVENCHY (1951), JOHN GALLIANO (1996), ALEXANDER MCQUEEN (1997), JULIEN MCDONALD (2001), RICCARDO TISCI (2005)
  GIVENCHY HOMME: OZWALD BOATENG (2003), RICCARDO TISCI (2008)
- YSATIS, ANGE OU DÉMON, ORGANZA, HOT COUTURE, VERY IRRESISTIBLE...

Givenchy haute couture show by Alexander McQueen, spring-summer 1997.

In 1988, Hubert de Givenchy sold his couture house to LVMH and retired from the helm in 1995, leaving his position as artistic director to a succession of brilliant young designers: first, the Brits John Galliano and Alexander McQueen, and then the Welshman Julien Macdonald. The British tailor Ozwald Boateng served as creative director of Givenchy Homme from 2003 to 2008. He has been succeeded by Riccardo Tisci, lauded by the fashion press since his arrival in 2005 at Givenchy Femme.

Tisci's enigmatically beautiful romantic-futurist collections have made the label one of the most watched and copied in the fashion world. His first collections had a mysterious and somber allure. He draped black veils over his models, recalling the religious processions observable in Italy.

Historical references do not scare Tisci, and he knows how to interpret them without copying them directly from the museum. An eighteenth-century whalebone corset, for example, might develop a cartoonish aesthetic in Tisci's hands. His haute-couture collections take advantage of this graphic edge. When combined with his vitrtuoso draping and cutting, Tisci presents a baroque approach to dressing with a purist's sensibility. Although his references to the house's tradition are equally present alongside his own flourishes, they remain unnoticeable except to the trained eye. Today the house is a jewel in the crown of LVMH, made newly contemporary by Tisci's anointment of the model Maria Carla Boscano as the twenty-first century successor to Hubert de Givenchy's muse, Audrey Hepburn.

! Audrey Hepburn. Created in January 1957, only the actress had the right to wear it. The perfume was not available for sale until December 1957.

Givenchy haute couture show by Riccardo Tisci, spring-summer 2007.

THE FASHION GAZETTE

CURRENT AFFAIRS AND NEWS

• Will the an-atomic bomb hit the beaches?

The bikini, the super-small two-piece swimsuit (named by its creator, Louis Réart, after the atoll where the United States conducts its nuclear tests), has experienced a difficult start: no model would agree to wear it, so on June 23rd it was presented by a nude dancer from a Paris casino. The demonstration's conclusion? An explosive effect! (1946)

• A New Art
"Pronounce the words 'cosmetic surgery' and you will be astonished by the lively reactions of those in earshot.
And yet, cosmetic surgery is not just for aging flirts resisting the work of time on their bodies.
It may have a useful role, especially among the young. Parents should consider it for their children: an ugly face will be of no help in life. (…) What can cosmetic surgery accomplish? (…) Breast corrections are the most frequently requested operations. (…) For flappy ears, ablating a crescent-shaped piece of cartilage from the ear will suffice." (excerpt from *Vogue*, 1939)

• Swimsuit a no-no
"Those women must put their clothes back on!" The municipality of Juan les Pins wants to keep swimsuits on the beaches! Summer-goers to the French Riviera will perhaps soon no longer be allowed to leave the beach while wearing this outfit, which flouts decency. (1928)

• A red, white and blue collection! In this difficult year of 1941, Alix Grès presented her first collection in the colors of France. This act of bravado against the German occupier was good enough to have the authorities shut down her house for the year to come. (1941)

• 1940: Parisian couture continues…

Jeanne Lanvin
who has never closed her house, presents her new designs, dresses and hats
22, Faubourg Saint-Honoré

Lucien Lelong
is currently showing his midseason collection
16, Avenue Matignon

Hermés
Will send its 1940 RECOMMENDATIONS on request
24, Faubourg Saint-Honoré

RUMORS AND SCANDALS

- **Summer 1934.** Fashion is showing us quite beautiful legs, in outfits that are more elegant than a simple swimsuit: women's shorts are worn with a polo shirt, a swimsuit top, or for the more audacious, a simple scarf knotted over the bosom.
- **Summer 1940.** The couturier Norman Hartnell has just been summoned by the Queen of England to revise her requirements for dress in light of the upcoming hostilities. He has been instructed to follow governmental laws concerning the austerity of uniforms and must now propose designs with a limited number of cuts, straight belts, and as few frills as possible. Lace is henceforth forbidden!

March 1947.
Not everyone is happy about the *New Look*

A photo session for Christian Dior dresses turned into a riot on Rue Lepic, in the very heart of the Montmartre market. The photographer had intended to replace the usual photo-shoot settings of the edge of the Seine, the Champs-Elysées, or the Place de la Concorde with this typically Parisian location. However, he did not count on the housewives of this modest neighborhood, who were shocked by the luxurious spread in the depths of the rationing period. The outraged housewives turned on the models, ripping their long, flowing skirts, some of which required up to twenty-five yards of fabric to create!

American Women Never Fail

From war to sportswear

Paris, the historic capital of haute couture, is now off-limits to New York couturiers. Alas, will this spell the end of haute couture?
Not at all! Even now, across the Atlantic, proud America is revolutionizing our clothing fashions. Hattie Carnegie, Tina Leser, Vera Maxwell, and Clare Potter… these are the pioneers who, during this period of rationing, are shortening the skirts and reinventing the cardigan. It would even appear that McCalls, which sells sewing patterns to American housewives, has released patterns that will allow men's suits to be transformed into women's suits, and womens dresses into children's clothing! Ever mindful of propagating this "casual" style, a "Best Dressed List" has supposedly been created under the aegis of the publicist Eleanor Lambert to identify those clients that are the most elegantly clothed by these magicians of the economic style. (1940)

Haute couture

From World War II to the present

Opposite:
Spectacular shows capture the attention of the press: a Dior haute couture show in 2003.

The first show by Jean-Louis Scherrer in 1963; the intimate character of the show was intended to win over private clientele.

During World War II, the German occupation of Paris naturally curtailed the activities of haute couture houses and obliged them to establish regulated procedures. After dismissing an idea to move the couture houses of Paris to Vienna and Berlin, the Chambre Syndicale faced a new struggle to find raw materials. Couturiers had always derived a large portion of their revenue from the sale of toile patterns to export agents and were therefore particularly hard-hit by rationing. Fashion houses benefited from a special governmental dispensation in return for enforcing strict membership criteria, which are maintained today.

After the liberation, Parisian haute couture faced an urgent mission: the reconquest of foreign markets lost during the Occupation. The Petit Théâtre de la Mode (Miniature Fashion Theater), an exhibition of dolls dressed in tiny versions of couture gowns, embarked on a propaganda tour of Europe in 1945 and America in 1946. Cristóbal Balenciaga, Pierre Balmain, Jacques Fath, Hubert de Givenchy, Madame Grès, Jacques Griffe, and Madame Carven were the stars of 1950s Paris couture, with Norman Hartnell in London and Mainbocher, Hattie Carnegie, Charles James, and Norman Norell in New York. But it was Christian Dior, with his voluptuous designs, who reaped the greatest success from a public starved for fashion and decadence.

The 1960s marked the end of this postwar golden age and the rise of a new avant-garde couture, as represented by Yves Saint Laurent, Pierre Cardin, André Courrèges, Louis Féraud, Paco Rabanne, Emanuel Ungaro, Guy Laroche, Ted Lapidus,

Jean-Louis Scherrer, Valentino, and Philippe Venet. After the revolutionary uproar of 1968—when haute couture, as a symbol of the bourgeois establishment, suddenly seemed outmoded—few new houses were founded. The last were Torrente in 1970, Per Spook in 1977, and Christian Lacroix in 1987. The current "official members" of the Chambre Syndicale's haute couture division are: Adeline André, Anne Valérie Hash, Chanel, Christian Dior, Christian Lacroix, Dominque Sirop, Emanuel Ungaro, Franck Sorbier, Givenchy, and Jean Paul Gaultier. After losing much of its status during the 1970s, it would appear that haute couture is now poised to come back into fashion, with the interest in luxury on the rise.

? When was the first sewing machine designed?

Yves Saint Laurent

• (1936–2008) - ALGERIA
ART, LITERATURE, MODERNITY, SPORTS OUTFITS, MEN'S CLOTHING, IMAGINARY TRAVELS
OPIUM, ELLE, YSL PARIS, BABY DOLL, YOUNG SEXY LOVELY, L'HOMME, KOUROS…

Cover of *Life* magazine with a dress from the Pop collection by Yves Saint Laurent, fall-winter 1966–7.

Below: Black crepe and lace dress, fall-winter 1970 collection.

Known as the Little Prince of couture, Yves Saint Laurent was still very young when he entered fashion history and became a living link between the grand manner of old-style haute couture and the contemporary face of exclusive ready-to-wear.

Winner of the Woolmark prize of the International Wool Secretariat, Yves Saint Laurent was recruited by Christian Dior in 1954, aged just eighteen, and soon became Dior's right-hand man. Upon Dior's sudden death in 1957, the young prodigy took over the artistic direction of the house and enjoyed an immense success with his Trapeze collection. Meeting Pierre Bergé would prove a turning point in his career: after being released from his contract with Dior, Saint Laurent went into partnership with Bergé and founded his own couture house in 1962, YSL. Despite the modesty of Saint Laurent's premises and means, his collections stunned the fashion press with their combination of modernism and elegance. In 1965 his Mondrian collection, a tribute to the artist's work, received worldwide coverage. But it was the following year, with his dinner jackets, that Yves Saint Laurent entered the mythology of the great style revolutionaries. The tuxedo

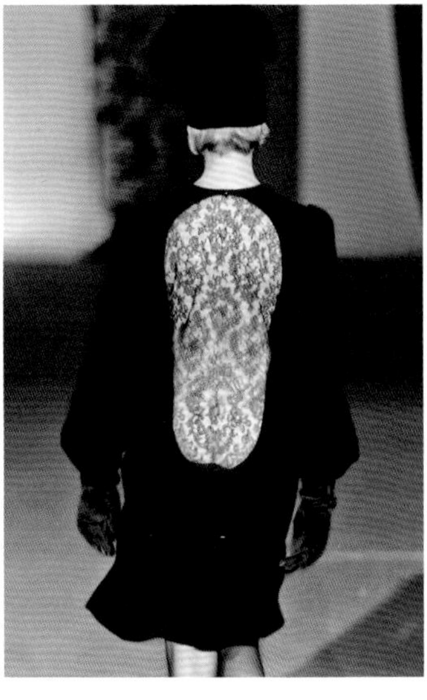

! In 1830, the Parisian tailor Barthélémy Thimonnier filed a patent for a wooden machine that would produce a chain stitch. The American Elias Howe, followed by Isaac Merritt Singer, improved the system.

Black-and-white striped wool pantsuit, spring-summer 1967 collection, the essence of the male-female style launched by Yves Saint Laurent.

introduced masculine elements into the female wardrobe and lent women's clothes a new dynamism and confidence. With his Pop and African collections, Saint Laurent sealed his position as the master of a new femininity, androgynous and liberated. These collections, along with the 1966 launch of his Rive Gauche ready-to-wear collection in a small gallery-boutique on Rue de Tournon in Paris, attracted worldwide attention.

In 1971, his 1940s-inspired collection caused a scandal, as its retro style reawakened memories of the Nazi occupation. But it opened the way to a seductively glamorous reinterpretation of the aesthetic of the period. Also at this time, he overturned the orthodox color palette to create unexpected combinations and sometimes violent clashes. Voyages of the imagination—to Spain, Morocco, India, China, Japan—lent the power of their mystery to his collections.

On January 7, 2002, Yves Saint Laurent announced his decision to shut down his couture house, marking the occasion with a retrospective show featuring 300 of his designs. However, the ultimate consecration of his work had come years earlier. In 1983 the Metropolitan Museum of Art presented an exhibition on the couturier, the first living designer whose work has been honored by a museum during his lifetime.

Boutiques
The style boutique

- STARTING FROM THE 1960s
- BIBA, DOROTHÉE, LAURA, VICTOIRE, LA PETITE GAMINERIE, PARAPHERNALIA, FIORUCCI...

Fashion boutiques appeared in the 1960s as pioneering outlets of the original designer prêt-à-porter collections. In order to attract the new youth market, these early boutiques did not merely display selections of the latest trendy clothes and accessories but rather invited their clientele into an all-enveloping world of fashion, where the style of the clothes was echoed by both the decor and the background music.

London's Carnaby Street and its boutiques—notably Lord Kitchener's Valet—became the epicenter of Swinging London. In 1964, Barbara Hulanicki opened her Biba boutique on Abingdon Road, Kensington, and by the early 1970s the new and bigger Biba boutique on Kensington Church Street had become a cult destination. Biba incorporated highly distinctive decor based on a mixture of Art Nouveau and Art Deco influences, a logo by Antony Little; and a highly desirable range of clothes, accessories, and makeup at affordable prices to attract a wide range of trendsetters, from students to rock stars. Paris had La Petite Gaminerie, made to resemble a white, labyrinthine grotto; Dorothée, founded by Elie Jacobson in 1958; Laura, at which Sonia Rykiel designed for a time; and Victoire, founded in 1964. In New York, Paraphernalia opened on Lexington Avenue in 1968. The previous year, Elio Fiorucci launched his first boutique in Milan, a sort of pop bazaar crammed with clothes and accessories in loud colors, gimmicky but indispensable for each passing season.

After 1966, psychedelic boutiques

Cher trying on a mini dress at Paraphernalia, circa 1967.

Opposite: Modeling a hat in the Biba boutique of Kensington in London, 1966.

multiplied under the influence of the hippie movement. Brothers Ron and Jay Thelin founded the short-lived Psychedelic Shop in the heart of San Francisco's Haight-Ashbury district. Though only in business from January 1966 to October 1967, the Haight Street shop was an essential part of the Summer of Love. The heart of psychedelic London, however, was alive and well on Newburgh Street, off Carnaby, and Jean Bouquin opened the Paris equivalent—an Aladdin's cave of fashion, where Brigitte Bardot and other chic hippies had outfits made to measure from fabrics brought back from exotic destinations.

?

Who is the only living couturier to whom Rei Kawakubo has paid tribute?

Leather

From Marlon Brando to Jean-Claude Jitrois

- FROM THE 1950S TO THE PRESENT
- SCHOTT BROTHERS, JEAN-CLAUDE JITROIS...
- PERFECTO, AVIATOR JACKET...

Leather, the ultimate embodiment of adolescent rebellion, didn't just enter the consciousness of a generation; it blazed through on an open road and took over its urban wardrobe. In 1928, Irving Schott of Schott Brothers, New York, designed the Perfecto, the first leather motorcycle jacket. In 1953, Marlon Brando immortalized the Schott Perfecto in László Benedek's *The Wild One*, sealing the leather biker jacket's the bad-guy reputation. In Britain, Lewis Leathers was soon producing its own faithful reproductions. In 1959, the French equivalent of the Hell's Angels were dubbed *les blousons noir* by the press. These were working-class rebels who rejected the mundane routine of everyday life and harbored no illusions about their future. Their black leather motorcycle jackets or sheepskin flying jackets were to become the symbol of their anger and their tribal identity, while popular opinion attributed to them a lurid and lawless lifestyle.

It took the Perfecto several decades to shake off this hell-raising reputation. Rock stars from Gene Vincent to Bruce Springsteen—including, the Ramones, Lou Reed, Jim Morrison and the Doors, the Clash, and George Michael—sported leather jackets as a sign of their street credibility. In 1960, Yves Saint Laurent anticipated the black leather jacket's move from rebellion to mainstream, causing a scandal in the hallowed halls of haute couture with his Beatnik collection for Dior. During the 1970s, the style reappeared on haute couture runways, this time on female models: Jean Paul Gaultier caused a sensation in his spring-summer 1977 collection with a black leather jacket, tutu, and sneakers, while Claude Montana and Thierry Mugler flirted even more thrillingly with the erotic connotations of all-over black leather. Azzedine Alaïa sheathed the female body in black leather, zipped or laced and hugging the curves of breasts and buttocks. In Gianni Versace's hands, it became shamelessly sexy. Today, these figure-hugging leather garments are also comfortable to wear thanks to the invention of stretch leather by Jean-Claude Jitrois.

! Azzedine Alaïa

The model Tuuli wearing a dipped lambskin jacket, croco-embroidery, fox collar, and gloves made of dipped lambskin.
Photograph by John Rankin for the Jitrois advertising campaign, fall-winter 2006–7 collection.

Yves Saint Laurent

To which artist is he paying tribute?

Answer

1. PIET MONDRIAN, fall-winter 1965–6 collection; **2. HENRI MATISSE**, fall-winter 1980 collection; **3. VINCENT VAN GOGH**, embroidery by Lesage, spring-summer 1988 collection; **4. GEORGES BRAQUE**, embroidery by Lesage, spring-summer 1988 collection.

1

2

GEORGES BRAQUE

•

HENRI MATISSE

•

PIET MONDRIAN

•

VINCENT VAN GOGH

3

4

The Trench Coat

• FROM THE 1930S TO THE PRESENT
BURBERRY, AQUASCUTUM...
TIELOCKEN, AIR-WARM, TRENCH COAT...

Opposite:
The famous Burberry trench coat, revisited once more for the spring-summer 2008 collection.

Audrey Hepburn in *Charade* by Stanley Donen, 1963.

Authentic, functional, indestructible, and constantly in fashion for more than a century, the trench coat is both ageless and timeless.

The design for the first trench coat for British officers was submitted to the War Office by Thomas Burberry in 1901. At the onset of fighting in 1914, the British army commissioned Burberry to supply a practical rain-coat that was more adaptable than the heavy wool greatcoat. Cut from a tightly woven, waterproof gabardine developed by Burberry in 1880, the first true trench coat featured a host of innovations, including a tongue to hold the collar closed, a deep back yoke to offer protection from the rain, front yokes to wedge a rifle butt, shoulder straps to accommodate a cap or an item of kit, buckled cuff straps to preserve body heat, and a belt with metal D-rings from which to hang grenades and a sword. During World War II, the design was adopted by the American, German, and Russian armies.

Cinema was instrumental in making the trench coat a fashion item; Humphrey Bogart was rarely seen without one, and numerous actresses were drawn to its heroic and slightly roguish chic. Marlene Dietrich, Greta Garbo, Lauren Bacall, Katharine Hepburn, Ingrid Bergman, and Catherine Deneuve exploited the trench coat's mannish glamour to devastating effect. And since Yves Saint Laurent introduced the trench coat into haute couture, few design-ers and couturiers have not attempt-ed a new spin on this wardrobe staple. Several outdoor-wear

companies, including Barbour and Aquascutum, have introduced variations on the theme, but Burberry remains the authentic label, instantly recognizable by its tartan lining, a registered trademark.

The trench coat has become one of fashion's most versatile items: short or long, in its original gray or beige or in bright colors, in day or evening versions, it has been adapted to all genres, from the most classic to the most avant-garde. In Burberry advertising campaigns since the year 2000, Kate Moss has restored its ineffably British charm, somewhere between tradition and cheekiness. In 2007, Lady Amanda Harlech, muse of John Galliano and subsequently of Karl Lagerfeld at Chanel, lent the trench a contemporary allure in a campaign for Gap.

? Where do the terms "jeans" and "denim" come from?

T-shirts

- FROM THE 1960S TO THE PRESENT
- FRUIT OF THE LOOM, GAP, HANES, AMERICAN APPAREL...
- TIE-DYED T-SHIRTS AND SLOGAN T-SHIRT...

! The fabrics used to make jeans probably come from the twill cotton from Nimes (*de Nimes*—hence “denim”) and *fustains* (a mixture of cotton and linen or wool) imported from Genoa and listed as “jean” or “jeane” in the logbooks of the Port of London, based on their port of shipment.

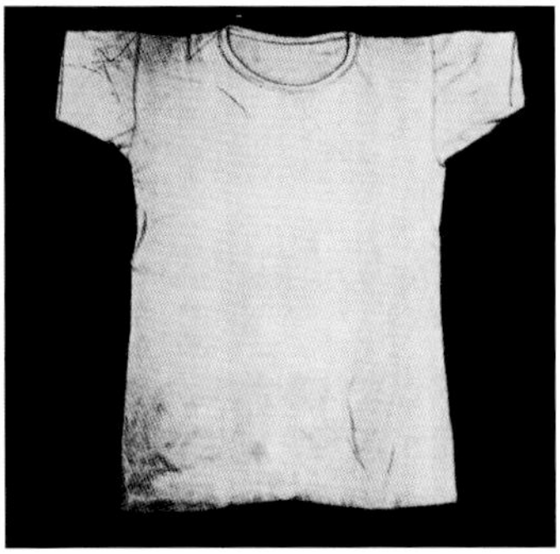

Named for its T shape, this most humble of garments, the T-shirt, shares with jeans the distinction of clothing three-quarters of the population of the planet.

Its modest origins lie in the singlet, or undershirt, to which manual laborers would strip down on hot days. In 1899, the undershirt became part of the regulation uniform for the U.S. Navy, and Europeans first discovered them as worn by G.I.’s in World War II.

It was the cinema of the 1950s that sealed the legend of the cotton jersey undershirt. In 1951, Marlon Brando appeared in a sweat-soaked T-shirt in *A Streetcar Named Desire*, his glistening torso instantly endowing it with sex appeal.

In *The Wild Bunch* a few years later, James Dean established the T-shirt as the symbol of the rebellious teenager. In 1960, the *New York Herald Tribune* T-shirt worn by Jean Seberg as a newspaper seller in Jean-Luc Godard’s film *Breathless* raised it to the level of a cult object. Soon it was claimed by pop culture as a means of expression, a blank slate on which to print.

Tie-dyed T-shirts were all the rage among Woodstock-era hippies, who emblazoned revolutionary maxims across them, and Andy Warhol’s Factory crew, who printed them with advertising slogans. Tight and covering the hips during

The shocking combination of an archetypal Chanel-style braided jacket and a sailor's T-shirt illustrates how Karl Lagerfeld reforms the codes of couture.

Opposite:
Top:
Created for the American army, this shirt's T shape would give its name to this undergarment.
Bottom:
T-shirt designed by Agnès B.

this period, designs became looser in the late 1970s, before shrinking again in the 1990s to leave girls' midriffs bare.

After the ubiquitous rock-band motifs of the 1970s and '80s, fashion designers at houses such as Chanel and Dior (with "J'Adore") used the heretofore down-market T-shirt to emblazon their labels. In 1984, designer Katharine Hamnett, originator of the "Choose Life" antidrug T-shirt, wore a "58 Percent Don't Want Pershing" shirt to meet with then Prime Minister Margaret Thatcher, a protest against basing Pershing missiles in the Britain. Today's T-shirts are increasingly used to broadcast political or philanthropic messages, as in Gap's (Product) RED line or the "Fashion Targets Breast Cancer" campaign, sales of which benefit their causes.

Metal dress and headdress by Paco Rabanne worn by Maud Betelsen on the Diablerets glacier in 1968.
Photograph by Gunnar Larsen.

Paco Rabanne

- (1934–) - SPAIN
- SCULPTURE AND CONTEMPORARY ARCHITECTURE, AVANT-GARDE, UNCONVENTIONAL MATERIALS, JEWELS, EGYPT, METAL...
- CALANDRE, MÉTAL, PACO RABANNE POUR HOMME, LA NUIT, EAU DE SPORT, TÉNÉRÉ, XS POUR HOMME, BLACK XS, ULTRAVIOLET...

Francisco Rabaneda Cuervo, graduate in architecture from the École Nationale des Beaux Arts and prizewinner at the Paris Biennale of 1963, was an artist and sculptor before becoming the futurist couturier we know today. With the help of his sister, who worked for the costume jeweler Roger Jean-Pierre, and his mother, a former chief seamstress at Balenciaga, he started out in the fashion world by making accessories for haute couture houses. Soon his jewelry, made of Rhodoid plastic, and his sunglasses and visors, brought a contemporary éclat to the creations of his friends, "the girls": Emmanuelle Khanh, Christiane Bailly, and Michèle Rosier. Rabanne's first haute couture collection debuted in February 1966. His collection "Twelve experimental and unwearable dresses in contemporary materials" attracted a great deal of attention. To a soundtrack of *Le marteau sans maître*, by Pierre Boulez, barefoot models paraded in minidresses made from Rhodoid "chain mail" plates constructed by Paco Rabanne himself using jewelry techniques. Other unusual materials followed, including riveted leather; affordable "throwaway" paper dresses, assembled in three minutes; the "Giffo" garment in seamless molded plastic; knitted fake fur; lacquered aluminum "chain mail" tops; plastic-coated Calais lace; the KIT line in toile, assembled with press studs; "Nida" bubble material used in aeronautics; laser discs; optical fiber and more.

The conceptual aspect of Rabanne's creations often left the fashion world baffled. Françoise Hardy and her dress of a thousand gold plates brought his metallic dresses into fashion, and Jane Fonda injected them with sex appeal in Roger Vadim's 1968 film *Barbarella*, but few ordinary women dared to wear his creations. Rabanne—mockingly nicknamed "the metallurgist" by Coco Chanel—moreover built his reputation on experimental haute couture, supporting this loss-making activity through a variety of licensing agreements and ready-to-wear lines.

Although the company was incorporated into the Puig group in 1968, Paco Rabanne continued to be in charge of the creative side and today remains as provocative as ever, sparking headlines even outside of the world of fashion design.

?

Whom does Paco Rabanne claim to have been in his previous lives?

André Courrèges

• (1923–) - FRANCE
FUTURISM, BAUHAUS, LIGHT, DESIGN...
EMPREINTE, EAU DE COURRÈGES, COURRÈGES IN BLUE, SWEET COURRÈGES, COURRÈGES 2020...

! A priest in the court of Pharaoh Amenophis III and, prior to that, an inhabitant of the planet Altair.

The 1960s, with its fresh new focus on youth, the modern world, and building the future, is inextricably linked with the spirit of André Courrèges. In the summer of 1965, Courrèges exploded onto the fashion scene with his "bombshell" (*la bombe Courrèges*, as the French still describe it), and the press went wild. Courrèges dressed his models in minidresses and futuristic trouser suits, to the outrage of the fashion establishment.

In fact, Courrèges dressed women in types of clothing formerly reserved for young girls, spicing the looks up with trousers for both day and evening wear and pairing them with flat shoes instead of high heels. His predominantly geometric designs, precision-cut from stiff, double-sided wool, projected an image of dynamic, youthful energy, which he accentuated initially with white (the color of light, according to Courrèges) and then, from the summer of 1967 onward, with pink and sky blue.

Through his mastery of the relationship between body and fabric, Courrèges showed himself a worthy heir to the spirit of Cristóbal Balenciaga, whose atelier Courrèges had headed from 1950 to 1961. In 1961, in partnership with his wife and creative alter ego, Coqueline, he launched his own couture house. His experience as a sculptor of clothes would now be reinforced by his passion for architecture and his early training as a civil engineer. At the same time, he softened the austerity of this architectural approach with the use of sequins, simple flower appliqués, Rhodoid portholes, and puffs of mink or feathers. A pioneer in the democratization of luxury, Courrèges divided his activities into separate lines early on, launching Couture Future in 1967, followed by Hyperbole and Prototype in 1970. In 1972 he built a factory in his native Pau, France, where he perfected numerous innovations, including his famous "second skin" of white mesh worn over a microskirt in 1969.

Influenced by artists of the Bauhaus, Courrèges extended his creative activities to embrace a whole range of different domains, including accessories, design, gastronomy, and real estate. In 1972 he designed the French uniforms for the Munich Olympics, and in 2001 he was represented at the Foire International d'Art Contemporain. In 1985 the Courrèges couture house was sold to the Japanese group Itokin, though Coqueline continued to oversee its designs.

Ten years later, André and Coqueline Courrèges bought back all the shares in their couture house, followed in 1996 by Courrèges Parfums, and so regained complete freedom of action in both the financial and creative spheres.

"Future couture" coat, with combination knitted second-skin tights, mittens and hat with knit garter stitches, 1969. Photograph by Peter Knapp.

Opposite:
"Second skin" suit, vinyl jacket and accessories, 1970. Photograph by Peter Knapp.

Pierre Cardin

• (1922–) - ITALY
THE FUTURE, ARCHITECTURE, THE CONQUEST OF SPACE, DESIGN, AVANT-GARDE...
CHOC, CENTAURES, ÉNIGME, PIERRE CARDIN POUR MONSIEUR, BLEU MARINE, OPHÉLIE, REVÉLATION, ROSE, TRISTAN & YSEULT...

Pierre Cardin designs, 1968.

Opposite:
A Pierre Cardin design, 1971. Cardin's futuristic style is rife with skillful cuts and geometric motifs.

The grand old man of the fashion industry, Pierre Cardin has built a vast and multifaceted empire, marrying an acute sense of design with shrewd business flair. He is now the last major couturier to be the sole independent proprietor of his own label. And his place in fashion history is guaranteed as the inventor of unisex fashions and an innovative designer of menswear.

After being apprenticed to tailors in Saint-Etienne, in the Loire region, and in Vichy, in 1945 Pierre Cardin went to work with Jeanne Paquin, where he made the costumes for Jean Cocteau's 1946 film *Beauty and the Beast*. After a period with Elsa Schiaparelli and then with Christian Dior, where he was chief tailor, Cardin founded his own couture house in 1950. His first haute couture collection, three years later, was a triumph. To make his creations—notably his famous bubble dresses—more accessible, he opened two boutiques, Eve and Adam. This move toward the democratization of haute couture and the young designer's unprecedented system of licensing agreements led to his expulsion from the Chambre Syndicale. Despite this snub, he would be widely imitated.

These two ideas, accessibility and licensing, would form the bedrock of the Cardin company. With the manufacturer Georges Bril, Cardin organized the distribution of his menswear in Europe, the Middle East, and North Africa. He made news by opening a boutique within the Printemps department store in 1962, scandalizing the traditional clientele with futuristic ready-to-wear designs. However, *Elle* magazine enthusiastically supported the endeavor, which launched a press campaign for the democratization of fashion. Articles about Cardin

appeared in magazines, as the outfits he designed for the Beatles and his zippered "cosmocorps" suits became emblematic of 1960s modernity. His unmistakable style—featuring geometric motifs, asymmetry, oversized buttons and collars, hooped dresses, vinyl inserts, and other experimental ideas such as the "Cardine," an automatic dress manufacturing system—continues to influence numerous designers, including Marc Jacobs.

Pierre Cardin succeeded in appending his signature on a staggering range of products; everything from food to furniture via ballpoint pens, razors, and toilet paper bears the Pierre Cardin label. The Cardin offices on Place Beauveau in Paris now administer hundreds of these licences, and the company boasts a workforce of 200,000, 840 factories, and annual profits of 35 million euros.

?

What was special about the models who walked the runway for Pierre Cardin's first men's fashion collection?

Shoes
The birth of the luxury shoe

- FROM THE 1950S TO THE 1970S
- BALLY, CHARLES JOURDAN, ISRAËL MILLER, HERMAN DELMAN...
- SPIKE-HEELED PUMP, THIGH-HIGH BOOTS...

By the 1960s, the availability of ready-to-wear rendered made-to-measure craftsmanship obsolete, and bespoke shoemakers followed dressmakers and milliners into virtual extinction. High-class shoe manufacturers lost no time in assuming the mantle of their evocative craft, however. The Swiss firm Bally, founded in Schönenwerd in 1851, developed a marketing strategy focused on the alliance of respected, age-old traditions with the benefits of mass production. It was a bold claim, but Bally was able to live up to it, thanks to its control of the entire chain of production, from the leather-tanning process to the retail outlet, with its exclusive network of boutiques. Other successful shoemakers who combined craftsmanship and availability included Charles Jourdan, who started as a foreman in a shoe factory; in 1921 he founded his own shoemaking business in the town of Romans, in southeastern France. Jourdan would become one of the pioneers of luxury ready-to-wear shoes, enjoying huge success with his Séducta line. At the opening of his first Paris boutique in 1957, a long queue waited patiently on Boulevard de la Madeleine for a glimpse of Brigitte Bardot and the opportunity to buy the shoes on view in the mouthwatering window displays. The novelty of his approach lay in his concentration on a small number of styles, each

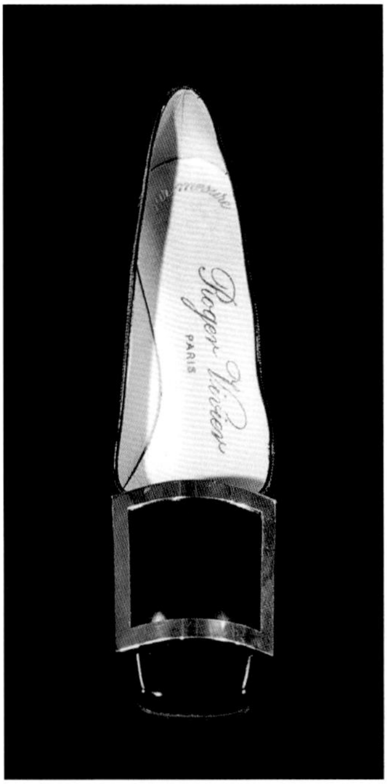

! They were students. Modeling agencies for men did not exist in 1960.

available in a wide range of colors. In 1959 the House of Dior licensed the firm to design and manufacture its shoes.

In the United States, major shoe designers such as Herman B. Delman and Israël Miller also made full use of their associations with famous names. Delman worked with Roger Vivier, and Miller commissioned shoe designs from the young Andy Warhol. One of Miller's former employees was David Evins, known as the inventor of the pump. A designer to celebrities and First Ladies, Evins's gift was the ability to create shoes with an inimitable handcrafted look. In Paris, François Villon de Boneviste, a former associate of André Perugia, set up his own business in 1960 to apply the principles of mass production to shoes that were quasi-made-to-measure, combining quality with the latest fashions and designs.

Above:
The photographer Guy Bourdin created the first advertising photographs of shoes, comparing the status of a fashion object to an incidental one in a surrealist framework, here for Charles Jourdan.

Opposite:
Roger Vivier created this shoe made of Corfam patent leather with a square heel and a large metal buckle for Yves Saint Laurent in 1965.
This legendary design remains one of the points of reference for the brand.

Shoes

Arrange the models in chronological order.

Answer

1. LACED BOOT, 1910s–1920s. **5. PUMP WITH T-STRAP**, 1920s–1930s. **2. HIGH-HEELED BROGUE**, 1930s–1950s. **4. PUMP**, 1950s–1960s. **6. PLATFORM SANDAL**, 1970s. **3. PUMP WITH HIGH HEELS**, 1990s. **7. TIGHT BOOTS WITH HIGH HEELS**, 2000s.

1

2

3

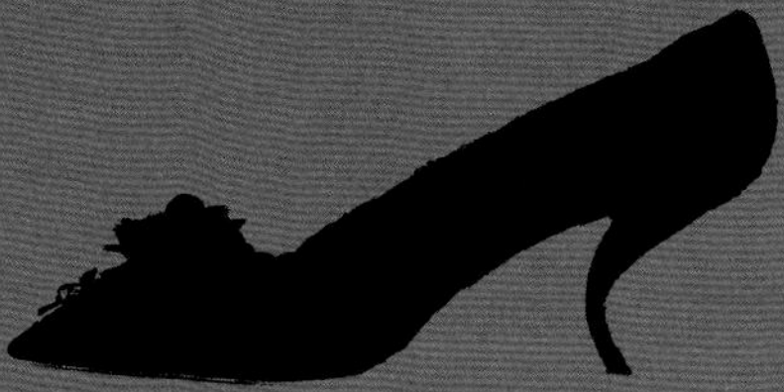

4

7

5

6

Mary Quant

• (1934–) - UNITED KINGDOM
SWINGING LONDON, POP CULTURE, YOUTH, AVANT-GARDE...
QUANT BY QUANT, HAVOC...

Mary Quant at home, reading *Vogue* magazine in 1967. The cover shows one of her designs worn by Twiggy.

Mary Quant was the quintessential fashion designer of Swinging London in the 1960s. But the credit for inventing the miniskirt, which so often goes to her, should in fact be evenly divided between Quant and her French counterpart, André Courrèges. The miniskirt phenomenon unfolded on both sides of the Channel simultaneously, with each designer bringing his or her interpretation to the wildly successful new style. Courrèges, with his architectural eye, redistributed the proportions of the minidress in order to achieve a new balance among the bust, waist, and legs, while Quant, the consummate stylist, offered the miniskirt as an affordable, off-the-peg garment with a distinctly youthful sensibility.

Quant studied fine art at Goldsmiths College of Art in London in the early 1950s, then went to work for the milliner Erik. She soon decided it was absurd to spend three days making a hat for a single client. In the brave new postwar world, it seemed indispensable to her that there should be a new and democratic form of fashion aimed at the teenage generation of the 1960s, the first to want to look different from their parents. Mary Quant's simple, bright, avant-garde designs were the perfect antidote.

In her first boutique, Bazaar, which she opened with her future

Mary Quant among models wearing her shoe designs in 1967.

husband, Alexander Plunket Green, on King's Road, Chelsea, in 1955, Quant sold a selection of ready-to-wear lines. For the shop's opening, Quant had designed what she called "mad house pajamas," and she was soon on the path to success. An American manufacturer copied the pajamas, and they were featured in *Harper's Bazaar*.

Confident in the talent she had to offer, Quant started to create other designs. From the early 1960s, she exported her collections, which caused a sensation in the United States. Miniskirts, microskirts, jersey tunics with geometric patterns, plastic raincoats, the notion of coordinates, giant polka dots: these mod accouterments were the perfect expression of pop culture. In 1966, Quant launched her make-up company, with a soon-to-be famous daisy logo and shades contained in paintboxes.

By the late 1970s, the label had begun to lose its quasi-mythical status in the fashion world. Yet today there are still 200 Mary Quant boutiques, and since 2000 Quant herself has once more been at the head of the cosmetics label, now owned by a Japanese company.

?

Who was Norman Hartnell?

Swinging London

- BETWEEN THE 1960S AND 1970S
- ZANDRA RHODES, OSSIE CLARK, JOHN BATES, THEA PORTER, GINA FRATINI, MARY QUANT, VIDAL SASSOON, FOALE & TUFFIN...

An influential moment in the history of pop culture, Swinging London erupted with Beatlemania in 1964 and drew to a close in the mid-1970s. During this heady period, London came to symbolize teenage hopes and aspirations; it was a city made by the young for the young. To the curious observer, the commercial aspect was perhaps the most obvious, embodied in the multifarious boutiques of Carnaby Street and King's Road, where trendy young things could find the latest looks: Mary Quant miniskirts and Vidal Sassoon haircuts for girls; tight-fitting suits, elastic-gored boots, and Beatles shags for boys. The most popular models of the time, Jean Shrimpton and Twiggy, so androgynous and uncompromisingly modern, were the incarnation of the aesthetic ideal of a generation dressed by Biba. London seemed to offer the progressive, open society that everybody dreamed of.

This explosion of energy fired exciting talent into every field: the Beatles, the Rolling Stones, and the Who in music; David Hockney, Peter Blake, and Allen Jones in art;

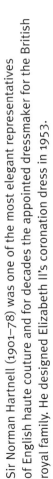

! Sir Norman Hartnell (1901–78) was one of the most elegant representatives of English haute couture and for decades the appointed dressmaker for the British royal family. He designed Elizabeth II's coronation dress in 1953.

and David Bailey in photography. When it came to fashion, Swinging London was a hothouse of young talent, much of it nurtured at the Royal College of Art, notably Zandra Rhodes, Ossie Clark, Antony Price, Graham Smith, Marion Foale and Sally Tuffin, John Bates (who designed under the name Jean Varon), Thea Porter, and Gina Fratini, to name only a few. The atmosphere of the Swinging Sixties is encapsulated in *Blow-Up*, Michelangelo Antonioni's cult film of 1966, in which a fashion photographer (David Hemmings) cruises the world of this young generation that flouted convention and invented a whole new lifestyle.

Twiggy, star model for Swinging London.

Opposite: The Rolling Stones (Charlie Watts, Bill Wyman, Mick Jagger, Keith Richards, and Brian Jones) walk in Green Park in London in 1967. Music as an incubator for modernity...

Emanuel Ungaro

• (1933–) - FRANCE
COLORS, ECLECTICISM, PAINTING...
DIVA, SENSO, UNGARO, UNGARO POUR HOMME, APPARITION...

Emanuel Ungaro well deserves his reputation as "the couturier who loves women." His collections have one aim: to make women more beautiful and desirable. "I'm obsessed with sensuality," he says with passion. First comes the sensuality of fabrics, of chiffon, lace, and passementerie; of a rich palette of colors inspired by bolts of fabric; and a simple cut. In 1965, Ungaro launched his couture house with Sonja Knapp, whose talents as an artist found dazzling expression in the creation of prints. Her designs and the sharp cut of his trapeze dresses and coats were geometrical in inspiration. Ungaro's novelty lay in his use of clashing prints—whether stripes on diamond patterns, plaid and polka dots on florals, or fur on Prince of Wales check. Soon leopard and polka dots had become his signature prints. Ungaro streamlined the cut of his designs, removed the seams from his coats, draped scarves as skirts, and created gypsy-inspired looks swathed in long shawls.

The 1980s saw the capstone of Parisian stylishness in Ungaro's signature polka-dot bustier dress voluminously draped at the shoulder. In the 1990s, painted silks were covered with fine beading, and the color choices and deliberate clashes exhibited a certain exoticism.

As a child in Aix-en-Provence, France, Ungaro used to play with his father's sewing machine and made ball gowns for his sisters. As a young man, he gradually climbed the ranks of the couture hierarchy, starting off as apprentice to a tailor in Aix before laboring in the tailoring workshop of his own father, Cosimo Ungaro, and for the Paris bespoke shop Camps de Luca. In 1958 he joined Balenciaga, and Ungaro's reputation was at last established when the Spanish couturier entrusted him with running the atelier in Madrid. Ungaro could finally claim the title of couturier, and the

Finale at the ready-to-wear show, spring-summer 1985.

Opposite: Stephanie Seymour photographed by Marc Hispard for *Elle*, 1987.

influence of his years under Balenciaga became apparent in his mix of textures and color.
Some of the most ravishing stars in show business have come to Ungaro for their dream gowns, including Penélope Cruz, Angelina Jolie, Lucy Liu, Sharon Stone, and Uma Thurman.
In advertising campaigns from 1983 to 1987, French actress Anouk Aimée embodied the essence of the Ungaro woman, defined by her charm, confidence, and power.
Thirty-nine years after founding his house, in 2004, he sold it to the Italian group Salvatore Ferragamo. The designer decided to leave to devote himself to the restoration of a Roman palazzo. The following year, the Ungaro company was bought by the American investment firm AIMZ, and Peter Dundas succeeded Vincent Darre as artistic director. The Norwegian Dundas left in 2007, and French designer Franck Boclet took over as artistic director of the Ungaro Homme collection.

?

Which designer used the ad “Who needs Paris when you can steal from yourself?”

Valentino

- (1932–) - ITALY
- THE EIGHTEENTH AND NINETEENTH CENTURIES, ARCHITECTURE, EXOTICISM, PAINTING, SCULPTURE, GLAMOUR...
- VALENTINO, VENDETTA, ROCK 'N ROSE, VERY VALENTINO, VALENTINO V, VALENTINO GOLD...

Valentino Garavani is the embodiment of Italian haute couture—a living link between French-dominated couture (the skills of which he learned at the École de la Chambre Syndicale de la Haute Couture) and the emerging couture elite couture of postwar Italy. He is also one of the last couturiers to have lived through this golden age. Valentino's career in fashion started at an early age, with training in Milan and Paris. Winning the Woolmark prize of the International Wool Secretariat earned him a job with Jean Dessès, and afterward at the young firm of Guy Laroche. In 1959 he opened his own couture house in Rome, based on the model of Ungaro in Paris—modest but with big ambitions. The elegance of his designs, refined and luxurious, quickly became clear, and in 1960 Elizabeth Taylor, in Italy at the time, commissioned Valentino to design her gown for the premiere of *Spartacus*. With Giancarlo Giammetti, Valentino soon launched a women's ready-to-wear line, followed by accessories and men's ready-to-wear.

The Valentino style rests on a strong sense of color, fabric, and pattern. Whether his patterns employ animal prints or graphic plays on black and white, Valentino set them off perfectly by the purity of his lines. The exclusive use of the color white in his famous White collection of 1968 also demonstrated his mastery and was his first major triumph in the press. Subsequently, fiery red became his signature hue. "Red is a fascinating color; it is life, the blood of death, passion, love, the absolute remedy for sadness," he explained. A favorite couturier of film stars and the jet set, Valentino designed Jacqueline Kennedy's wedding

! Bill Blass, who posed with a model for this 1965 advertisement.

Claudia Schiffer wearing a Valentino evening gown, spring-summer 1995. Schiffer stands in the Trevi fountain in Rome, an allusion to Anita Ekberg (in *La Dolce Vita* by Fellini).

Opposite:
An array of Valentino couture evening gowns in the designer's famous poppy red. From left to right: drape in the form of a petal, fall-winter 1989–90; vertical drape, fall-winter 1984–5; fabric shaped with running ribbon, fall-winter 1978–8; asymmetric drape, fall-winter 1989–90; line adjusted and lifted by two knots, spring-summer 1985; fringe-enriched pleats, 1983.

dress for her marriage to Aristotle Onassis in 1968. And over the years, his long career has been celebrated with numerous retrospectives and honors, including the 1967 Neiman Marcus Award in Dallas. In 2007, Valentino celebrated his 45-year career in high style at the foot of the Coliseum in Rome before announcing his retirement from fashion. Valentino continues to be publicly honored for the timeless elegance and classicism of his designs, at once the heritage and symbol of the glamorous Italy of la dolce vita—a unique point of view in today's fashion industry.

Detail
Who was the designer?

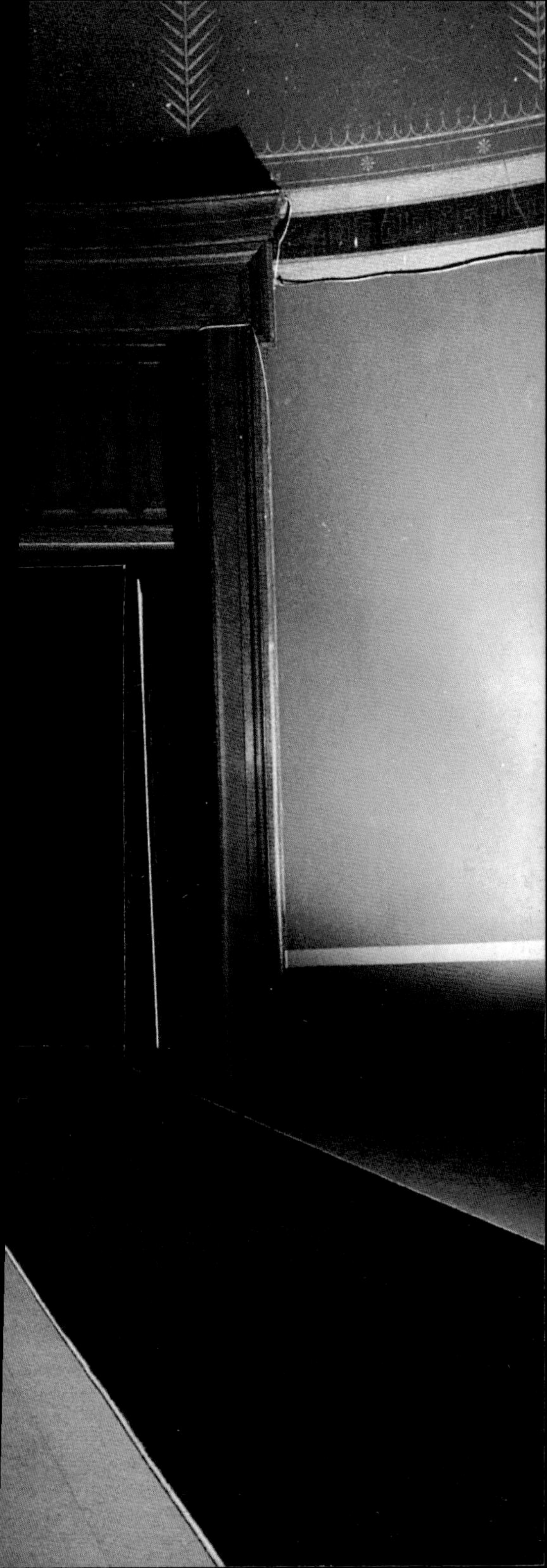

JE

This

by t

is no

Po

Sneakers

- FROM THE 1970S TO THE PRESENT
- ADIDAS, NIKE, REEBOK, CONVERSE...
- CHUCK TAYLOR ALL-STARS BY CONVERSE, AIR MAX BY NIKE, MICHAEL JORDAN BY NIKE, SUPERSTAR BY ADIDAS...

In 1875 the word "sneaker" entered the American vocabulary, followed by "basketball shoes" in 1891. Fashion would never be the same. One of the largest mass-market phenomena in the history of fashion, sneakers (or trainers) account for $25 billion in annual sales. Although 80 percent of these sales are now in the areas of street- or leisurewear, the origin of the sneaker lies, not surprisingly, in the world of sports. Athletic footwear dates back as far as 1839, when Charles Goodyear invented the process of vulcanization, which produced a form of rubber that was resistant enough to make soles for canvas uppers. The earliest examples of these canvas-and-rubber shoes were designed for playing croquet and lawn tennis. Keds were produced by the American firm U.S. Rubber, and plimsolls were made by the Liverpool Rubber Company in the U.K. But it wasn't until after the invention of basketball by Dr. James Naismith, a Canadian physical-education instructor at the Young Men's Christian Association Training School in Springfield, Massachusetts, that athletic shoes began to dominate.

Basketball, combined with the increasing professionalization of sport and the revival of the Olympic Games by Pierre de Coubertin in Athens in 1896, lent fresh impetus to the manufacture of sports shoes. In 1917, All-Star basketball shoes, launched by the American company Converse, rose to fame on the feet of the star player Chuck Taylor. Sports marketing was born. Adi Dassler, the founder of the German firm Adidas, subsequently exploited the idea by ensuring that champion sprinters wore his newly designed running shoes, which incorporated nails in their soles. The consummate athlete Jesse Owens ensured the celebrity of the Adidas name when he carried off four gold medals at the Berlin Olympics in 1936.

In the early 1970s, Bill Bowerman, cofounder of Nike, revolutionized

Opposite:
Adi Dassler, founder of Adidas, presents his revolutionary system for shoes with removable spikes.

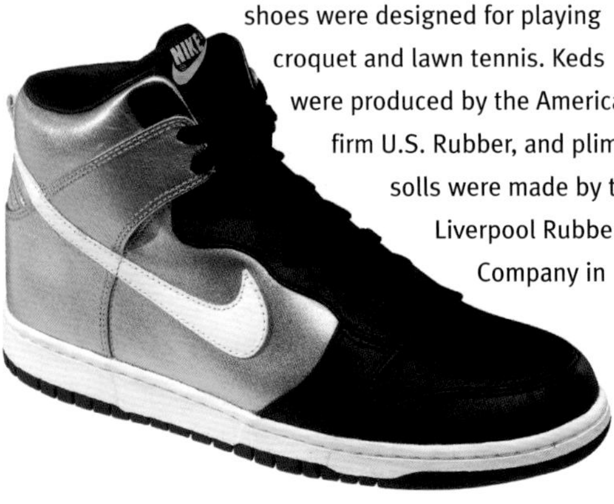

Nike Dunk metal blue basketball shoe, spring-summer 2008 collection.

running shoes with his tread design based on his wife's waffle iron, kicking off a running craze. The signature Nike "Swoosh," arguably one of the most recognizable logos in the world, was designed for the company in 1971 by Carolyn Davidson, a student at Portland State University. Technological advances such as air cushioning and reflective trim quickly distinguished world market leaders Nike and Reebok, with Adidas lagging in third place.

How did this sports accessory become a cult object par excellence? The idea of turning athletic shoes into street wear originated in America: students had long worn them on college campuses, and as jogging became fashionable, office girls wore sneakers on their way to work. Shoes linked to sports stars and other celebrities ensured instant success for certain styles: Michael Jackson wore Nikes, Run-DMC sported Superstars by Adidas, and Madonna showed off her kicks with leggings and skirts.

In the 1980s in Europe, couturiers Jean Paul Gaultier and Vivienne Westwood provocatively teamed sneakers with dresses. It wasn't long before no one batted an eyelid at the sight, and in 1997, Prada launched Prada Sport, a perfect hybrid of sport and style that earned worldwide fame.

Today's sports labels are no longer wary of high fashion: Adidas has lines designed by Stella McCartney and Yohji Yamamoto; and since being bought by the Pinault-Printemps-Redoute group in 2007, Puma (founded by Adi Dassler's brother Rudolf) has developed models on the cutting edge of design, including a collection by Alexander McQueen.

?

When was Nike's famous "Swoosh" logo created?

Jeans

- FROM THE 1950S TO THE PRESENT
- LEVI'S, WRANGLER, LEE, DIESEL, MARITHÉ + FRANÇOIS GIRBAUD...
- 501'S, STONEWASHED, BLACK DENIM...

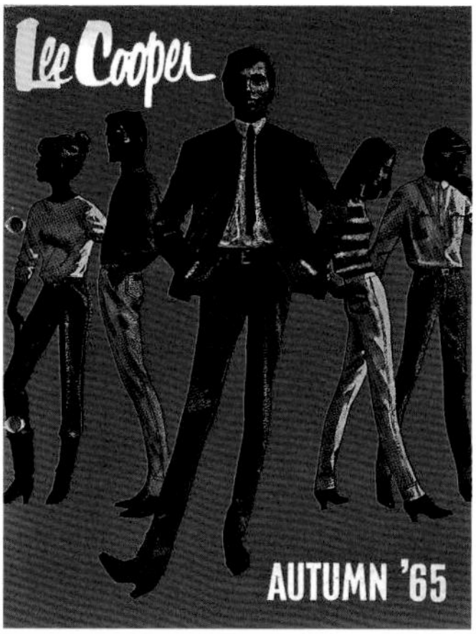

If any single garment could stand as an emblem of modern civilization, it would be a pair of jeans. Since the second half of the twentieth century, jeans have crossed all boundaries—geographical, climatic, and cultural. More than simply something to wear, they symbolize a rejection of the traditional European dress codes that dominated the globe until World War II. So weakened was postwar Europe that its cultural models lost their authority, and in their place rose fashions like the quintessentially American garment, jeans, to become the universal form of dress.

Over the course of their history, jeans have alternated between being a functional basic of the working wardrobe and a desirable fashion item. Originally, these tough denim trousers were designed for miners and cowboys. By the 1930s, wealthy West Coast ranch owners had adopted jeans for their built-in authenticity. In 1955, James Dean wore jeans in *Rebel Without a Cause*, elevating them to a symbol of youthful rebellion. This, combined with the image of the cowboy immortalized in Westerns, made a potent myth ripe for exploitation by the original manufacturers of jeans: Levi's, Wrangler, and Lee.

Toward the end of the 1960s, jeans embarked on a conquest of the world. From this point on, each fashion wave—rocker, biker, hippie, punk, New Wave, grunge, rap—would produce a new variation on the basic jeans shape. The presence of jeans in pop music during these years attests to their longevity: In 1971, Janis Joplin sang, "I's feelin' nearly as faded as my jeans." Madonna responded thirty years later, "Girls can wear jeans and cut their hair short / Wear shirts and boots 'cause it's OK to be a boy." Adapting to all new alternative

! In 1971. Its creator, Carolyn Davidson, received $35 in payment.

fashions, by the 1980s jeans had become an institution and had lost something of their mythical aura. But it returned in the 1990s, however, with the vogue for vintage and the development of exclusive designer jeans. The Marithé + François Girbaud label, pioneers in this field, explored new technologies in order to revitalize the jeans market. In America, the demand for premium denim took off in the early 2000s, spurred by a craze for hand-finished, meticulously tailored jeans by specialist labels. These jeans, by such makers as Seven for All Mankind, Frankie B, Adriano Goldschmied, Rogan, Hudson, Paige, and Sass & Bide—quickly raised the bar for original details—and prices. Today jeans are indispensable once more, worn by everyone in the fashion world, and in dressier contexts than ever before.

François Girbaud, in 2004, surrounded by jeans processed using the "Imagine" laser technology by Marithé + François Girbaud.

Opposite: Lee Cooper advertisement, fall-winter 1965–6 collection.

Air France Uniforms
Who made what?

Answer

1. BALENCIAGA, terelyne and wool summer suit with sky blue or pale pink flames, kimono-style arms, at the neck, a marine blue knot known as a "had her stop" keeps the jacket open along the bias, 1969.
2. PIERRE CARDIN, coat, 1968. **3. CHRISTIAN LACROIX**, dress with a belt knotted like a gift ribbon, and suit jacket with shoulders "Air France," 2005. **4. ANDRÉ COURRÈGES**, faux-leather jacket, 1973.
5. RODIER, following the uniform designed by André Courrèges, Air France introduced slacks into the wardrobe in 1976. **6. DIOR**, winter suit with a blue Marceau basketweave center cut, flat shirt knot made of terylene or white "ceylon," appears in the collar of the jacket, 1963.

1

2

3

COURRÈGES

•

CHRISTIAN LACROIX

•

DIOR

•

BALENCIAGA

•

RODIER

•

PIERRE CARDIN

4

5

6

The designer, photographed by Arthur Elgort, posing for her 2006 advertising campaign.

Carolina Herrera

• (1939–) - VENEZUELA
GLAMOUR, JET SET, SPLENDOR...
CAROLINA HERRERA, HERRERA FOR MEN, HERRERA AQUA, CHIC, 212 MEN...

Carolina Herrera's understanding of couture began from a client's perspective: She saw her first fashion collection at the age of thirteen, when her grandmother took her to a Balenciaga show. Born into the highest echelons of Venezuelan society, Carolina spent a glamorous and carefree youth in the world's wealthiest playgrounds, surrounded by celebrated friends such as Mick Jagger and Andy Warhol. Innumerable appearances on the International Best Dressed List (started in 1940 by fashionista Eleanor Lambert, now drawn up every year by *Vanity Fair*) cemented her reputation as one of the most elegant figures of the jet set.

Yet Herrera was not content to simply wear the fashions of others, and after a first collection, which received encouragement from Diana Vreeland, Carolina Herrera opened her ready-to-wear house in New York in 1981. Her designs reflected her early exposure to high fashion. She creates clothes of haute couture quality, classic but with contemporary touches. She herself says, "I make clothes that are classic, but with a modern twist." Her business has expanded to include women's wear, bridal wear, cosmetics, accessories, and perfumes, and Herrera has opened boutiques in the United Arab Emirates, Spain, Mexico, Portugal, and Switzerland. Her four daughters and her husband, Reinaldo, are as important to her as her work as a designer, and one of her daughters, Carolina Adriana, now works with her as both muse and associate.

Herrera is noted particularly for the understated elegance of her evening gowns and her bridal wear. In both her clothes and her perfumes, she is careful to remain a realist, but she also injects a note of fantasy into her work. "I love the idea of elegance and intricacy, but whether it is in a piece of clothing or a fragrance, the intricacy must appear as simplicity," she says. Her designs appeal not only to women of her own social milieu but also to such women as Jacqueline Onassis (whom she dressed for the last twelve years of her life), film star Renée Zellweger, and society figure Ivana Trump, one of her most faithful clients.

Which airline had a new style of uniform created for it by the American designer Halston?

Geoffrey Beene

• (1927–2004) - UNITED STATES
THE HAUTE COUTURE TRADITION ALLIED WITH MODERNITY, SCULPTURE, FUTURE, SPORT-CHIC...
GREY FLANNEL, COLOGNE BOWLING GREEN BY GEOFFREY BEENE...

Occupying a prominent place in the history of American couture, Geoffrey Beene created a style that was at once sophisticated and unfussy, simple, and easy to wear. Born in Haynesville, Louisiana, Beene gave up his medical studies at the University of Tulane in 1946 and, convinced that he was better suited to fashion, went to Los Angeles to work for the exclusive department store I. Magnin. Encouraged by one of his supervisors to make a career in fashion, Beene moved to New York in 1947 to study at the Traphagen School of Fashion. After completing his training at the Académie Julian in Paris, he worked for a variety of fashion houses in both Paris and New York, from Molyneux to Teal Traina.
In 1963 he launched his own fashion house and showroom on New York's Seventh Avenue. The success that greeted his first collection would continue unabated throughout a career that spanned sixty years. Although Beene will always be associated with the baby-doll look, his talent was distinguished by his perfectionism, his highly sophisticated feel for cut, the purity of his proportions, and his graphic use of black and white. His whole approach was aimed at extreme simplification: banishing unnecessary accessories, he surprised the fashion world by using modest fabrics for luxury garments. Wool, jersey, and flannel were his favored materials, softening a style that might otherwise have tended toward austerity. In the 1970s, he even created evening gowns in denim and sweatshirt fleece.
Beene's prominent clients, including Lady Bird Johnson, Pat Nixon, Nancy Reagan, Faye Dunaway, and Glenn

! Braniff Airlines in 1977.

Close, were attracted not only by his legendary style but also by his gentlemanly manner and his sense of humor. These qualities helped to seal Beene's reputation for sophisticated elegance.
Geoffrey Beene died in 2004, but his legacy is kept alive notably by the designer Alber Elbaz, who developed an understanding of fabrics and learned the techniques of cutting at his side.

Jersey dress by Geoffrey Beene, circa 1975.

Opposite: Portrait of Geoffrey Beene posing in front of an ornate wall of fashion figures, 1999.

Fashion Icons

From the 1960s to the 1980s

The preadolescent allure of a young girl who refuses to grow-up: Twiggy wearing a dress from her own house, around 1968.

Below:
Crosses, fingerless gloves, and disheveled hair were the basis for the bad-girl panoply: Madonna in *Desperately Seeking Susan* by Susan Seidelman, 1985.

Many trends of this period were directly influenced by popular music. Among the Saint-Germain milieu in postwar France, Juliette Gréco was already a picture of existential ennui in the earliest manifestation of the "teenage" look, all sloppy-joe sweaters, flat shoes, long hair, and eyeliner. And for hip young things in Left Bank cafés, Carnaby Street, and Kings Road, pants, bikinis, and miniskirts became the latest wardrobe essentials. French 1960s pop culture was electrified by the impish Sylvie Vartan, who launched her own fashion label, and the worldly-wise Françoise Hardy. With her trademark T-shirts, jeans, and straw basket, Jane Birkin became an icon of the Swinging Sixties on both sides of the Channel.

In America, Joan Baez, Cher, and the Mamas and the Papas embodied the cool ethnic look, while the model Veruschka, indisputable ambassadress for the jungle look, posed in Yves Saint Laurent safari suits. Nico of the Velvet Underground, Janis Joplin, and Patti Smith presented an astonishingly modern image of rebel outsiders. And the icons of R&B, personified by Diana Ross and Tina Turner, exuded a new, flashier sensuality.

On the heels of the 1980s New Wave came Madonna's miniskirts, wild blouson jackets, lace, and crucifixes, while Chrissie Hynde of the

Pretenders and Annie Lennox of the Eurythmics immortalized the punk look for girls. But in fact the tastes of the decade swerved between Debbie Harry of Blondie, the B-52s' thrift-store chic, the glamorous high-heeled retinue of Roxy Music, and the avant-garde eccentricity of Nina Hagen, whose mantle would be taken up in the '90s by Björk.

Above:
Beautiful with almost nothing! Jane Birkin in 1968.

When did the first issue of *Elle* appear?

Oscar de la Renta

• (1932–) - DOMINICAN REPUBLIC
THE TRIUMPHANT WOMAN, LUXURY, GLAMOUR, STRONG COLORS...
OSCAR SIGNATURE, RUFFLES, VOLUPTÉ, INTRUSION, OSCAR CELEBRATION, TROPICAL COLORS, OSCAR RED SATIN...

! On November 21, 1945, this innovative women's magazine addressed the generation of women coming of age after the war. The American title was introduced in 1981, and is today published in 27 countries.

As a young man, Oscar de la Renta, a native of Santo Domingo, in the Dominican Republic, studied art in Madrid. When a dress he designed for the daughter of the American ambassador to Spain was featured on the cover of *Life* magazine in 1956, his future in fashion was decided. After completing an apprenticeship under Cristóbal Balenciaga in Madrid, he became an assistant to Antonio Canovas del Castillo at Lanvin in Paris before joining Elizabeth Arden in New York in 1963. In 1965, de la Renta launched his ready-to-wear label, and his style, combining the haute couture spirit of Paris and Madrid, soon attracted attention. The fashion press raved about his long, romantic dresses and his Gypsy collection of 1967. That same year, he married his first wife, Françoise de Langlade, editor in chief of French *Vogue*, who introduced him to his first celebrity clients.

With his luxurious collections mixing classicism and extravagance, his opulent evening gowns, and his sense of color and decoration, Oscar de la Renta was soon dressing "everyone who was anyone" in America, becoming the couturier to First Ladies, society figures, and celebrities, including Jacqueline Kennedy Onassis, Hillary Clinton, Laura Bush, the Duchess of Windsor, Sarah Jessica Parker, and Beyoncé.

De la Renta has made the union of European and American elegance his signature. Like the master Balenciaga, the cuts of his gowns and clothes are designed to flatter the silhouette, giving them a timeless appeal.

Above:
The dynamism of the '80s, captured by an article in *Women's Wear Daily* about Oscar de la Renta and illustrated by Antonio.

Oscar de la Renta surrounded by models wearing his designs during a trip to Japan in 1981.

Creation by Tobias Konrath, a student at the Institut Français de la Mode, 2007. Following the system implemented by the school's director, Francine Pairon, companies produce prototypes of student projects. This experience prepares the students for the reality of the profession. Here, the prototype for the dress was produced by Simon Fonlupt, and the coat made of blue fox (Saga Furs & Bodin Joyeux Leather) by Walter Lecompte.

Opposite: The illustrious Parsons The New School for Design in New York.

Fashion Schools

- ESMOD, STUDIO BERÇOT, FASHION INSTITUTE OF TECHNOLOGY, PARSONS THE NEW SCHOOL FOR DESIGN, BUNKA GAKUEN, CENTRAL SAINT MARTINS, ANTWERP ROYAL ACADEMY OF FINE ARTS, ÉCOLE LA CAMBRE...
- PARIS, LONDON, NEW YORK, ANTWERP, TOKYO...

Though the vocations of individual fashion schools vary, overall the field has expanded greatly since the 1980s. In France and Italy, for example, fashion schools have filled the void left by the apprenticeships abandoned by businesses and see their role as primarily vocational. In the U.K., Belgium, and the Netherlands, by contrast, they are often attached to and developed from art schools, with a particular focus on design. American colleges, such as the Fashion Institute of Technology in New York, are more business oriented and train students to adapt their designs to commercial constraints. In Japan, establishments such as Bunka Fashion College at Bunka Gakuen introduce students to the latest manufacturing processes.

Over the past fifteen years or so, these national identities have been shaken up by global developments in fashion. The rise of luxury conglomerates combining several brands, the entry of many businesses into the stock market, the growing need for profitability, and the relocation of the bulk of production processes to Asia have created new needs in terms of recruitment and careers.

These changes have been matched by a fundamental shift in students' attitudes. Whereas fashion students of the 1980s dreamed of becoming star designers, many of their counterparts today hope to work within an established fashion business. The most ambitious see themselves as artistic directors; most will become studio or product managers, unnamed designers, or designers specializing in image,

Which couturier created a new uniform for the French police in 1985?

publicity, or merchandising. Young candidates nowadays are expected to offer more professionalism and less vague "artiness." In response to this new demand for dialogue and harmonization between management and designers, Pierre Bergé and Didier Grumbach founded the Institut Français de la Mode in 1986. The 1990s marked the coming of age of British and American schools, such as Central Saint Martins College of Art and Design in London and Parsons The New School for Design in New York, which bathed in the reflected glory of spectacularly successful graduates, including John Galliano, Alexander McQueen, and Marc Jacobs—all now included under the umbrella of the French conglomerate LVMH. Belgian and Dutch schools have also produced personalities who have founded independent design labels. Currently, the fashion schools that enjoy prestigious reputations are the Atelier Chardon Savard, the Institut Supérieure des Arts Appliqués (LISAA), and Studio Berçot in France; and the Istituto Marangoni and Polimoda Fashion School in Italy. In Belgium, two schools have benefited particularly from the prestige of talented former students: the Royal Academy of Fine Arts in Antwerp, alma mater of Martin Margiela, Ann Demeulemeester, and Dries Van Noten; and the fashion department of La Cambre, founded by Francine Pairon, which includes among its former students Xavier Delcour, José Enrique Oña Selfa, and Olivier Theyskens. Meanwhile, in the United States and Canada, a perhaps less prestigious but far more

! French designer Pierre Balmain replaced the peaked cap and peacoat with a flat hat and jacket.

Design by Ruth Leach, a graduate of Central Saint Martins College of Art and Design in 2007.

Opposite:
Photograph created by Esmeralda Patisso, student at the Istituto Marangoni, as part of a competition for the launching of a new product for L'Oréal.

well known "school" of design is beamed to viewers every week, as aspiring fashion designers compete to prove themselves on television's *Project Runway*.

Models
Who's who?

Answer

1. JEAN SHRIMPTON, photographed by Peter Knapp for the cover of *Elle*, May 27, 1965.
2. VERUSCHKA, for the cover of *Life*, August 18, 1967. **3. TWIGGY**, for the cover of *Queen* in the 1960s.
4. MARISA BERENSON, for the cover of *Vogue*, July 1970.

1

2

MARISA BERENSON

•

TWIGGY

•

JEAN SHRIMPTON

•

VERUSCHKA

3

4

Céline

• HOUSE FOUNDED IN 1945
SAINT-GERMAIN-DES-PRÈS, SPORT AND COUTURE, EQUESTRIANISM, PARISIANS...
CÉLINE CÉLINE, CÉLINE MAGIC ROUGE, CÉLINE POUR FEMME...

In 1945, Céline Vipiana took over a family-owned leather-goods workshop. Her made-to-measure children's shoes bore the label *Céline, bottier pour enfants*, and with each purchase, she included a charming red elephant toy. Her shoe shop proved successful, encouraging Vipiana to branch out into ranges of shoes for older girls and then, in 1959, for adults, in the manner of Jeanne Lanvin. To her boutique at 52 Rue de Malte she added more exclusive addresses on Rue du Faubourg Saint-Honoré and Rue de Rennes, at which she received clients as distinguished as Princess Grace of Monaco and her children. Soon Vipiana broadened her merchandise to include gloves, followed by scarves, hats, jewelry, perfume, and bags. Céline's reputation as a high-quality luxury brand was thus established. Indeed, it had come time to update the brand's elephant emblem, and in 1967 the firm's new logo was derived from a drawing of an American sulky. Combined with the "C" of Céline, this logo provided the pattern for the brand's exclusive fabric, introduced in 1970. (Later, the motif of the Arc de Triomphe inside a chain link became another of the brand's logos.) In 1969, Vipiana launched a Couture Sportswear line that applied an up-to-the-minute take on classic wardrobe basics and proved a rival to Hermès. She became known for her moccasins, bags, blouses, leather vests, pleated skirts, trench coats, and daywear with a thoroughly Saint-Germain-des-Prés elegance. In 1976, Céline embarked on its worldwide expansion with the opening of seven boutiques. Bernard Arnault's Financière Agache acquired the brand in 1987 and brought in the designer Peggy Huyn Kinh, formerly an associate of Madame Grès, as creative director. The sporty sophistication of Kinh's leather garments restored the label to

An advertisement published in 1967 that shows a New Wave girl with a style representative of Céline's clients.

Opposite: Céline minidress and riding boots by Ivana Omazic. Fall-winter 2005 collection.

the dynamism of its early days. When the house was bought by LVMH in 1996, the American designer Michael Kors was put in charge of women's ready-to-wear, and three years later he became the brand's artistic director. Leather goods continued to attract attention with such "It" bags as the Boogie, Poulbot, and Verdine in the early 2000s. After a brief tenure as creative director in 2004, the Italian Roberto Menichetti was succeeded the following year by Ivana Omazic. Trained at the European Institute of Design in Milan, this young Croatian had gained valuable experience as a designer at Prada for seven years, working on the Jil Sander, Prada, and Miu Miu labels. She seeks to lend a more cosmopolitan dimension to this quintessentially Parisian brand while following in the footsteps of Vipiana, who created a multifaceted look that respects each client's personality.

?

Who designed the wedding gown for the future Duchess of Windsor in 1936?

Bridal wear

YVES SAINT LAURENT, CHRISTIAN LACROIX, VERA WANG, NARCISO RODRIGUEZ...
WHITE WEDDING DRESS SINCE THE NINETEENTH CENTURY

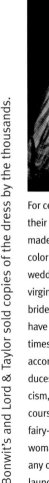

! The American couturier Mainbocher (1890–1976). After a photograph of the dress appeared in American newspapers, the department-store chains Bonwit's and Lord & Taylor sold copies of the dress by the thousands.

For centuries Western brides wore their best or prettiest dress, perhaps made for the occasion, and often in the color red. Only after Queen Victoria's wedding to Prince Albert in 1840 did virginal white become de rigueur for brides. Ever since, wedding dresses have followed the fashions of the times, with hemlines rising and falling accordingly. Yet each period also produces its version of timeless romanticism, in sweeping, rustling gowns. Of course, not every bride yearns for a fairy-tale wedding dress, and one woman knew this perhaps better than any other designer. In 1990, Vera Wang launched more than just a bridal salon; she created an entirely new look for millions of brides-to-be, incorporating fashionable sophistication into bridal wear. Even today shoppers fly to New York from across the United States to attend her annual sample sale.
Until recently, all haute couture shows culminated with the appearance of the bridal gown, the climax of the spectacle, generally worn by the youngest model or the couturier's favorite. Traditionally, in the ateliers, single young seamstresses would wish for a husband by sewing one of their hairs into the hem of the gown. But as the institution of marriage has lost its aura of sacred duty, haute couture wedding gowns have cast the solemnity and respectability of the wedding ceremony to the winds, as evidenced by Yves Saint Laurent's bridal bikini, modeled by a pouting Laetitia Casta in 1999, or the bridal bouquet failing to disguise Kate Moss's naked back in the finale of a Vivienne Westwood show.

Above:
Vivienne Westwood wedding dress worn by Kate Moss, fall-winter 1993–4 collection.

Opposite:
A reincarnation of Loïe Fuller and her dance of veils: wedding dress by Jean Paul Gaultier made of silk tulle and feathers, photographed by Solve Sundsbo.

THE FASHION GAZETTE

CURRENT AFFAIRS AND NEWS

• Madame, please cover your breast and hide it from my view! Molière's famed hypocrite Tartuffe might have said that to the young lady who was walking along the Cabourg dike in a monokini. This type of swimsuit held up by suspenders, which leaves the breasts bare, comes to France from the United States, where it has caused a scandal since being released by the designer Rudi Gernreich in the month of June. (1964).

• **Universally adopted, never equaled!** On February 5, 1954, Mademoiselle Chanel reopened her house of couture after 15 years of inactivity. Its new collection offers a jersey suit. (1954)

• **A sizable surprise…** The designer Roy Halston made a model of the voluminous actress Pat Ast (weighing in, we are told, at 220 pounds), having her walk the runway for him—a first for this universe obsessed with thinness.

• **Peace-and-Love Style** In 1968, the hippie life has taken over fashion. Make love, not war—in flowered dresses, tie-dyed T-shirts, and bell-bottom jeans. (1968)

• **1969: "mini," "midi," or "maxi"?** The war over hemlines continues to rage among the major designers.

• **Rebel in white?** After being worn blue by Dean and Brando, jeans are now white. The new director of Levi Strauss and Company, Walter Haas Jr., has decided to release jeans more focused on the youth market. It has even been announced that …corduroy jeans will be making their appearance. (1960)

• **More than a model, a supermodel!** The model Lauren Hutton has just signed an exclusive contract with the Revlon cosmetics brand for $1 million! This has never been seen before in the world of beauty products! (1974)

RUMORS AND SCANDALS

The Philadelphia Story

On this beautiful morning of April 12, 1956, the magnificent actress Grace Kelly has just debarked the *Constitution* steamship, which brought her to Monaco with four enormous trunks and 56 suitcases. The future princess had purchased three fur coats, fourteen dresses, and twenty hats, for the modest sum of $25,000, before leaving New York. Her wedding dress, created by the MGM stylist Helen Rose, traveled in a steel case—sheltered from prying eyes. (1956)

Scandalous perfume at YSL

Yves Saint Laurent posed naked in front of Jean-Loup Sieff's lens for the release of his first men's perfume, YSL Pour Homme. (1971)

Jerry Gischia, wife of the painter Léon Gischia, banned from the nightclub!

It must be said that the sexagenarian was definitely indecent in her ensemble of a white mesh bodysuit accompanied by a microskirt 18 centimeters wide! One woman shouted at her, "Pornographia!" and Jerry retorted, "No, Madame, Courrèges!"

NAN KEMPNER IS NOT LACKING IN CLASS!

The "most elegant woman in the world" according to Yves Saint Laurent was refused entrance to a restaurant because she was in a tunic-and-pants ensemble, even though they were signed by the great couturier. She reappeared a few minutes later without the reprehensible object, her tunic transformed into a mini dress! (1968)

Kenzo

- HOUSE FOUNDED IN 1970
- FOLKLORE, FLOWERS, THE WORLD, COLORS...
- KENZO AMOUR, FLOWER BY KENZO, TOKYO BY KENZO, L'EAU PAR KENZO, SUMMER BY KENZO, KENZO PARFUM D'ÉTÉ, KENZO JUNGLE, KENZO AIR...

Kenzo Takada has created a world culture of fashion, drawing his inspiration from the four corners of the globe, in a synthesis of world traditions. One of the first male students to study at the Faculty of Fashion Science of the Bunka Women's University, in Tokyo, Japan, after it opened its doors to men, he graduated with first prize. In 1964, the arrival of this young designer in Paris, then the undisputed capital of haute couture, caused a stir in the fashion world, where Japanese designers were still a rarity. But, armed with his good humor and enthusiasm, Kenzo completed his training as an assistant at catwalk shows and succeeded in selling five designs to Louis Féraud. After a meeting with Jacques Delahaye, his designs were published in the magazine *Le Jardin des Modes* and placed with Dominique Peclers, head of design at the Printemps department store. With this encouragement under his belt, he continued to develop his talents in the thriving Paris design scene, working for Pisanti and Relations Textiles, the first style bureau, founded in 1957 by Claude de Coux.

Kenzo advertising campaign: "The world is beautiful" by the photographer Hans Feurer, fall-winter 1975–6 collection.

Opposite:
The finale of the show "The English Garden," fall-winter 2005–6 collection. Kenzo by Antonio Marras: the designer's rich imagination is obvious in the elaborate sets of his shows.

It was in 1970 that the Kenzo story began to take shape, in a boutique in Galerie Vivienne that he had financed with two friends. Under the Jungle Jap label, and amid a decor of Rousseau paintings, Kenzo created five collections a year, which he made on the first floor using inexpensive fabrics from Marché Saint Pierre. In 1976, he moved the boutique, offices, and studio to Place des Victoires, creating a new magnet for Paris shoppers. His fresh, youthful style, spirited and fun, with its exuberant combinations of prints and bright colors, quickly attracted the trendsetters of the younger generation. On a deeper level,

Kenzo also created new shapes for his clothes, borrowing freely from folk traditions throughout the world to instill his designs with a heady freedom of movement. In 1983, he launched his first menswear collection. Greeted enthusiastically by the press, this collection helped to introduce color and prints (and, daringly, floral patterns) into the masculine wardrobe. At the same time, numerous Kenzo boutiques were opened worldwide.

In 1993 the House of Kenzo joined the luxury group LVMH and continued to grow, with an ambition reflected by the creation of signature products, such as the Pagodon bag, in 1998. Inspired by baskets used by Asian rice carriers, this bag, like all Kenzo creations, combines tradition and modernity. In 1999, at the height of his thirty-year tenure as artistic director of a major brand, Kenzo Takada left the house he created. Since 2003, the House of Kenzo has orchestrated its renaissance with the arrival of Antonio Marras. A self-taught designer of Sardinian origin, Marras's artistic sensibility was nurtured by a youth spent amid the remnants and fabrics of his father's shop. His aesthetic, borrowing from Arte Povera and poetry, leads to sensually feminine creations, weaving a medley of cultures and styles.

In 2006, Marras marked the house's rebirth by introducing a new jewel to the Kenzo collection: the concept store KENZO Renouveau, located at Place des Victoires in Paris. This "room of wonders" is the embodiment of the Kenzo boutiques.

How many spectators saw the show organized by Pierre Cardin at the Place Rouge in 1991?

Jean-Charles de Castelbajac

• (1949–) - MOROCCO
ART, MUSIC, CINEMA, CONTEMPORARY DESIGN, POP CULTURE, ROCK 'N' ROLL, THE HISTORY OF HEROES, COMIC-BOOK ART, UNCONVENTIONAL MATERIALS...
CASTELBAJAC, CASTELBAJAC LE COMPAGNON...

Invitation by Keith Haring for the women's show, fall-winter 1990–1.

Below: Castelbajac with the actress Farrah Fawcett, whom he dressed for the TV series *Charlie's Angels*.

The scion of an aristocratic French family, Jean-Charles de Castelbajac has always sought the timeless in the everyday. Not for him the quest for fame and fortune—indeed, Castelbajac's passions lie in the exploration of untrodden paths and unexpected back roads and in the decompartmentalization of forms of artistic expression, exhibiting a Warhol-like temptation to bring together art, design, music, and clothes. This constitutional need to dabble in every discipline has sometimes led to his being underestimated by the fashion press, which tends to overlook Castelbajac's pioneering contribution in many different fields. In 1971, influenced by the Situationists and by the support-surface movement, the young designer embarked on a mission to rescue materials that were either disposable or held in little regard. His first garment, a coat that he cut out of a blanket when he was at boarding school, became an emblem of his label; humble Velpeau bandages were turned into tunics and dresses; floorcloths embarked on new lives as T-shirts; straw, raffia, twigs, and sponges all lent organic texture to his jackets and coats. He dressed a rock band in bulletproof vests and used recycled cheesecloth to make chasubles. By combining experimental materials with a play on colors,

! More than two hundred thousand.

Castelbajac established an unmistakable style. He uses primary colors like building blocks to create dynamic garments, and transposes the world of comics and graphic novels onto evening dresses.
In 1982 Castelbajac started to use clothing as a canvas. Artists such as Jean-Charles Blais, Robert Combas, Annette Messager, and Keith Haring contributed to his painting-dresses, risking derision for their involvement in such a commercial venture. Now the number of collaborative ventures between artists and luxury conglomerates that followed in Castelbajac's wake is too numerous to list. But he also challenged the traditional world of fashion. One of his most controversial creations was an emblematic T-shaped garment based on a liturgical vestment, the linen shirt of Saint Louis on view in the treasury of Notre Dame cathedral. Critics complained that it masked the curves of the female body; Castelbajac claimed, by contrast, that its fullness was subtly suggestive of the body beneath. In the simplicity of their forms, Castelbajac's clothes are theoretically adaptable to all body shapes, cultures, countries, and ages. In 2007 the Victoria and Albert Museum in London and the Musée Galliera in Paris mounted retrospective exhibitions of his work.

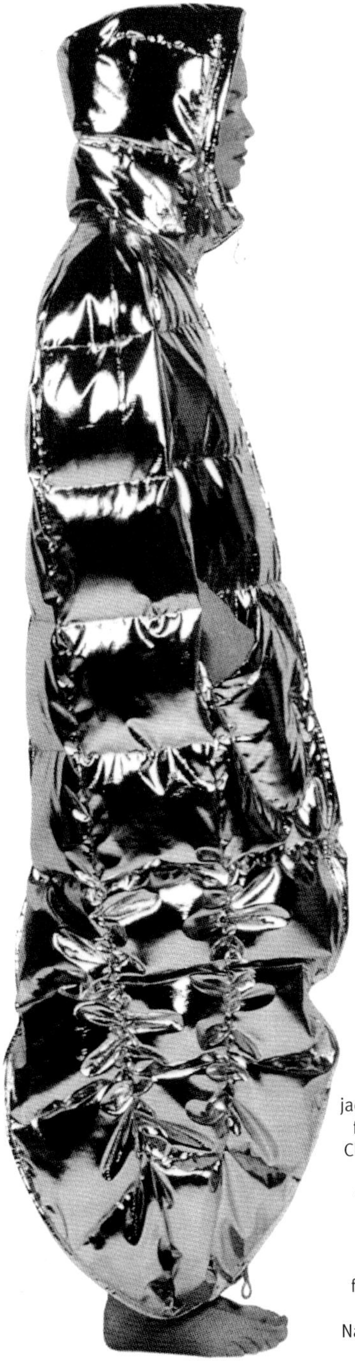

The Cocoon down jacket, one of the iconic fashion items by Jean-Charles de Castelbajac, presented during the fall-winter 1999–2000 State of Emergency show, in which three hundred male and female models walked the new Bibliothèque Nationale Metro station in Paris.

Sonia Rykiel

• (1930–) - FRANCE
PERSONAL STYLE, RETRO, LITERATURE, DESIGN, GRAPHICS, GASTRONOMY, SAINT-GERMAIN-DES-PRÉS, WOMEN'S LIBERATION...
SONIA RYKIEL LE PARFUM, L'EAU DE SONIA RYKIEL, RYKIEL WOMAN, RYKIEL HOMME, RYKIEL ROSE, RYKIEL GREY, RYKIEL WOMAN NOT FOR MEN!, BELLE EN RYKIEL...

Sonia Rykiel, photographed by Peter Knapp, backstage at the spring-summer 1981 show.

Opposite:
Finale of the spring-summer 1984 show. Sonia Rykiel's much-awaited finales are known to be highlights of spectacle.

In the 1960s, Sonia Rykiel created a relaxed style that was the polar opposite of that of the great couturiers: she produced fashion for herself, designed for women by a woman.

Her career as a fashion designer began when she was pregnant. "When I was pregnant, I made my first dress...that dress was filled with all the babies in the world, because I wanted [my pregnancy] to show," she explains.

Encouraged by her design, and unable to find clothes that she felt were modern in the shops at that time, she commissioned the sweater of her dreams from an Italian supplier who worked with her husband's boutique, Laura. In 1962, this gray sweater, simple and close-fitting, found shelf space at Laura, and six years later, Rykiel struck out on her own. She opened her first boutique on Rue de Grenelle in Paris, and in 1970, the American trade newspaper Women's Wear Daily enthroned her as the "Queen of Knits."

Sonia Rykiel's knits are sensual and clinging, hugging the body's movements in fluid fabrics such as jersey and crepe. Their long, elegant lines make women look taller and thinner. Beginning in the 1970s, Rykiel embarked on experimental techniques that were positively iconoclastic. She dispensed with hems and linings, not in order to shock, but for the sake of comfort. In 1974, she started to turn her garments inside out, allowing the seams to show "as a reflection of the body." More provocative still were inscriptions in rhinestones on her knits, outerwear in deep-shear

velour, and the contrasting stripes that were to become her signature. Sonia Rykiel always trusts her intuition, whatever the field. She designed the interiors of the Hôtel de Crillon in 1982 and the Hôtel Lutétia in 1985, a Nintendo Xbox video-game console in 2006, and a pocket dispenser for Canderel sweeteners in 2004.
Her daughter, Nathalie Rykiel, is now artistic director and chief executive of the Sonia Rykiel brand. In 2005, Nathalie created the sportswear line Rykiel Karma Body and Soul, dedicated to the harmony of body and spirit. She remains faithful to the ideals of her mother, who once declared, "For me, chic is really a question of attitude. And because of that, chic is an expression of the individual. She might be sensuous or mysterious, boyish or feminine. It's the way you walk, the way you speak, and the way you play with your body and what it can do."

How did Issey Miyake's "Pleats Please" line come about?

Issey Miyake

• (1938–) - JAPAN
EAST MEETS WEST, TRADITIONAL TEXTILES MEET CONTEMPORARY TECHNOLOGY, THE JAPANESE *MA*, COMFORT, SCULPTURE, DESIGN...
L'EAU D'ISSEY, LE FEU D'ISSEY, L'EAU BLEUE D'ISSEY...

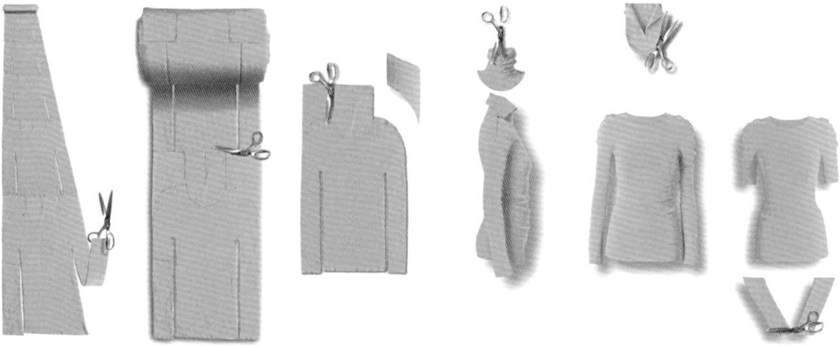

! He was approached by Frankfurt Ballet director William Forsythe about creating costumes for the company. The line made its commercial debut in spring-summer 1993.

At Issey Miyake's first New York show, in 1971, he wore a T-shirt bearing a tattoolike image of Jimi Hendrix and Janis Joplin. The look encapsulated Miyake's sensibilities—an East-West crossover combining traditional Japanese tattoos and American rock culture.

After graduating in graphic design from Tama Art University in Tokyo, Miyake continued his studies in Paris and was an apprentice to Guy Laroche and to Hubert de Givenchy before going to New York to work with Geoffrey Beene. When he returned to Tokyo in 1970, Miyake opened up avant-garde Japanese design, demonstrating the country's liberation from a passive imitation of Western fashion. Steeped in the culture of both hemispheres, Miyake married the two in symbiotic fashion in his 1978 book *East Meets West*.

Interested more in design than in fashion as such, Issey Miyake has always sought a fresh approach to the conception of Western garments.

His work has been the subject of numerous exhibitions in great museums throughout the world, including "Issey Miyake Bodyworks" (1983), "Issey Miyake A-UN" (1988), and "Issey Miyake Making Things" (1998). At the Miyake Design Studio, he experimented with combining Western-style, figure-hugging tailoring with the flat cut of the Japanese kimono. Collaborations with Japanese textile manufacturers enabled him to create innovative fabrics. His One Piece of Cloth collection in 1976 laid the basis for a whole career of innovation. This concept of the quintessential garment cut from a single piece of fabric led to the launch in 1998 of the A-POC (A Piece of Cloth) range, in which the client could choose to cut out one of a range of garments outlined on a single length of cloth. In the intervening period, he had also, in 1993, founded the Pleats Please line, based on a concept he had invented in the 1980s that allowed a hot press to permanently pleat a garment after it is cut and sewn. Miyake clothes designed according to this principle combine creativity and comfort, suit all body shapes, and confer a feeling of modernity.

In the late '90s and early 2000s, Miyake turned his energies principally to design projects, entrusting the artistic directorship of the collections to his associate Naoki Takizawa, until the latter launched his own label in 2007. Dai Fujiwara succeeded Takizawa in the men's and women's ready-to-wear collections, Issey Miyake Men and Issey Miyake Women, as well as the Issey Miyake Fête collection, launched in 2004.

Finale of the spring-summer 1994 collection.

Opposite:
Top:
A-POC Baguette, design that is meant to be cut.
Bottom:
Installation view of "Issey Miyake Making Things" at the Museum of Contemporary Art in Tokyo.

Fashion illustrators
Who drew what?

Answer

1. **ANTONIO**, Paloma Picasso in her wedding dress created by Yves Saint Laurent, for *Vanity*, Italy, 1983.
2. **THIERRY PEREZ**, suit made of Alaïa butterfly Fair Isle mesh, spring-summer 1992 collection.
3. **TONY VIRAMONTES**, haute couture ensemble by Jean-Louis Scherrer, fall-winter 1984–5 collection, for *La Mode en Peinture*.
4. **RUBEN TOLEDO**, Isabel Toledo design around 1990.

1

2

RUBEN TOLEDO

•

TONY VIRAMONTES

•

THIERRY PEREZ

•

ANTONIO

3

4

Lingerie

• UNDERGARMENTS SINCE THE APPEARANCE OF CLOTHING; LINGERIE SINCE THE 1920S

Opposite:
Lingerie as an accessory to seduction: Chantal Thomass's underthings offer the allure of a pin-up, photographed by Ellen Von Unwerth, spring-summer 2006 collection.

The seductive little slips of nothing now sported by women confident in their powers of seduction bear a marked departure from the roomy, practical undergarments once worn by their forebears. Nineteenth-century women's lingerie formed impregnable defenses designed to protect a lady's modesty. Chemises, corsets, and petticoats together conspired against sheer fashions and instead cloaked women under layer upon layer of clothing. But in the early twentieth century, as women began to emerge from the cocoon of their traditional role as wife and mother, the first signs of less-restrictive underwear appeared.

As early as 1907, Paul Poiret designed dresses to be worn without the crippling corsets then in fashion, substituting instead a girdle and an early form of brassiere (American *Vogue*, which used the word in 1907, is often credited for the terminology's acceptance in the United States). In the 1920s, two-piece garments with divided legs were worn under dresses, while bust flatteners produced a fashionable flat-as-a-board figure. Rubberized girdles took the place of corsets and were worn with short knickers or bloomers. In the 1930s, girdles became softer and more fluid thanks to the development of the revolutionary Lastex, an elastic fabric made from covered latex thread, which helped to shape the bust. Bias-cut and figure-hugging dresses that skimmed the body's curves like a second skin were now in in style. In 1931, Warner launched Le Gant, the first elastic girdle, and in 1935 the same company developed a system for grading the size of bra cups, from A to D. In the 1950s, the hourglass shape promoted by Christian Dior brought back into fashion the corsetry and frothy petticoats that had become the uniform of pinup girls. The basque, launched by the French couturier Marcel Rochas in 1945, and the serre-taille became indispensable for nipping in the waist. And when at last American nylons arrived in Europe after World War II, peace and luxury seemed back to stay. Yet the miniskirts and trousers of the 1960s banished the retro lingerie of the 1950s once more. Two new items of underwear appeared: Dim produced the first tights in 1966, and panties helped to avoid visible lines under trousers. But in 1976, Chantal Thomass gave traditional lingerie a new lease on life by investing it with risqué connotations inspired by the

punk movement, which had adopted erotica in fashion as a form of visual provocation. The 1980s brought the bodysuit (indispensable under leggings) and glossy black tights by companies like Wolford. The 1990s saw a craze for thongs. This was also the decade of the push-up bra and padded panties. In a publicity campaign that caused a sensation, the image of supermodel Eva Herzigova wearing a Wonderbra was splashed over giant billboards above the knowing tagline "Hello, boys." At the same time, Calvin Klein produced a range of sports-inspired cotton underwear in response to the new minimalism. And since 2000, the use of microfiber has ushered in lingerie with cosmetic effects that aim to eliminate visible lines and bulges under clothing.

Romantic, sexy, sensual, or sporty, a wide variety of styles and trends now accommodates all tastes. Today's lingerie market rivals the outerwear market in size; the transformation of the undergarment from a utilitarian commodity to a multifunctional fashion accessory is complete. Perhaps the most notable new development has been the creation of a high-end erotic market addressed by such companies as Agent Provocateur, the British company founded by Vivienne Westwood's son Joseph Corré, and Victoria's Secret. In chic boutiques such as Sonia Rykiel and Yoba, lingerie rubs shoulders with sex toys, and onstage performers such as Dita Von Teese and Arielle Dombasle have raised burlesque and its lingerie to an art form.

?

What lingerie bottom gives the illusion of a naked body and was created by Emilio Pucci?

Vivienne Westwood

• (1941–) - UNITED KINGDOM
MUSIC, ECCENTRICITY, ENGLAND, ART HISTORY, TRADITION AND MODERNITY...
BOUDOIR, ANGLOMANIA, LIBERTINE, LET IT ROCK...

Portrait of Vivienne Westwood by John Rankin.

Vivienne Westwood has lived at least two separate lives: the first as the Queen of Punk, the second as the highly respected and publicly honored doyenne of the British fashion scene. The story began when Westwood, then a young teacher, met Malcolm McLaren, an art student, and they discovered a shared desire to break away from the hippie aesthetic. The successive identities of the boutique they founded on King's Road in 1970 continue the story of their iconoclastic approach. Opening under the name Let It Rock, the store sold vintage clothes from the 1950s, Teddy Boy suits, records, and clothes of Westwood's own design. In 1972 the shop became known as Too Fast to Live, Too Young to Die, and started selling zoot suits and leather gear festooned with chains. After a brush with the law regarding the explicit images on T-shirts displayed in their window, Westwood and McLaren changed the shop's name to Sex, and passersby would freeze at the sight of Westwood in bondage gear, ripped T-shirts, towering stilettos, and vinyl leggings.
By this time, McLaren was putting together a band from the young men who hung around the shop. The Sex Pistols would embody the spirit of punk in the 1970s, notably in the form of Johnny Rotten, with his aggressive vocals, spiky green hair, and "I Hate Pink Floyd" T-shirt. After the band's first concert in 1976, the boutique, now renamed Seditionaries, became a temple of punk.
The 1980s marked a turning point for Westwood, as she expanded her focus and set out to revolutionize couture. The Pirates collection of her autumn-winter 1981 show offered a romantic, unisex world inspired by buccaneers and dandies. The boutique's name changed to World's End.
After separating from McLaren in

! The Viva panty, made of stretch silk.

"Rock chicken bone" T-shirt, embroidered with chicken bones and sold at the boutique Let It Rock in 1971.

Below:
The blue platform shoes worn by Naomi Campbell during her famous fall on the runway in 1993.

1983, Westwood began to build on a style of startling originality, based on contemporary reworkings of traditional garments and cuts. Her Mini-Crini collection of 1985 marked a milestone in fashion history, with its impertinent reinterpretations of demure Victoriana. The restrictive cut of her suits and shirts thrust the bust forward (spilling over "like milk jellies," she would say), nipped in the waist and arched the back and hips, while high waists and shoulders free of padding reinvented Regency fashions. Her Harris Tweed collection of 1988 dusted off the corsetry of the seventeenth century, while her 1990 collection brought historic portraits to life. Now a living legend, Westwood inspires respect and admiration from couturiers and fans alike, dazzled as much by her technical skill as by her creative excesses. World's End, meanwhile, has become a place of pilgrimage for those who want to see where the legend began.

How many Wrap dresses did Diane von Furstenberg sell at the beginning of her career?

Answer

Five million wraps were sold between 1973 and 1976. Introduced in 1973, these comfortable dresses made of jersey responded to the desires of women in the 1970s. Here, Diane von Furstenberg poses for her first advertisement with her slogan „Feel like a woman, wear a dress."

Feel like a woman, Wear a dress

Fur

• THE MIDDLE AGES, 1950 TO 1960, THEN STARTING FROM 1990–2000
RÉVILLON, SAGA FURS, YVES SALOMON, SPRUNG FRÈRES...

A sophisticated look with a fox collar and kimono sleeves. Drawing by Paul Colin, 1928.

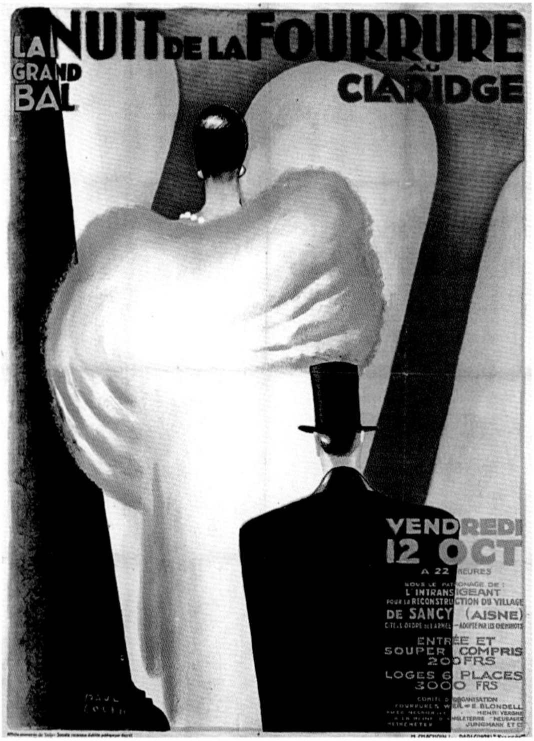

Until the twentieth century, fur, the earliest form of human clothing, had a comparatively low fashion profile. With the exception of the medieval period, it has virtually always remained invisible, concealed as a lining or reserved for decorative trim on scarves, collars, and cuffs. However subtle, fur has always been a symbol of wealth and power: the robes of kings and emperors were lined in ermine for centuries.

In the 1950s, fur came out of the closet as Hollywood stars flaunted their luxury lifestyles by cocooning themselves in swaths of white mink.

During these years, actresses enveloped in shimmering fur wraps sashayed up the stairs at Cannes, and Brigitte Bardot wore a sumptuous panther coat as nonchalantly as if it were an ordinary sweater.

At this time, the fur coat entered women's wardrobes as a sign of wealth and status on a par with the latest automobile. A mink or Astrakhan coat was a costly purchase meant to last a lifetime, and could be lengthened or shortened as fashions came and went. Then the hippie styles of the 1970s brought in the ubiquitous Afghan coat or vest in reversed and embroidered sheepskin.

The 1980s and '90s saw a growing backlash against the fur industry. Bardot cast off her furs and devoted herself to animal-rights activism upon her retirement in 1974. Organizations such as PETA (People for the Ethical Treatment of Animals) protested vociferously and some-

times violently against the cruelty of the fur trade; model Christy Turlington posed naked below the slogan "I'd rather go naked than wear fur" on behalf of the group. Designer Stella McCartney renounced the use of fur and other animal products in her designs. The use of fur declined and was in some cases replaced by the flashiness of fake fur.

While fur has virtually disappeared from both the runway and the street, in Europe it has resurged as a fashion phenomenon in recent years.

Between 1996 and 2006, the turnover of fur has increased at a rate of 10 percent annually. The House of Revillon Frères, founded in 1723, was sold in 2006 to the furrier Yves Salomon, principal supplier of fur for luxury goods and haute couture. The largest fur supplier, however, remains Saga Furs, founded in 1954 by a group of Scandinavian fur farmers; Saga is largely responsible for fur's renaissance. Today innovative ways of curing the skins to make them lighter and tighter, transforming fur into a more versatile and less rarefied material, appears in new guises with each season.

Above:
Christy Turlington strikes a pose for the famous (and controversial) ad campaign by PETA (People for the Ethical Treatment of Animals).

?

Which designer created a collection of erotic objects?

Thierry Mugler

• (1948–) - FRANCE
FUTURISM, HOLLYWOOD, THEATER AND OPERA, POP CULTURE...
ANGEL, A*MEN, ANGEL ÉTOILE, VIOLETTE ANGEL, ALIEN, EAU DE STAR, INNOCENT...

A showman and former dancer with the Opéra National du Rhin in Strasbourg, Thierry Mugler creates a world of theatrical illusion, with heroines inspired by the ultra-feminine, vampish glamour of 1940s and 1950s Hollywood. From first sketch to finished creation, these visions of sexy, stylish beauty have a fantasy appeal, while their technical perfection sets them firmly in the world of great couture.

With his first fashion line, Café de Paris, launched in 1973, Mugler paid homage to the classic *Parisienne* look, complete with little black dresses, tailored suits, and trench coats. Adopting an exaggerated vision of feminine elegance, he proposed fur-trimmed evening gowns with plunging necklines and figure-hugging suits that transformed his clients into stars. In the late 1970s, Mugler was at the forefront of the return of an engineered, structured look with padded shoulders, handspan waists, skirts molded to the thighs, and stiletto heels.

In 1992, Mugler left the world of ready-to-wear and entered haute couture. At the same time, he launched his perfume Angel in conjunction with Clarins. Angel would become one of the greatest successes in the history of perfume, staying at the top of the world sales charts for nearly a decade. Ten years later, Mugler retired from fashion. He now devotes his time to decorative art and theatrical costume design: in 2003 he created costumes for Cirque du Soleil and designed one of the tableaux for the company's "cabaret érotique" show.

Today the Mugler company, renamed Thierry Mugler Mode and Patrimoine, is owned by Clarins, which presents men's and women's ready-to-wear lines in the spirit of their founding father. Thomas Engelhart, a talented young figure of the New York fashion scene, has been appointed artistic director of men's fashions, with a brief to reinterpret the unique style of Mugler Homme. The same sense of drama and the spectacular united the two designers: the world of the night and its happenings for Engelhart, the magic of Hollywood for Mugler.

In February 2008, Rosemary Rodriguez replaced Englehart as head of Mugler Homme.

!

In 2002, Sonia Rykiel incorporated sex toys in her "Rykiel Woman" line.

Fencing corset with black vinyl stockings, photographed by Thierry Mugler for the fall-winter collection catalog, 1996–7.

Storing more than fifty tons of supplies, this stockroom allows the House of Lesage to recreate any of the more than sixty thousand samples of embroidery designs that were created and archived over the course of a century.

Suppliers

• EMBROIDERER, BOOT MAKER, TUCKER...
LESAGE, LEMARIÉ, MASSARO, MICHEL, GOOSSENS, DESRUES, GRIPOIX, LOGNON...

Until the 1980s, craftsmen and manufacturers working in the field of fashion used the tradesmen's entrance. Certain trades have always been dependent on the vagaries of fashion and tastes in clothing. When hats were no longer a required item of dress, for instance, the associated workers became increasingly rare, from high-fashion milliners to the makers of the wooden forms on which the hats were shaped. Above all, the slightest changes in formal dress, especially in evening gowns, can cause the disappearance of skills such as embroidery, passementerie (braids, cords, tassels, and beads), and lacemaking. Of the three hundred *plumassier* establishments specializing in ornamental feathers and plumes in Paris in 1900, for instance, only fifty remained in 1960, and a mere handful by the beginning of the twenty-first century.

With the arrival of Karl Lagerfeld at Chanel in 1983 and the opening of the house of Christian Lacroix in 1987, new impetus was given to these fast-disappearing trades. The spectacular style of the 1980s—the baroque designs of Lacroix and the highly accessorized look of Chanel—

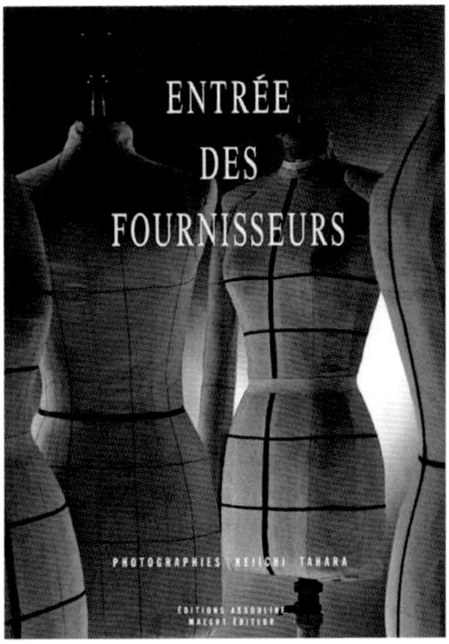

The book *Entrée des founisseurs,* Assouline, 1990.

brought them back into fashion. In addition, François Lesage, heir to the prestigious embroidery business, led a media campaign to draw attention to the precariousness of their position. In 1990 Lesage inspired a book entitled *Entrée des fournisseurs* (Tradesmen's Entrance), which championed the excellence of these fashion trades in which "ancestral skills exist side by side with the latest technologies." Most importantly, he sounded the alarm by listing the rare survivors: lace by Marescot, embroidery by Lesage, passementerie by Pouzieux, millinery by Michel, feathers by Lemarié, costume jewelry by Gripoix and Desrues, pleating by Lognon,

? Who was Elsa Schiaparelli's preferred embroiderer?

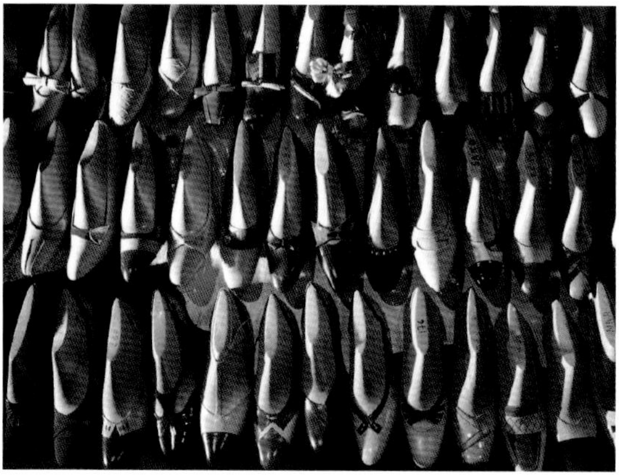

dyeing by Perrochon, and fabrics by Gustav Zumsteg. Without these arcane trades, he argued, haute couture and luxury industries would not exist, and Paris fashion would lose its excellence and individuality. After the threat of extinction, these suppliers enjoyed a newly indispensable status.

When Alexander McQueen grabbed the reins at Givenchy in 1996 and John Galliano took over Dior in 1997, the demand for embellishments and trimmings rose even further and began to trickle down to the high street. Soon the need to establish the distinction between true luxury and its newfound egalitarian iterations obliged couture houses to raise the stakes, vying with one another in the elegance and extravagance of their decorative details, and so keeping these specialist firms in business. During preparations for the spring and fall shows, only these craftsmen are capable of interpreting the desires of artistic directors in keeping with tight deadlines. But the cost of this work brought them to their knees, and in 1997 the house of Chanel bought a number of trade firms in order to save them from bankruptcy and to preserve their skills. Thus, Lemarié, Desrues, Michel, Lesage, Massaro, Goossens, and even the florist Guillet were absorbed into the Chanel fold through its Paraffection subsidiary.

The initiative of Chanel was not an isolated one. The quest for true luxury and individualized fashions has unleashed a return to objects and works of beauty and unique quality. Jewelry, bespoke shoes, made-to-measure suits, personalized perfumes, and gloves and leather

!

Albert Lesage. His son, François, has preserved all of the original designs from his embroideries.

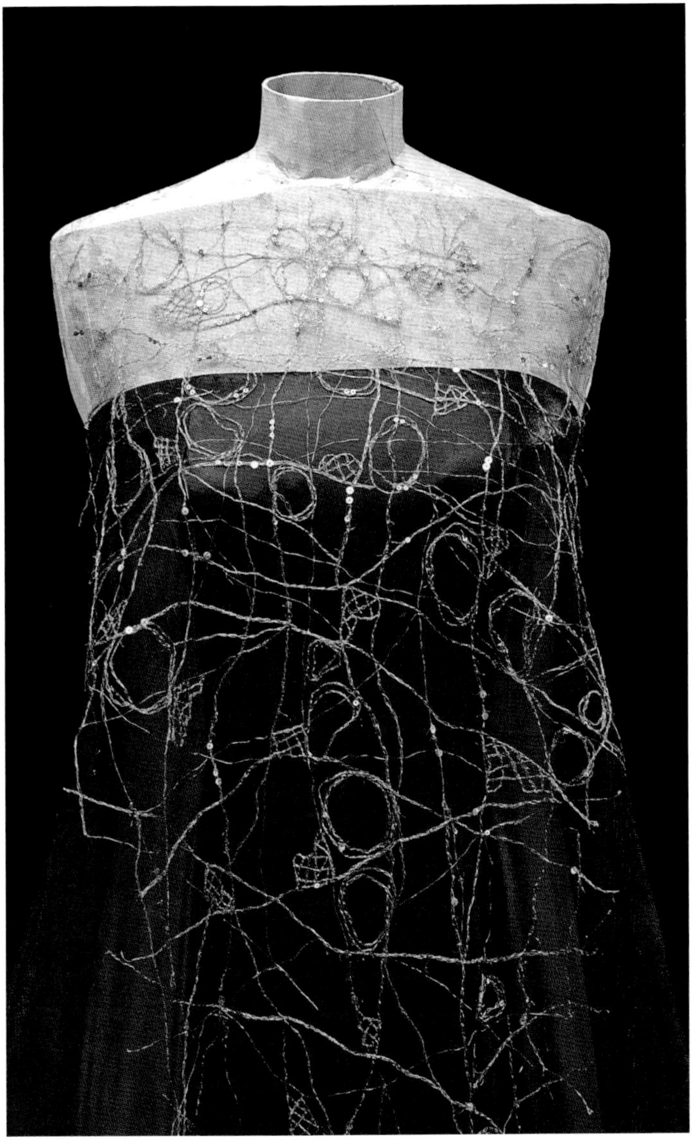

A Dominique Sirop dress formed of a crocheted mesh for summer 1999.

Opposite:
Top:
Massaro designs.
Bottom:
A cardboard mold with pleated stuffing inside.

goods made on commission are indicators of this reborn interest in luxury. Goods made by hand are valued once again, shops selling jewelry supplies are multiplying, and haberdashery counters—such as Entrée des Fournisseurs in the Marais district of Paris, created in 1993 by Lisa and Patrick Aboukrat, founders of Abou d'Abi Bazaar—are waking from their long slumbers.

Pioneers of Ready-to-Wear

• BEGINNING IN THE 1940S AND 1950S

CLAIRE MCCARDELL, BONNIE CASHIN, VERA MAXWELL, GHISLAINE DE POLIGNAC, JACQUELINE BÉNARD, CLAUDE DE COUX, FRANÇOISE VINCENT, DENISE FAYOLLE, EMMANUELLE KHANH, SONIA RYKIEL, BETSEY JOHNSON, MARY QUANT...

"Disposable" mini dresses by Daniel Hechter in 1966, the epitome of cheap and replaceable clothes generated by fashion's accelerated rhythm.

Opposite: Emmanuelle Khanh and her famous sunglasses in 1991.

When ready-to-wear finally cut the umbilical cord by which it had been attached to haute couture, the emerging figure that did so was the fashion designer. As the twentieth century progressed, the ready-to-wear business boasted designers with the ability and skill to produce collections that would be influential in carving out new directions in fashion.

In the United States in the 1940s, and '50s, Claire McCardell, Vera Maxwell, and Bonnie Cashin led the ready-to-wear charge with their streamlined, versatile separates for the modern woman. Although their eponymous lines were sold by department stores and other mass retailers, it was common among this generation of designers to be personally involved in their designs at every level, from gowns to galoshes: McCardell was the first to license her name to an industrial manufacturer, Accessocraft, in the 1940s. These pioneering designers defied the excesses of Parisian haute couture and sought to make clothing that was both chic and wearable, forging an innovative path for American fashion.

In France a nascent class of fashion consultants and agencies, rather than the designers themselves, played a leading role in establishing the ready-to-wear category. The initiative came from department-store owners, who observed that—in direct contrast to American women—no Frenchwoman of style or elegance ever bought her clothes at their establishments. Max Heilbron of Galeries Lafayette was a pioneer in this field, hiring Princess Ghislaine de Polignac, the

famously elegant grand-niece of Jeanne Lanvin, as a fashion adviser in 1952. Impressed by the inverted snobbery of *chic et pas cher* ("chic and cheap"), the Duchess of Windsor ordered two coats. The Printemps department store soon followed suit, hiring the editor in chief of *Femina*, Jacqueline Bénard, as the style director in 1958. Under the Bénard regime, in-house designers and stylists were exempted from the system of clocking in, a sign of a new aristocracy within the fashion industry. Many prominent designers, including Karl Lagerfeld, Agnès B., Jean-Charles de Castelbajac, Corrine Sarrut, and Jacques Delahaye, got their start as freelancers for the industrial manufacturers who produced lines for department stores. The endorsement of major stylists gave these designers the name recognition they needed to found their own successful lines in the 1960s and 1970s.

? What is "Nylon Day"?

Jean Paul Gaultier

• (1952–) - FRANCE
CINEMA, ART, EXOTICISM, GENDER BENDING, PARIS, ROCK 'N' ROLL, TRADITIONAL CLOTHING...
GAULTIER, LE MÂLE, LE BEAU MÂLE, FLEUR DU MÂLE, FRAGILE, UNISEXE, CLASSIQUE...

!

On May 15, 1940, when the Du Pont de Nemours company released nylon stockings, it triggered riots in the stores. Nine million pairs were sold that year, and American G.I.'s would later offer nylon stockings as gifts in Europe during the Liberation.

A veteran enfant terrible of fashion, Jean Paul Gaultier has demonstrated that an ultracreative label can also be an enduring one. The trajectory of his career is similar to an independent musician who one day finds himself an international superstar. Gaultier is the designer who, by opening up new directions, styles, and media opportunities, laid the foundations for contemporary fashion design. The mix-and-match principle so prevalent in today's haute couture was launched by Gaultier in his first show in, 1976, when he paired prima ballerina tutus with biker jackets.

Fashion magazines immediately latched on to the popular image of Gaultier as a boy from the suburbs who came to Paris to conquer the world capital of fashion. But this image obscures a different Gaultier—the Gaultier who was strongly influenced in his youth by his admiration of the golden age of couture, from the 1930s to the 1950s, and by his fashionable grandmother. Wanting to breathe new life into haute couture, he paired it with punk and added his own interpretation of Parisian chic, a combination of man-about-town, working-class lad, and aristocrat. In his spring-summer 1988 collection, impeccably cut suits met jaunty scarves and berets.

Witty irreverence became a hallmark of Gaultier's style. His fall-winter 1984 show recast the corset as outerwear, with an exaggerated conical silhouette, while spring-summer 1985 explored the theme of androgyny. Sexual ambiguity—putting men in skirts, for instance—has been an enduring theme. His provocation is aimed at destroying the traditional

Madonna wearing a Jean Paul Gautier bodysuit, which was inspired by traditional lingerie, for her Blonde Ambition tour in 1990.

Opposite:
Long "sailor's sweater" dress, Les Indes Galantes collection, 2000.

masculine and feminine wardrobe and all the social snobbery and conventions that go with it.

For many years, Gaultier collections enchanted the press, who marveled at these chic and shocking spectacles but saw them only as expressions of an unwearable avant-garde vision of fashion. Some fifteen years elapsed before his skills as a couturier received recognition. Only then did it emerge that the enfant terrible had apprenticed with Pierre Cardin and Jean Patou. Gaultier's official entrance into haute couture, in 1997, was a triumphant demonstration of his mastery of the subtleties of tailoring, of the delicacy of his color ranges, and of the beauty of his fabrics and ornaments. This recognition was crowned by his appointment as artistic director of the venerable House of Hermès.

Fashion and Cinema

Which designer goes with which film?

Answer

1. **JEAN PAUL GAULTIER**, *The Fifth Element*, directed by Luc Besson, 1997. 2. **EMILIO PUCCI**, *The President's Analyst*, directed by Theodore Flicker, 1967. 3. **CHANEL**, *Last Year at Marienbad*, directed by Alain Resnais, 1961. 4. **ELSA SCHIAPARELLI**, *Every Day's A Holiday*, directed by Edward Sutherland, 1937.

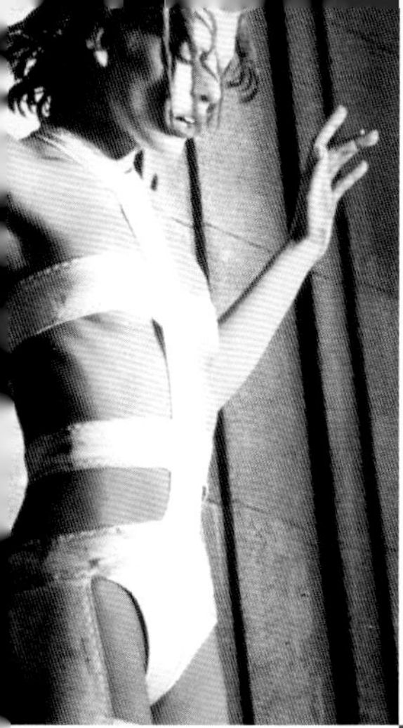

1

2

ELSA SCHIAPARELLI

•

CHANEL

•

JEAN PAUL GAULTIER

•

EMILIO PUCCI

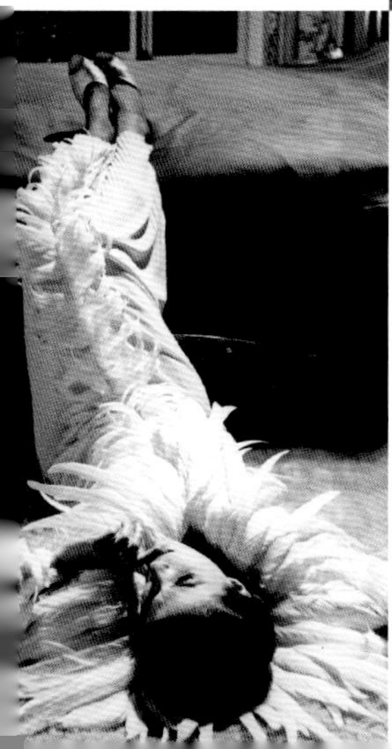

3

4

Paul Smith

- (1947–) - UNITED KINGDOM
- THE TAILORING TRADITION MEETS MODERNITY, ROCK MUSIC, THE STREET, POP CULTURE, GRAPHICS, COLOR, DESIGN…
- PAUL SMITH WOMAN, PAUL SMITH MEN, FLORAL, LONDON FOR WOMAN, PAUL SMITH STORY, EXTREME FOR MEN, LONDON FOR MEN, PAUL SMITH ROSE…

Sir Paul Smith, who fell into the world of fashion by pure chance, completely overhauled and revived the male wardrobe in the 1980s.
He engineered the rediscovery of the British tailoring tradition while injecting it with touches of humor and modernity.
In 1964, Paul Smith was seventeen and had his sights set on a career as a professional cyclist. An accident put an end to that ambition, and when he came out of the hospital he met a group of art students in a pub in his native Nottingham. They introduced him to the world of contemporary art and the rock scene. Encouraged by one of the students, Pauline Denyer, whom he would later marry, Smith opened a small boutique in 1970 while taking evening classes in tailoring. Soon he started to create his own designs, and so became both a couturier and a retailer. In 1976 he showed his first Paris collection, and three years later he opened a boutique on Floral Street in Covent Garden, helping to launch the area as the epicenter of the London fashion scene.
Smith's boutique offered an eclectic range of merchandise, a mixture of menswear and such accessories as Filofaxes, to which he added personal flourishes. But the success of his style was based on, as he described it, "Savile Row meets Mr. Bean." Smith's blend of classic British style with bright colors conveyed a spirit that was offbeat to the point of eccentricity; multicolored stripes became his signature motif and could be found on a plethora of designs.
With a multidisciplinary approach and a finely tuned business instinct,

Fall-winter 2002–3 show in London

Opposite: Fall-winter 2008–9 collection, Paris.

Paul Smith has expanded into women's wear, children's wear, furniture, office supplies, jewelry, books, and art. His boutiques, meanwhile, have evolved in the direction of concept stores. Today Paul Smith sells twelve lines throughout the world (including 200 boutiques in Japan alone): a formidable achievement for British fashion.

What is the origin of the "4239 shirt," a characteristic shirt in Paul Smith's line?

Comme des Garçons

- HOUSE FOUNDED IN 1973
- DECONSTRUCTION, ASYMMETRY, INCOMPLETENESS, CONTEMPORARY ART, MINIMALISM, THE POOR LOOK...
- COMME DES GARÇONS EAU DE PARFUM, ODEUR71, ODEUR53, COMME3, WHITE, ODEUR71, CDG2, CDG2 MA RED SERIES, INCENSE SERIES, COLOGNE SERIES, SHERBET SERIES, SYNTHETIC SERIES, SWEET SERIES...

! It is a shirt with a unique cut (42 inches in the back, 39 inches in the front) created by the tailor Newbold for farm workers in Lincolnshire. When Paul Smith took over the company, he integrated the cut of these shirts into his collections.

The rejection and ridicule to which Rei Kawakubo was subjected when she launched Comme des Garçons in Paris in 1981 have been equaled only by the devoted admiration accorded to her today: elevated to the status of mother goddess of the fashion world, she has become the unwitting muse to countless young talents and the disinterested inspiration to numerous luxury labels. Her raw edges, distressed fabrics and layering, and montages that seemed to defy common sense have become givens of contemporary fashion. When they first appeared on Paris catwalks in 1981, these features were viewed as revolutionary; Kawakubo's winter 1982 show was denounced as "post-nuclear;" and her summer 1997 show was notoriously dubbed the "lumps and bumps" collection. With hindsight, her creative approach would be defined as deconstructionist, an aggressive rhetoric for a bold manifesto that flew in the face of European sensibilities. But what appeared as merely a mission to destroy the tradition of Western clothing was in fact quite the opposite: Kawakubo's approach set out to analyze and scrutinize components of fashion before reconstructing them in more interesting and exciting ways. This avant-garde approach was influenced by the Japanese tradition and notably by the wabi-sabi philosophy and aesthetic derived from Zen Buddhism, which finds beauty in imperfection and impermanence. A Comme des Garçons garment is defined by its resistance to definition: whether asymmetrical, intricately draped, or outlandish, it defies simple description.

Kawakubo has also hijacked the methods of the art world for the benefit of fashion. Her boutiques in Paris and New York re-created the ambience of an art gallery, with each item presented as a unique piece—and so raised industrial creation to the level of an art form. Her current boutiques—such as her red boutique in the Faubourg Saint-Honoré in Paris, with shiny scarlet-lacquered sliding walls that hide doors and windows, and her store in London's exclusive Dover Street Market—make few evident concessions to the requirements of the retail world. In her flagship store, which opened its doors in Aoyama, Tokyo, in 1989, Kawakubo gave prominent space and carte blanche to contempo-

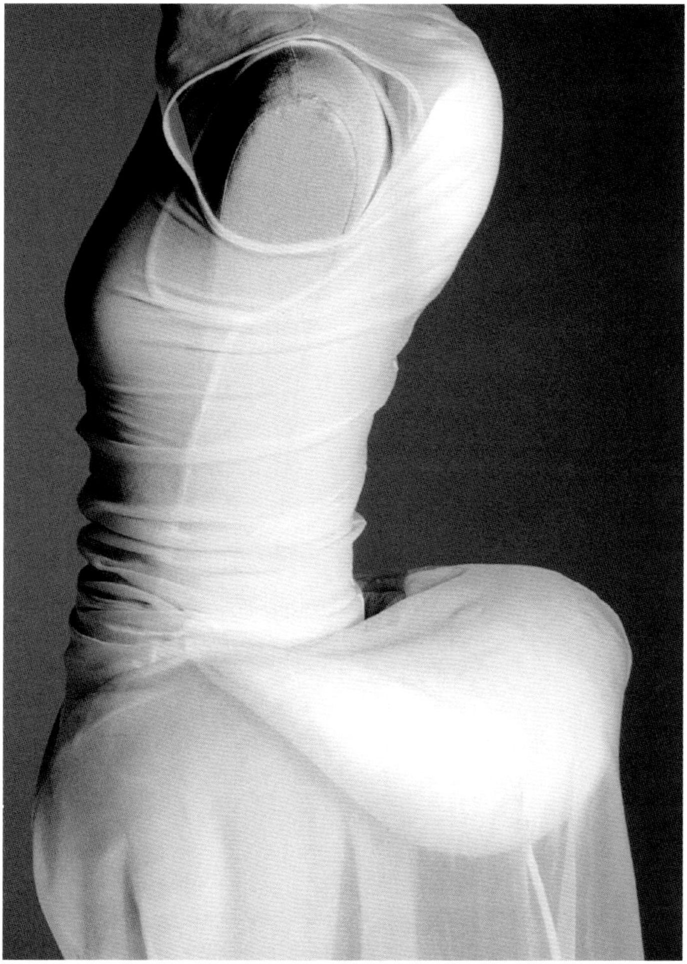

"Six 1/2".
The dress and its components redefined codes of beauty. Insert created for *Visionaire* No. 20—a special edition album devoted to Comme des Garçons in 1997. Photograph by Kishin Shinoyama.

rary artists, such as Alison Berger, Daniel Buren, Jim Gary, Kaeseberg, Jesús Rafael Soto, and Line Vautrin, to exhibit their work. And the Comme des Garçons perfume, launched in 1994 with the collaboration of French artist and designer Christian Astuguevieille, turned the traditions of perfumery on their head. Notes of everything from rotting undergrowth to photocopier ink evoke unexpected places, memories, and sensations.

Many admirers view Kawakubo as a pure artist, detached from the commercial realities of fashion. Nothing could be farther from the truth: she learned the ropes of distribution in 1969, when she sold her own collections. Even now, despite her rise to success, Kawakubo insists on doing her own photocopying, hardly ever takes a holiday, and demonstrates iron will and exemplary eye for detail.

Yohji Yamamoto

• (1943–) - JAPAN
THE NINETEENTH CENTURY; WABI-SABI; "CODED" DESIGNS OF CHANEL, DIOR, GRÈS, AND VIONNET; BLACKNESS; OLD PHOTOGRAPHY; WORKING CLOTHES...
YOHJI, YOHJI HOMME, ESSENTIEL...

Portrait of Yohji Yamamoto by Koichi Inakoshi.

Opossite: The fall-winter 1996–7 show exhibited Yamamoto's talent as a sculptor of felt dresses.

Yohji Yamamoto and his former partner, Rei Kawakubo, are the two chief protagonists of deconstructionism. In 1981, Yamamoto persuaded Kawakubo to go with him to Paris to show their collections, with an eye toward placing Japan on the map of world fashion. The event was a publicity coup: fashionistas talked of little else, and the press was stunned.

The Tokyo-born Yamamoto was well situated to appreciate the strength of the European hold on Japanese fashion. His father had been killed in World War II, and the young Yohji helped his mother, a dressmaker, make copies of Paris couture models for her clients. When he displayed little interest in his law studies, his mother sent him to Bunka Gakuen in Shinjuku, Tokyo, in order to broaden his knowledge of couture. On a trip to Paris in 1969, he realized that his future lay in creating ready-to-wear designs that would shake up both the European and the Japanese traditions. In 1972 he set up his own business, Y's, in Tokyo, and launched his first attack on a great bastion of fashion: the suit. For men, he broke down its traditional appeal as a protective cloak of respectability; for women, he introduced a striking encounter between austere tailoring and pretty, loose-fitting softness. Yamamoto reinterpreted the classics with fullness, draping, and asymmetry. Black was revealed as a true color, rich in warm and cool nuances, with the simplicity of a white shirt as its luminous counterpoint.

As a springboard for his collections, Yamamoto looks to real people, the way they live and think. Then he allows himself to be guided by the sensuality of fabrics, and finally the shape of the garment emerges, disposed around a point of equilibrium situated in the middle of the back. His aim is to create a "pre-worn" look, ennobled by the

patina of time. The spirit of Japanese dress is the foundation of Yamamoto's style. His clothing incorporates a loose fullness and often conceals the body to increase its mystery. And of course, he has reworked the kimono numerous times. As the culmination of his desire to bring fashion within the parameters of daily life, in 2002 Yamamoto signed a contract with Adidas to launch his Y-3 line. Yamamoto is also celebrated for his involvement in the arts. He challenged the aesthetics of fashion photography, for example, by recruiting Marc Ascoli as artistic director of his shoots. A charismatic figure, Ascoli inaugurated collaborative ventures with photographers such as Paolo Roversi, David Sims, and Nick Knight. Their photos are a measure of Yamamoto's impact on a milieu that often clings to a comfortable but shallow charm.

What is the favorite color of couturier Yohji Yamamoto?

Chloé

- HOUSE FOUNDED IN 1952
- PARISIANS, BOHEMIAN BOURGEOIS, YOUTH, JET SET....
- CHLOÉ, NARCISSE, CHLOÉ INNOCENCE...

The Raglan raincoat photographed by Peter Knapp.

Opposite: Ready-to-wear show, fall-winter 2006–7.

! Black. He believes that this color outlines the silhouette most precisely.

With Chloé "bohemian chic" style, the house was a pioneer in luxury ready-to-wear, filling the gap between the ready-made market and haute couture in the years after World War II.

The story of Chloé is that of a young woman who could find nothing to her taste and who decided to create her own fashions. In 1945, Gaby Aghion, an Egyptian intellectual with a Western education, left Alexandria for Paris, where she mixed with the writers and existentialists who frequented the cafés of Saint-Germain-des-Prés. Determined to rescue Parisians from the postwar dearth of stylish clothes, she offered six dresses in youthful styles to local clothes shops. In 1952, she called her label Chloé after one of her friends, writing it in salmon pink on a sand-colored background—the colors of her desert childhood. Her first show, in 1956, was at breakfast time in the Café de Flore, and it introduced the idea of using unusual venues for presenting couture collections. Aghion and her brand were at the cutting edge.

In 1953, Aghion brought in Jacques Lenoir as a business partner, and in 1957 she recruited the designer Gérard Pipart, who designed an original collection based on loose, straight lines and fluid, slippery fabrics. The entire first generation of designers then emerging in Paris—Christiane Bailly, Maxime de la Falaise, Graziella Fontana, Tan Giudicelli, Carlos Rodriguez, and Michèle Rosier—worked for Chloé, transforming the label into a factory of fashion ideas. Hand-painted chiffon dresses, printed or embroidered silk jerseys, billowing smocks, and tunics were all notable successes. With the arrival of Karl Lagerfeld in 1965, Chloé gained an international reputation, and for the first time a designer played a starring role in a ready-to-wear house.

The walls of the Chloé boutique in the seventh arrondissement in Paris were covered with cartoon-strip images; outside, fleets of Rolls Royces disgorged a galaxy of stars, including Lauren Bacall, Brigitte Bardot, Maria Callas, Grace Kelly, Jacqueline Kennedy, Christina Onassis (who bought thirty-six silk blouses in one go), and Sylvie Vartan and her son David. One iconic image symbolizes the contemporary spirit of Chloé: Paloma Picasso photographed by Helmut Newton in a sheath dress, one bare breast hidden behind a glass.
In 1983, Karl Lagerfeld left Chloé for Chanel. In 1985, the founding partners sold Chloé to Dunhill Holdings, part of the Richemont group, and the young and up-to-the-minute designer Martine Sitbon created an offbeat look of severe navy and white suits and black dresses. In 1992, Karl Lagerfeld made a triumphant return, with a soft palette and unstructured shapes. The arrival in 1997 of Stella McCartney, daughter of ex-Beatle Paul and his muse Linda, was a major media event worldwide. She brought with her a contemporary take on pop culture, a passion for vintage detail and for "feminine things" that women (such as her friends Madonna, Kate Moss, and Liv Tyler) wanted to wear.
With Ralph Toledano at the helm, the brand has diversified and launched numerous must-have bags. In 2000, the launch of a second ready-to-wear line, See By Chloé, was a notable hit. Then in 2001, McCartney's assistant Phoebe Philo took over, with equal success. By then the Chloé style—a mélange of sensuality, freedom, and confident femininity—had made it an indispensable part of the modern young woman's wardrobe. In 2008, Hannah MacGibbon replaced Paulo Melim Andersson at the helm.

The designs of the young genius of men's fashion,
Hedi Slimane, collection for men, fall-winter 2004–5.

Menswear

- FROM THE 1960S
- HUGO BOSS, PIERRE CARDIN, CERUTTI, JEAN PAUL GAULTIER, KENZO, YOHJI YAMAMOTO, COMME DES GARÇONS, THIERRY MUGLER, PAUL SMITH, JOSÉ LÉVY, MARTIN MARGIELA, DRIES VAN NOTEN, HELMUT LANG, RAF SIMONS, PRADA, GUCCI, HEDI SLIMANE...

Since the late 1980s, the twice-yearly fashion-show calendar has featured menswear as prominently as women's wear. The first menswear shows by Yohji Yamamoto, Comme des Garçons, Jean Paul Gaultier, Thierry Mugler, José Lévy, Martin Margiela, Dries Van Noten, and Helmut Lang represented a minor revolution in the world of fashion design. In a field well known for its traditionalism, making a show out of men's fashions and applying creative design principles to them was a startlingly new approach. Amused female fashion editors attended these early shows in a spirit of novelty but without placing much faith in the future of fashion design for men.

While it could not be denied that alternative styles had filtered up from the street to enliven traditional male clothing in the second half of the twentieth century, the effects were limited to the younger generation. Following the rigid codes of dress inherited from the nineteenth century, the ubiquitous suit and tie still reigned supreme, with jeans, polo shirts, T-shirts, and sweaters permissible for leisure wear.

Designers were therefore setting out on a formidable challenge to shake the status quo of the masculine wardrobe to its foundations, especially when it came to everyday wear. Due to fears of ridicule and of jettisoning all signifiers of masculine respectability, it took a long time for the wildest eccentricities, including lace suits, skirts for men, and eye-watering colors, to make their appearance on the catwalk. In the '80s, only a few of these outfits would penetrate beyond the rarefied circles of fashion victims: Yohji Yamamoto's black suits, Giorgio Armani's softly draped tailoring, and Paul Smith's revivals of the spirit of Savile Row.

The minimalism of the 1990s, led by Helmut Lang and taken up by Prada, was much more convincing to a male audience. Its austerity, as well as its combination of urban and sporty looks, ushered in a spasm of change that produced echoes on the high street, in stores like Zara and Celio in Europe and Club Monaco in North America.

Gradually, men accepted the mixing

Who invented the polo shirt?

Above:
Men also wear Prada. Left: a Zegna coat, Rag & Bone hooded sweatshirt, John Varvatos Star USA crew neck, CK39 jeans, and Ralph Lauren shoes. Right: a Prada shirt, Filippa K tie, and John Lobb shoes. Photograph by Richard Burbridge for *GQ*.

of genres, such as a parka worn over a suit or a sweatshirt under a jacket, like the "college boy" models of the Belgian designer Raf Simons. Classic feminine attributes migrated toward male attire, with the embroidery of José Lévy and the "total look" (suit, shirt, and tie in the same color) of Gucci, while Walter Van Beirendonck offered an arty take on streetwear with his comic-strip characters. By the end of the decade, the suit was only worn when necessary for work; the rest of the time, sportswear dominated the male wardrobe. At the start of the twenty-first century, under a powerful media spotlight, Hedi Slimane took over as artistic director of Dior Homme. Former assistant to José Lévy, Slimane looked to the world of young collegians for inspiration. Mixing with rock bands such as the Libertines and Franz Ferdinand, Slimane breathed a sensual, romantic, dandified charm into his "slim look," his snake-hipped, narrow-chested line. Designed to restore attitude and a confident bearing to men, the clothes proved equally attractive to women, who were known to buy his tight-fitting dinner jackets for themselves. Slimane was credited with reviving the suit, and the entire menswear sector benefited from this return to favor of masculine elegance, embraced with fervor by a new generation.

! The tennis player René Lacoste, at the end of the 1920s. Nicknamed "The Alligator," he adopted the reptile as his logo.

Photograph by Nathaniel Goldberg for the Costume National campaign, fall-winter 1996–7.

Brand patterns
What do they represent?

Answer

1. CACHAREL. 2. BURBERRY. 3. DIANE VON FURSTENBERG, "Twigs" motif, from a Wrap dress.
4. CHANEL. 5. PAUL SMITH. 6. EMILIO PUCCI.

1

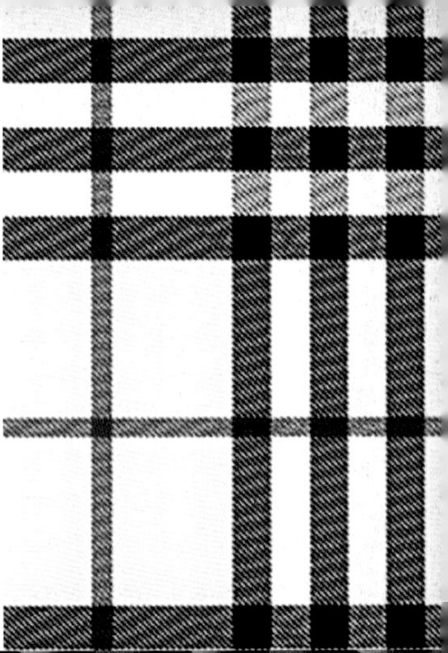

2

3

PAUL SMITH

•

EMILIO PUCCI

•

BURBERRY

•

CACHAREL

•

CHANEL

•

DIANE VON FURSTENBERG

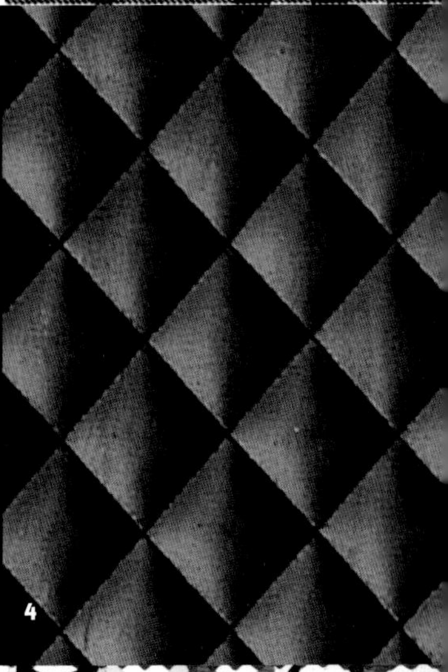

4

5

6

Martin Margiela

• (1957–) - BELGIUM
DECONSTRUCTION, MEMORY, RECYCLING, ECONOMY OF RESOURCES...

Martin Margiela doesn't allow photographs, unless you count the passport photo displayed in his atelier. His labels do not bear his name—only a number. And for many designers working today, he has created an alternative approach to fashion. From 1984 to 1987, when Japanese designers were experimenting with deconstructionism, Margiela was Jean Paul Gaultier's assistant, leading the second stage of this revolution but also broadening it with his artistic, poetic, and sensual sensibility.

From the outset, Margiela's themes were absence, traces, memory, and recycling. His propensity for analysis and pragmatism allows him to delve deeper with each collection into the art of tailoring and drapery in quest of new expressions of balance and proportion. A tailor's dummy takes pride of place in his atelier.

For his Flat collection, armholes and necks were flat as in a kimono; for his Stockman Dummy collection, as Tamsin Blanchard reported in the London *Independent,* he "chose not to show on the catwalk and showed a video in his showroom instead. The collection is based on the Stockman tailor's dummy, which Margiela has fashioned into a foundation garment. An ingeniously simple square of black silk is pinned onto it to make an elegant evening dress, while a yellow velvet half-dress or half-skirt is tied around as a 'work in progress.'"

Several of his lines are designated by numerals: Artisanal is 0, women's wear is 6, menswear is 10. Another line is devoted to authentic costumes, including an airplane stewardess's jacket, a priest's cassock, an eighteenth-century man's shirt, and a 1930s coverall. In addition, he recycles clothes that he has bought at flea markets. Every part of the original garment is used: The sleeves become mittens; the collars, handsome necklaces; the linings, pretty dresses. In the same spirit, Margiela's spring-summer 1994 show featured a collection of designs from previous seasons, unified by the color gray.

Margiela is a master of unsettling the world of fashion with his avant-garde shows. For his spring-summer 1990 show, fashion editors were invited to take their seats on a rubbish-strewn wasteland, to watch a parade of designs made out of plastic bags and sticky tape.

His arrival at Hermès in 1997, where

Opposite:
Stockman jacket, spring-summer 1997 collection. Margiela carved into actual Stockman tailor's dummies, then attached half-draped garments onto the forms to create jackets, vests, and dresses. The collection is an homage to the work of haute couture.

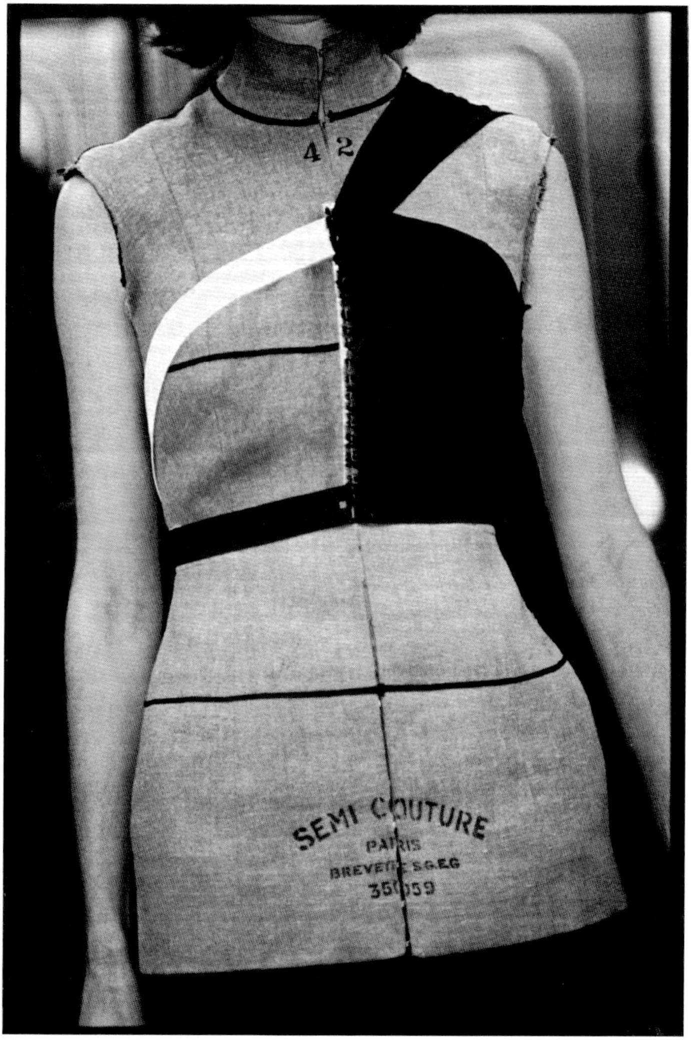

he designed collections until he was replaced by Gaultier in 2003, reinforced his reputation as a trailblazer. In 2003, the Italian group Diesel invested in Margiela's fashion house, enabling him to develop his lines and organize astonishing catwalk presentations, such as his 2005 show, in which models glided down the runway on dollies, their necklaces of colored ice gradually melting over their evening gowns; and his fall-winter 2007 show, which included a system of magic mirrors, as in a peep show.

Margiela is a free spirit in a world constrained by monetary concerns. Despite this, he continually turns out beautiful clothes that are on a plane all their own.

?

Martin Margiela's signature shoe design echoes the shape of what Japanese footwear?

Calvin Klein

• (1942–) - UNITED STATES
SIMPLICITY, SENSUALITY, LOVE, PURITY, ADOLESCENCE...
OBSESSION, ESCAPE, ETERNITY, CK ONE, EUPHORIA, CONTRADICTION, TRUTH...

Margiela's signature design draws inspiration from *tabi*, traditional split-toe socks and boots.

In 1980, Brooke Shields, then barely fifteen, purred, "Nothing comes between me and my Calvins." From that moment on, America knew the name Calvin Klein.

Born in the Bronx, in 1942 to Hungarian immigrant parents, Klein was always a prolific sketcher and was encouraged by his mother and grandmother to go into fashion. After attending the New York High School of Art and Design, he studied at the Fashion Institute of Technology until age twenty. In 1968, just six years later, he set up a small fashion studio with a childhood friend, Barry Schwartz, and made six coats and three dresses. Even in this microcollection, the Klein sense of design was conspicuous, catching the eye of a buyer from the Bonwit Teller store on Fifth Avenue: The collection went into its windows, and Klein gained the confidence to design a complete line of sportswear.

In the early 1970s, Klein launched the concept of designer jeans—immaculately cut and sporting his label—that was to be taken up by all his rivals. The scandal that erupted surrounding his now-infamous ad campaign featuring the young Ms. Shields helped to distinguish his brand and significantly boosted the label's street credibility among the young—and in the process, helped to sell Calvin Klein jeans by the thousands. A fashion show featuring a parade of models in briefs also shocked the public, but not as deeply as a 1990s campaign featuring adolescents in provocative poses. In these campaigns we see not just one of the first and most successful exponents of designer jeans and branded underwear but also an outstanding player in fashion marketing. Indeed, his 1992 campaign by Herb Ritts, with Kate Moss and Mark Wahlberg, ensured the success of the unisex fashion that had become a Calvin Klein specialty.

The unisex application of his designs was aided by the simplicity of form, color, and fabric that had become a hallmark of his work. The sensuality that imbued the photographs used in advertising campaigns for his perfumes further emphasized the stylistic connections with his underwear line. In

1982, when his boxer shorts hit the streets, thousands of young men began showing off the distinctive waistbands of the boxers—the "CK" logo peeking out just above their baggy jeans. Klein had established the concept of sexy male underwear. In the 1990s, his women's lingerie would again reinvent a wardrobe staple, this time lending a more sophisticated twist to traditional cotton underwear. Klein's career, a marriage of two opposing forces, contrasts the understated minimalism of his clothes with the controversial provocation (some would say exploitation) that marks his publicity strategy. He has been showered with honors, and has been among the top twenty-five on *Time* magazine's "most influential" list. Klein sold his business to the Phillips-Van Heusen Corporation in 2003.

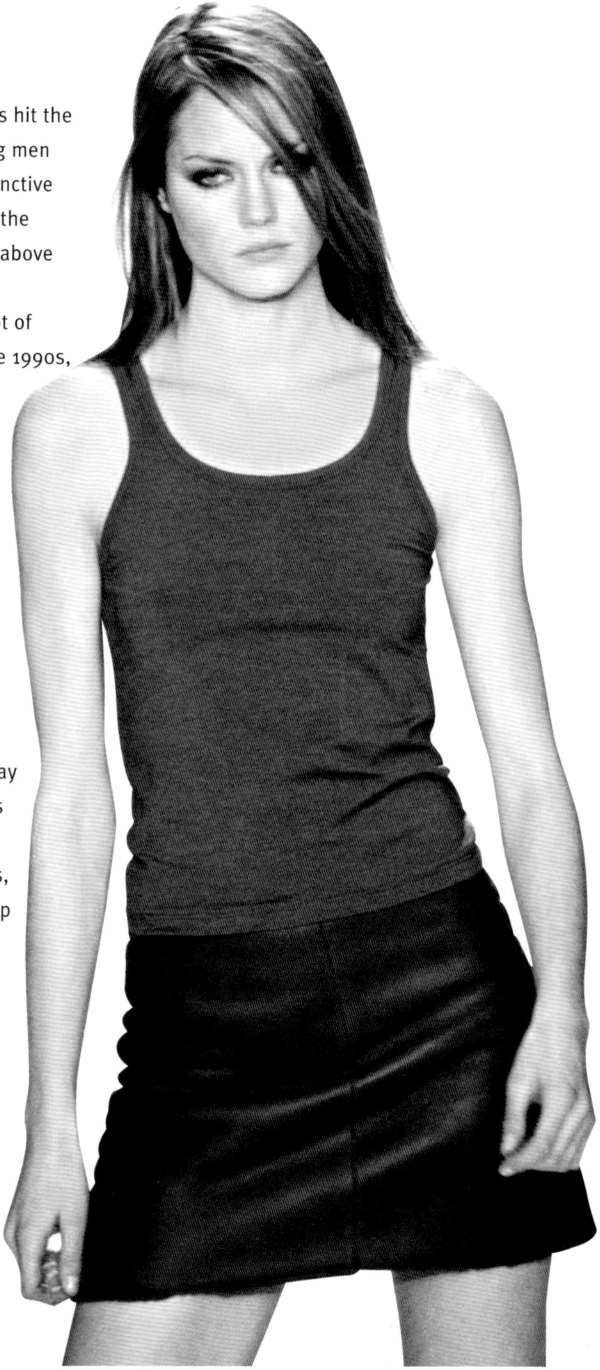

From the Calvin Klein fall-winter 2001–2 show in New York.

Designers' words
Who said what?

Gianni Versace

Christian Dior

Manolo Blahnik

Tom Ford

Geoffrey Beene

Elsa Schiaparelli

Stefano Gabbana

Miuccia Prada

Oleg Cassini

Hubert de Givenchy

Fashion Magazines

- SINCE THE EIGHTEENTH CENTURY
- *VOGUE, HARPER'S BAZAAR, ELLE, MARIE CLAIRE, GLAMOUR, COSMOPOLITAN, L'OFFICIEL, ESQUIRE, GQ...*

Vogue magazine, March 1912, illustrated by Gayle Porter Hoskins.

Opposite: *Harper's Bazaar* cover, February 1952.

Although Paris is the modern capital of the fashion press, the earliest precursor to a fashion magazine was published in Germany in 1586 by Swiss artist Josse Amman. Called *Gynasceum*, or *Theater of Women*, it featured hand-painted plates showing the styles of the day.

Starting in the eighteenth century, however, France took the lead. *La Galerie des modes et costumes Français* was published from 1778 to 1787 and featured colored engravings and descriptions of costumes worn by ladies of the court. By the end of the next century, photography had become available as an aid to disseminating the latest looks: The monthly *Les Modes* (launched in 1901) made a specialty of the new medium with its full-page portrait plates of mannequins and celebrities. The fortnightly *Femina,* launched the same year, addressed a broad readership with varied editorial content, including fashion, reporting, a society gossip column, and, in a tentative manifestation of early feminism, profiles of exceptional women.

In 1912, the French publisher Lucien Vogel launched *La Gazette du bon ton,* illustrated with engravings by well-known artists and accompanied by texts from writers including Jean Cocteau. Vogel's next venture, *Le Jardin des Modes* (founded in 1922), together with the weekly *Marie Claire* (started in 1937 by Jean Prouvost, who also launched *Paris Soir*) and *Elle* (founded in 1945 by Marcelle Auclair and Hélène Lazareff) formed a trio of titles that expressed the postwar desire for modernity.

In the United States, the women's press modeled itself on the pioneering *Harper's Bazaar,* a weekly launched in 1867. This and other elite titles developed by Condé Nast Publications, including *Vanity Fair* and *Vogue*, introduced the work of many of the great names in photography, including Irving Penn, Richard

Avedon, David Bailey, and Helmut Newton. The powerful editors of these glossy magazines sought not only to showcase the latest fashion trends but to shape them as well, and they continue to play a role in making or breaking a designer's career. John Fairchild, the publisher of *Women's Wear Daily* from 1960 to 1996, famously banned any mention of certain designers in his pages.

In the 1990s, the magazine *Purple* opened up a new genre, somewhere between contemporary-art review and fashion magazine. Publications such as *Citizen K*, *Self Service*, *View on Colour*, *Visionaire*, and *W* sprang up to occupy this challenging territory. Other new titles moved in the opposite direction, specializing in a particular category of fashion, such as shoes or jewelry. Recently, in addition to the niche publications, the financial and daily newspapers have begun vying with the dedicated glossies to offer informed perspectives on the fashion industry—proof of fashion's influence beyond its own sphere.

?

Who created the first fashion "series" in 1911 for the magazine *Art et Décoration*?

Versace

- HOUSE FOUNDED IN 1978
- GLAMOUR, BAROQUE, ECLECTICISM, SENSUALITY, JET SET, ROCK 'N' ROLL...
- VERSACE WOMEN, VERSACE HOMME, VERSUS, RED JEANS, METAL JEANS FEMME, CRYSTAL NOIR, BLONDE, THE DREAMER, BLUE JEANS, TIME TO RELAX, TIME FOR ENERGY, TIME FOR PLEASURE...

! The couturier Paul Poiret and the photographer Edward Steichen.

Gianni Versace had no fear of provocation or paradox when he proclaimed, "I dress the nouveaux riches. So what?" Two of his red-carpet gowns stand out as milestones in his high-profile career: The safety-pinned column (fondly known in the British press as "That Dress") worn by Elizabeth Hurley and the corseted and fishtailed black gown chosen by Catherine Zeta-Jones for the 2001 Oscars. And of course, who could forget Jennifer Lopez's dramatic appearance at the 2000 Grammy Awards in a certain green Versace dress? These quintessentially Versace apparitions showcased a carefully calculated balance between a full-frontal celebration of feminine allure and a sense of sheer spectacle. Versace offered his fans a mélange of pure, unadulterated Italian style, culled from every part of the peninsula, repackaging the idea of the overdressed stars of Italian Cinecittà with a dash of the most celestial and beautiful figure in Italy—the *Pietà*.

Indeed, Versace found inspiration all over his home country, from his apprenticeship with his couturiere mother in Calabria to the Byzantine mosaics in the city of Ravenna; from Bernini's baroque Roman splendor to the colors of the duomos and the magnificence of Michelangelo; and in the elegance and immaculate cuts of Emilio Pucci and the Sisters Fontana. Versace's decorative sense, meanwhile, drew from the city of Como, the Borromeo palazzi, and the villas of Palladio. The structure of his business was Italian, too—a family firm with his businessman brother, Santo, and his sister and muse, Donatella, at its center. In Versace's world, baroque exuberance exploded into unfettered eclecticism, Roman history mingled with a colorful miscellany of references as diverse as Alexander Calder, Wassily Kandinsky, Gustav Klimt, Andy Warhol, ancient Egypt, Neoplatonism, and psychedelia. Alongside all this, Versace pursued a campaign of accumulating estates, labels, and boutiques in the fields of fashion, accessories, and home decoration, while living like a Renaissance prince in sumptuous

Top models photographed by Michel Comte in the Versace house of couture for the fall-winter 1994–5 collection.

Medici-era palazzi to which he gave Hollywood-style makeovers. His response to criticism of his taste for excess was clear: "I can't bear half-measures. I believe in making definite choices."

This riveting life story, from impoverished origins to the pinnacles of fame and success, was to come to a tragic end. On July 15, 1997, Gianni Versace was murdered outside Casa Casuarina, his mansion in Miami Beach. He was fifty. His funeral in Milan Cathedral was attended by two thousand guests and was on a scale normally only seen for heads of state. The reasons for his murder remain unclear. Most certainly, it was a family tragedy. As speculation swirled, the fashion industry mourned its loss. But the spirit that Gianni Versace embodied would not be broken, and following her brother's death, Donatella took over the creative direction of the House of Versace, remaining true to Gianni's belief that female sensuality is the expression of female power.

Giorgio Armani

- (1934–) - ITALY
- THE SPIRIT OF THE TIMES, PERSONAL STYLE, THE ELEGANCE OF WELL-BEING...
- ACQUA DI GIÒ, ARMANI CODE, EMPORIO ARMANI POUR LUI, ATTITUDE, ARMANI, ARMANI MANIA, CITY GLAM, SENSI, EMPORIO ARMANI DIAMONDS, EMPORIO ARMANI WHITE, EMPORIO SHE...

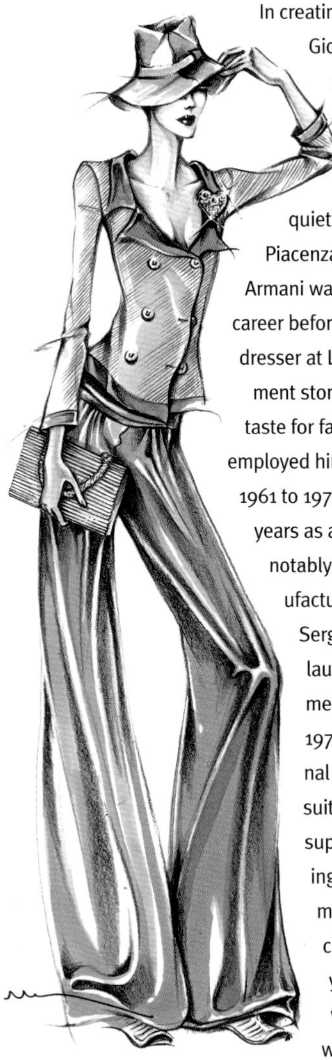

In creating his luxury empire, Giorgio Armani launched a revolution in menswear that changed the way men view black-tie style. Born in the quiet provincial town of Piacenza, in northern Italy, Armani was set on a medical career before a job as a window dresser at La Rinascente, a department store in Milan, gave him a taste for fashion. Nino Cerruti employed him as a designer from 1961 to 1970; he then spent a few years as a freelance designer, notably for a men's jacket manufacturer. With his partner, Sergio Galeotti, Armani launched his own menswear collection in 1974, founded on the original concept that men's suits should possess the suppleness and fine tailoring that was more commonly found in women's clothing. The following year, he launched a women's collection in which he gave the suits a contemporary edge by borrowing from men's tailoring.

In his early men's suits, Armani removed all interfacings and stiffeners from the jackets, which he wanted to have a softly worn-in look; the cut, meanwhile, was semifitted to give greater freedom of movement. A single button replaced the traditional four or five. In making the male silhouette more fluid and pliant, Armani created a new ideal of masculinity, epitomized by Richard Gere's character in the 1980 film *American Gigolo*, written and directed by Paul Schrader. In it, Gere donned more than thirty Armani suits, and the coolly stylish eroticism of the film appealed to a new generation of men who wanted an alternative to the stiff and starchy connotations of the traditional suit. The brand Emporio Armani, launched the following year, was a massive success among young people, who could now buy high-quality suits at reasonable prices. The growth of the Armani empire has continued, expanding to include furniture and restaurants.

Undoubtedly, Armani's focus on realistic fashion, wearable and far removed from the theatricality of the haute cou-

ture shows, has ensured the outstanding success of his empire. As the innovator himself says, "The reason I do runway shows is so that the press can talk about what will be in the stores." Even on the runway, Armani believes in practicalities.

Richard Gere wearing Giorgio Armani in Paul Schrader's *American Gigolo*, 1980. The actor greatly contributed to the success of Armani's men's suits.

Opposite:
Sketch by Giorgio Armani for his spring-summer 2007 collection.

?

Who was Jacques Doucet?

Ralph Lauren

• (1939–) - UNITED STATES
POLO, GENTLEMEN, SPORTS, WASP STYLE, BOURGEOIS CHIC...
POLO, LAUREN, POLO EXPLORER, POLO SPORT, PURE TURQUOISE, ROMANCE, SAFARI...

Known throughout the world, the Ralph Lauren look is based on an all-American lifestyle, a WASP-inspired version of casual gentrification. Buying a Ralph Lauren garment is like buying into the American dream. This was the basic concept, formulated forty years ago by a former glove salesman named Ralph Lifshitz, upon which the massive success of the label would rest. But the spirit of the label also reflects its founder's personal trajectory. The son of Jewish immigrants from Belarus, the young Ralph worked after school in order to buy smart clothes, and at sixteen changed his name from Lifshitz to Lauren in order to better fit into American society. Studying business at night school, he worked for Brooks Brothers and then Beau Brummell Ties, where in 1967 the company's president gave Lauren carte blanche to run his own tie division. The Polo label was born.
Lauren wanted to make the necktie into a style statement. As he explained years later, "A tie was the way a man expressed himself. I believed that men were ready for something new and different. They didn't want to look as if they worked for IBM. A beautiful tie was an expression of quality, taste, style." Instead of the narrow ties dictated by convention, Lauren proposed wide, handmade ties in flamboyant designs and colors. His small necktie company, Polo Fashions, would eventually become a vast multinational enterprise.
Gradually, Lauren explored all the archetypes of Ivy League male elegance, taking inspiration from such traditionally aristocratic sports as polo, golf, tennis, sailing, and rugby, as well from as preppy campus life. He also produced women's wear versions of his menswear lines, adapting the house style to current trends: He went high-tech with the RLX label, and urban with Purple Label, for example. In the 1980s, Lauren opened boutiques that were forerunners of his flagship stores, conceived as comfortable and luxurious living spaces through which clients were invited to wander at their leisure.
The embodiment of classic style adapted to contemporary life, Ralph Lauren remains one of the most prominent and successful of American ready-to-wear designers.

! A patron of the arts, an aesthete, and a collector (he was the first to buy *Les demoiselles d'Avignon* from Picasso), this couturier (1853–1929) invented the "tea gown"—the indoor robe worn to "receive people"—and discovered Paul Poiret.

From the Ralph Lauren fall-winter 2005–6 collection.

Models
Who's who?

Answer

1. **CHERYL TIEGS**, cover of *Time*, March 6, 1978. 2. **JANICE DICKINSON**, photographed by Duffy, cover of *Elle*, June 2, 1975. 3. **LAUREN HUTTON**, cover of *Esquire*, December 1968. 4. **MARGAUX HEMINGWAY**, photographed by Dick Halstead, cover of *Time*, June 16, 1975.

1

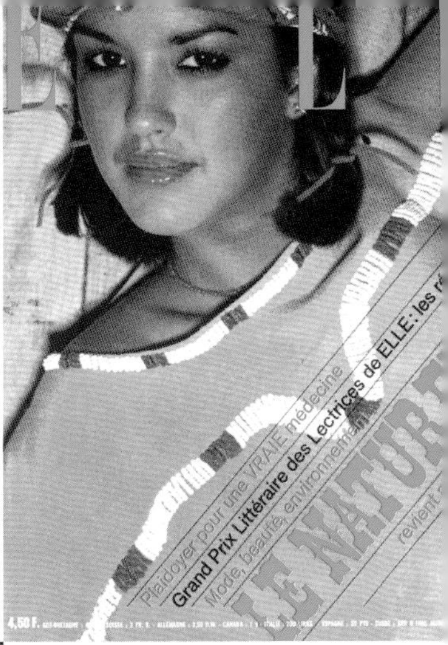

2

CHERYL TIEGS

•

LAUREN HUTTON

•

MARGAUX HEMINGWAY

•

JANICE DICKINSON

3

4

Fabrics

Opposite:
A manufacturing facility in the Lyonnaise region of France.

A designer's studio. Photographed by Keiichi Tahara.

Textile fibers, in the form of woven threads, are the raw materials used to make fabrics, which in turn are used to make clothing. How the warp and weft yarns intersect defines the weave by which fabrics are categorized.

Weaves fall into three principal types: plain, twill, and satin. Plain weave is the oldest of these, with the earliest surviving fragments, found in Turkey, dating back to 6,000 BC. Twill weaves, such as serge and tweed, appeared in the first millennium BC, while satin weave appeared in Europe in the fourteenth century. The variety of textures derives from the nature of the yarn, the weave, and the colors used; in Europe, this variety developed as a result of the meeting of East and West during the time of the Crusades. Trade with India and China introduced coveted silks to Europe.

The earliest fiber to be used in human history was of vegetable origin; wool made its appearance around 4,000 BC. It was not until the early twentieth century that artificial fibers were introduced, revolutionizing the textile industry and allowing the development of synthetic fabrics. Artificial fibers are in fact derived from natural substances—whether animal (protein), vegetable (cellulose), or mineral (glass)—that undergo a chemical change. In 1885, the French chemist Hilaire de Chardonnet developed an artificial thread that looked and felt like silk. Later known as rayon, it was widely used in lingerie, but artificial silks were not introduced

in fashion until the 1920s, when couturiers such as Coco Chanel and Elsa Schiaparelli used them to make evening dresses.

Synthetic fibers, meanwhile, are products of organic chemistry and do not exist in nature; they are compounds derived from substances such as coal, petrol, and castor oil. In 1931, the American chemist Wallace Carothers developed the first synthetic fiber, polyamide 6/6. Beginning in 1938, it was marketed as nylon, and the material advertised as “strong as steel and as fine as a spider’s web” quickly supplanted silk in the hugely successful postwar stocking industry.

Today the vast choice of available fabrics is constantly enriched by new inventions, but natural fibers remain popular. Indeed, the interest in organic and unbleached cottons, as well as in fabrics made from hemp or bamboo, has only increased in an ecologically aware age. In the luxury market, Lyon silk dominated for centuries, but fashion designers are increasingly turning to innovative Italian and Japanese textiles.

Who invented the first machine for weaving fabrics?

Azzedine Alaïa

• (1940–) - TUNISIA
ANATOMY, SENSUALITY, THE 1930S, GRECO-ROMAN ANTIQUITY, CONTEMPORARY ART, DESIGN....

In 1769, the English inventor Richard Arkwright patented a hydro-powered weaving machine.

Little known among the general public but unanimously respected by his fellow designers, Azzedine Alaïa is often regarded as the greatest living couturier. He combines creative excellence with technical virtuosity and will personally make a garment from start to finish. And Alaïa is more than capable of inventing new couture techniques along the way. His immense couture house on the corner of Rue de Moussy and Rue de la Verrerie in Paris brings together a mélange of fashion and industry. This hive of activity functions along similar lines to the concept store at 10 Corso Como in Milan, the brainchild of Carla Sozzani, who has advised Alaïa since he joined the Prada group, in 2000. In both locations, couture and prêt-à-porter collections jostle with exhibitions and galas in a never-ending whirl of activities.

The Alaïa phenomenon is not easily explained, and the couturier himself is at pains to sustain the mystery: How did this student of sculpture at the Ecole des Beaux-Arts in Tunis become known as the most Parisian of all couturiers? He arrived in Paris in 1957 and worked for just five days at Dior and then for two seasons at Guy Laroche, always laboring in the shadow of admiring clients, such as the actress Arletty, the writer Louise de Vilmorin, Simone Zehrfuss, and the Comtesse de Blégiers. The fashion press can take some credit for offering encouragement to the young designer: One of his designs for Les Fourrures de la Madeleine was featured in *Elle* in 1979, and a coat perforated with metal eyelets appeared in *Dépêche Mode* in 1980. And so Alaïa was launched; he showed his first collections in 1981 in his small apartment on Rue de Bellechasse, attracting a galaxy of stars that included Grace Jones, Madonna, and Tina Turner. But beyond this enigmatic life story lies one unde-

Helena Christensen in a long chain lacy nightgown, over a black demicup bra and panties made of cotton satin, spring-summer 1992 collection. Sculpting the body was intended to give it dreamlike proportions.

Opposite:
Azzedine Alaïa adjusting the waistline of a skirt for the spring-summer 1992 collection.

niable truth: Azzedine Alaïa has invented a new way of making women beautiful and desirable. Alaïa exalts the female body without artifice and with no weapons other than skillful cutting and innovations such as sinuous seams that snake around the body's contours. In the 1980s, when he became known as the King of Cling, he created figure-hugging bodysuits and leggings that accentuated the waist, hips, buttocks, and breasts while disguising imperfections. The use of stretch fabrics, later to be adopted by the high street, marked his tenure at 17 Rue du Parc-Royal. Since 2000, collection after collection has featured innovative variations on corsets, skirts, sleeves, and jacket and coat collars, notably perfecting a subtle system of articulated seams. The secret of Alaïa's allure can be found in his lavish celebration of female beauty, combined with austere restraint in his choice of palette and decoration.

Donna Karan

• HOUSE FOUNDED IN 1984
THE CORPORATE WORLD, FUNCTIONALISM, SENSUALITY, WOMAN OF ACTION...
CASHMERE MIST, BE DELICIOUS, DONNA KARAN GOLD...

Donna Karan advertising campaign: "In Women We Trust," spring-summer 1992 collection. Photograph by Peter Lindbergh.

Opposite:
The model Beri Smither posing for a DKNY NYC advertising campaign, fall-winter 1994. Photograph by Peter Lindbergh.

Born and bred in New York, the daughter of a model and a Seventh Avenue tailor, Donna Karan—known as the Queen of Seventh Avenue—is the quintessential American fashion designer, largely responsible for the international reputation of American ready-to-wear collections.
Her fashion story began with a quest for her own personal style: "What do I need? How can I make life easier? How can dressing be simplified so that I can get on with my own life?" Karan was looking for a mix between sportswear and urban chic. Reinventing the code of the working woman's wardrobe, she added notes of seductiveness and sensuality, dressing women in soft, clinging jersey, cashmere, and stretch crepe, and sheathing their legs in tights. In Karan's publicity campaigns, Isabella Rossellini personified career women who were also successful wives and mothers—consummate women of action. The spring-summer 1992 "In Women We Trust" campaign featured a model posing as the first female U. S. president, dressed in a Donna Karan suit.
After attending the Parsons School of Design, Karan started work as a designer for Anne Klein in 1967. In 1974, the week that Karan's first child was born, Klein died of cancer. Karan had hardly brought her baby home before she was swamped by rail upon rail of half-completed clothes needed for an imminent show, accompanied by models and the atelier staff en masse. Though she had intended to stop working in order to look after her newborn, Karan suddenly found herself running the company, and the *New York Times* declared, "A Star Is Born."
In 1984, Karan struck out on her own and founded Donna Karan New York with her second husband and business partner, the sculptor Stephan Weiss. She launched her famous "Seven Easy Pieces" collection—in

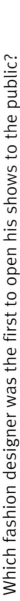

her signature color black, naturally. Practical and interchangeable, it formed the basis of a complete capsule wardrobe. With coordinates for men, she also freed the male wardrobe from the stranglehold of convention.

Her brand has grown to encompass beauty products, perfume, accessories, furniture, home accessories, children's wear, and jeans and is now sold in sixteen Donna Karan boutiques and forty-seven DKNY boutiques throughout the world. Quoted on the New York Stock Exchange in 1996 and sold in 2001 to the LVMH group for $643 million, the company is now run by Mark Weber, chief executive of LVMH in America.

?

Which fashion designer was the first to open his shows to the public?

Evolution of Fashion Designers

- BEGINNING IN 1950–60
- CHRISTIANE BAILLY, EMMANUELLE KHANH, MICHÈLE ROSIER, SONIA RYKIEL, KENZO, ISSEY MIYAKE, THIERRY MUGLER, JEAN PAUL GAULTIER, AGNÈS B., ANNE-MARIE BERETTA, CHANTAL THOMASS, CLAUDE MONTANA...

! Thierry Mugler. In 1984, he presented a show and concert to six thousand spectators.

The term "fashion designer" was coined in the 1960s to describe the new activity of creating collections for ready-to-wear manufacturers. Before this time, manufacturers had worked with dress designers, who looked to press pictures of haute couture models for inspiration to make garments that both conformed to the dictates of the couturiers and were suitable for mass production. Fashion designers enabled manufacturers to extricate themselves from this dependence on haute couture and to produce autonomous ready-to-wear collections. As haute couture lost momentum, young designers who were engaged with this experiment gained confidence. They launched ready-to-wear lines under their own names, becoming influential figures in the latest developments and trends.

Prominent among this first generation of designers were Azzedine Alaïa, Agnès B., Anne Marie Beretta, Jean-Charles de Castelbajac, Jean Paul Gaultier, Kenzo, Issey Miyake, Claude Montana, Thierry Mugler, Sonia Rykiel, and Chantal Thomass.

During the 1980s, many of the haute couture fashion designers placed an increasing emphasis on their unbridled creativity, comporting themselves like artists and celebrities, sometimes to the point of forgetting the ultimate purpose of their work: to sell clothes. The archetype of the "mad genius" Paris couturier eventually lost its luster, tarnished by a spate of bankruptcies and failures to develop viable labels.

By the late 1980s, young fashion students who ten years earlier would have dreamed of launching their own businesses and becoming the next Gaultier were fewer and fewer. Today's ambitious young design graduate instead aspires to helm a luxury conglomerate as an artistic director, orchestrating all the departments—from conception to merchandising—and defining the artistic and media profile of the brand.

The concept of fashion design, meanwhile, has broadened to embrace two kinds of stylists: those who set up shots for maga-

zine and advertising shoots, and those who advise the artistic director on the development of each new line, with the power to exert considerable influence on the collection's direction and concept.

Yohji Yamamoto lost in thought, imagining the spring-summer 1991 show in Paris.

Designers' sketches
Who made what?

Answer

1. CHRISTIAN LACROIX, haute couture collection, spring-summer 2008. **2. GIANFRANCO FERRÉ FOR DIOR**, Dior haute couture collection, fall-winter 1989–90. **3. YOHJI YAMAMOTO**, Poupées Russes (Russian Dolls) collection, spring-summer 1989. **4. VALENTINO**, haute couture collection, fall-winter 1989–90.

1

2

GIANFRANCO FERRÉ

•

YOHJI YAMAMOTO

•

CHRISTIAN LACROIX

•

VALENTINO

3

4

Christian Lacroix

• HOUSE FOUNDED IN 1987 BY CHRISTIAN LACROIX (1951–) - FRANCE
ARLES, THE BAROQUE, SPAIN, ART HISTORY, PAINTING, COLORS, THEATER...
C'EST LA VIE !, TUMULTE, BAZAR, EAU FLORALE...

Spring-summer collection, 2008.

Opposite:
The couturier Christian Lacroix with models for his first collection in spring-summer 1988, including Marpessa, Marie Seznec, and Kadija.

When he founded his fashion house in 1987—with Bernard Arnault's Financière Agache, later to become the LVMH group—Christian Lacroix restored haute couture to its place in the fashion galaxy. Lacroix didn't just revamp haute couture, he also signaled a return of fashion as a whole to luxury and sophistication. Six months after his label's debut, his baroque style was the trend to follow for ready-to-wear collections, featuring strong, contrasting colors; exuberant combinations of polka dots, stripes, and floral patterns; and petticoats, puffball skirts, and bolero jackets. It was a look of elegant flirtation.

Lacroix's rich variety of design influences stems from memories of his childhood in Arles, France; his voracious reading and studies in the history of art and fashion; his fascination with the eighteenth and nineteenth centuries; and his interest in Spain and folk culture. In addition, three professional experiences paved the way for his glittering career: First, he worked as a designer at Hermès; then as an assistant to Guy Paulin in 1978; and finally as artistic director at Jean Patou in 1981. In each position Lacroix consistently impressed the fashion press with the brilliance of his designs. One of the factors that set him apart was his realization that luxury haute couture had no chance of survival without suppli-

ers of quality, and he gave the latter a prominent place in his collections. The public gazed in wonder at the beauty of his embroideries and passementerie, at the feathers and flowers that had been neglected by haute couture for the two prior decades. Through his attention to such details, Lacroix established a fine balance between tradition and modernity.

During the 1990s, Lacroix began to explore the world of theater and dance, designing costumes and sets for numerous productions. Theater techniques now began to enrich his fashion designs, with paints, dyes, embroideries, and patinas lending intensity and vibrancy to the surfaces of his garments, while hair and accessories also became more dramatic and expressive. In 2007, an exhibition entitled "Christian Lacroix: Costumer," held at the Centre National de Costume de Scène et de Scénographie in Moulins, France, paid tribute to thirty productions costumed by Lacroix. Gradually, he focused all his theatrical research on fabrics and cuts into haute couture, while his ready-to-wear designs became more practical for everyday.

In the spring of 2008, Lacroix's twenty years in haute couture were celebrated in an exhibition entitled "Collexposition" at the Musée de la Mode et du Textile in Paris.

?

What does "prêt-à-porter" mean?

Dolce & Gabbana

- HOUSE FOUNDED IN 1985
- BAROQUE, ECLECTICISM, SENSUALITY, ROCK 'N' ROLL...
- DOLCE & GABBANA, D&G FÉMININE, SICILY, LIGHT BLUE, THE ONE...

! It is French for "ready-to-wear," a term that was originated by American fashion designers and later adopted by French manufacturers to describe noncouture clothes sold in standard sizes.

The label Dolce & Gabbana combines the two extremities of the Italian peninsula, fusing the fashion of the north with the passion of the south. Domenico Dolce was born in Polizzi Generosa, near Palermo, Sicily, and Stefano Gabbana is from the northern city of Milan. Touches of Sicilian life and folk traditions have always informed their designs, which often reflect or incorporate Sicilian cross-stitch embroidery, shawls, bustiers modeled on 1920s singlets, liberty bodices, crucifixes, cameos, ex-votos prints, the color black, and floral motifs inspired by the gardens of Palermo. Indeed, popular and aristocratic life in Sicily came together in the company's 1988 manifesto collection. In it, the designers drew inspiration from the proud, passionate female characters of the writer Leonardo Sciascia, whose Sicilian tales celebrate women in their many roles: wives, mothers, and lovers who carry their rosaries as trophies of life and death.

Mingling with these influences is the duo's unconditional love for Italian cinema—for *La Dolce Vita*, the stars of Cinecittà, the dignified sensuality of film icons such as Anna Magnani, and the directors Federico Fellini, Pier Paolo Pasolini, and Luchino Visconti. The Dolce & Gabbana heroine, as embodied by the androgynous "Saphico chic" collection of 1994, shared with her male counterpart a neorealist style featuring the cap of the Sicilian mafiosi, singlets, and striped trousers.

Dolce & Gabbana invokes the past without nostalgia and projects it against an ultracontemporary context. A 1995 collection, for example, inspired by the Aeolian Islands, offered images of elegant women wearing head scarves and rosaries at their throats—but even against this austere background, leopard and zebra prints, corsets, and Grace Kelly–inspired chignons were never absent for long. As confirmed admirers of the baroque, Dolce and Gabbana revel in eclecticism: Their "hippie chic" collection of 1992 was all flashiness and kitsch, with basques worn under suit jackets, dresses with suggestively exposed décolletages, an abundance of fur, and bra-revealing necklines.

In 2007, photographs by Steven Klein for the American fashion magazine *W* laid Dolce & Gabbana bare, both literally and metaphorically, revealing a world of decadent and morbid fantasy, a Pasolini-like universe of languidly beautiful young men. Yet Dolce & Gabbana has an impressive list of glamorous women, actresses, and female celebrities as clients, including Beyoncé, Gisele Bündchen, Kylie Minogue, Madonna, Elizabeth Hurley, and Monica Bellucci.

With a dual instinct for the popular and the baroque, the pair occupies the place held in the 1990s by Gianni Versace. At their nineteenth-century minipalazzo in Milan, they would recreate la dolce vita, throwing sumptuous parties amid a decor described by the *Guardian*'s Jess Cartner-Morley as a "gorgeously kitsch romp."

Cindy Crawford wearing Dolce & Gabbana at the spring-summer 1992 show.

Opposite: Stefano Gabbana and Domenico Dolce at the Dolce & Gabbana gala at the 57th Cannes Film Festival, in 2004.

From the Dries Van Noten spring-summer 2007 collection.

Opposite: Portrait of Ann Demeulemeester.

The Belgian School

- FROM 1986 TO THE PRESENT
- MARTIN MARGIELA, ANN DEMEULEMEESTER, DRIES VAN NOTEN, WALTER VAN BEIRENDONCK, DIRK BIKKEMBERGS, RAF SIMONS, VERONIQUE BRANQUINHO, A. F. VANDEVORST, KRIS VAN ASSCHE, OLIVIER THEYSKENS, HAIDER ACKERMANN, LUTZ, BRUNO PIETERS, DIRK VAN SAENE, MARTINA YEE...

In the 1980s, the famous Antwerp Six succeeded in revolutionizing Belgian fashion and securing a place for the city on the map of world style. However, just ten years earlier, in the late 1970s, Belgian textile manufacturing companies were struggling, despite their professionalism, to compete with rivals in France, Italy, and Britain. Try as they might to boost their fortunes by adopting Italian- or American-sounding names, Belgian labels simply lacked credibility on the international fashion scene. Against this background, the Belgian government decided to take action, founding the Instituut voor Textiel en Confectie van België, inaugurating the Gouden Spoel competition, organizing trips to Japan for fashion students, and launching the magazine *Mode, dit is Belgisch* (*Fashion Is Belgian*). In 1986, a group of six designers who had graduated from the Royal Academy of Fine Arts in Antwerp several years earlier, supported by state subsidies, exhibited their

work at London Fashion Week. Within a few years, their names—Dirk Bikkembergs, Ann Demeulemeester, Walter Van Beirendonck, Dries Van Noten, Dirk Van Saene, and Martina Yee—would become common parlance in the fashion world. A seventh designer, Martin Margiela, who graduated from the same school in 1980, sealed Belgium's new reputation and prominence in the field. Although the members of this Belgian avant-garde repudiate the idea of a homogeneous artistic group, observers outside Belgium have identified them as creators of an alternative style

?

For whom did Jean-Charles de Castelbajac create liturgical clothing?

The Belgian School

distinguished by its subtle combination of austerity, hidden luxury, art, pragmatism, and perfectionism. From experienced Japanese designers they learned the lessons of fashion and developed the ability to break down the traditional elements of a garment to create new and arresting designs. As the reputation of the Belgian School has grown, several generations of designers have received attention and immediate recognition in the international fashion press. Following in the wake of the Antwerp Six came another group of young designers: Haider Ackermann, Veronique Branquinho, Lutz, Bruno Pieters, Raf Simons, and An Vandevorst and Filip Arickx. Doubtless because Belgian design is distinguished by originality, an independent spirit, and an uncompromising attitude that is not easily compatible with the philosophy of the big luxury labels, the most exclusive firms have only recently started to employ their talents, with Dior putting Kris Van Assche in charge of Dior Homme and Nina Ricci selecting Olivier Theyskens as artistic director in 2007. Though major brands have been slow to adopt these designers, the Belgians are masters at developing their own labels and making them commercial without compromising their creative dynamic.

Above:
Dries Van Noten designs.

Right:
An Ann Demeulemeester design.

! For the Pope, on the occasion of the twelfth World Youth Day, in 1997.

Detail

Who was the designer?

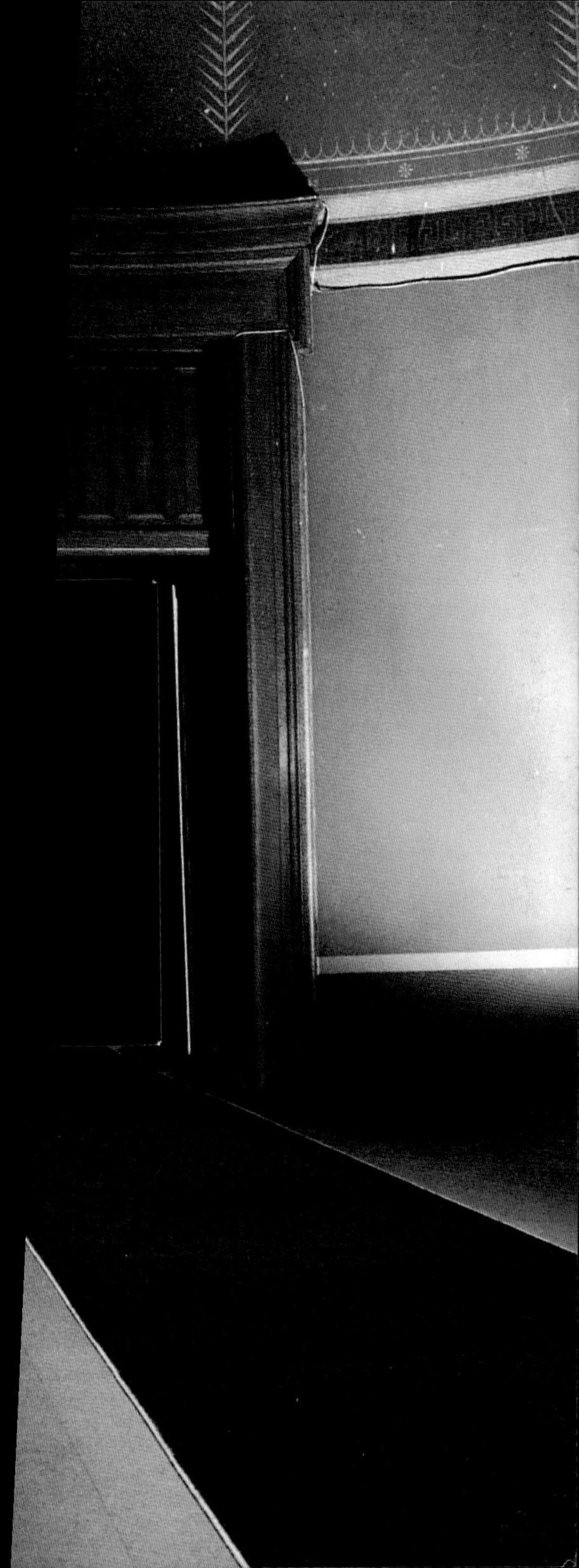

ELSA SC

Schiaparelli create
with Salvador Dalí. Dalí c
lobster on the front of th
designer on silk, transposed
Dalí wanted to sprea
finished dress

Handbags

- THE UTILITARIAN BAG SINCE FOREVER, THE "IT" BAG SINCE THE 1990S
- THE 2-55 BY CHANEL, THE KELLY BY HERMÈS, THE BAGUETTE BY FENDI, THE LADY DI BY DIOR, THE JACKIE O. BY GUCCI...

An edition of the Fendi Baguette handbag.

Below:
Speedy Bag in Graffiti Monogram canvas, created in 2000 in collaboration with New York artist Stephen Sprouse.

It was not until the past two decades that the handbag—a simple accessory—came to embody the quintessence of each season's fashions. Historically, designers of leather goods had been content to combine elegance with practicality, and women chose sturdy handbags designed to last for a number of years. When it came to choosing day bags that might be kept for a lifetime, quality was the prime consideration. A touch of frivolity might be permitted for evening bags, but it had to be borne in mind that most women only owned one, which had to go with every evening outfit.

The arrival in the world of fashion of the great leather-goods firms, such as Gucci, Prada, and Louis Vuitton, brought about a fundamental change in the traditional status of the handbag. Because the luxury firms could not turn a fast profit on their ready-to-wear collections, they began to focus on developing their handbags, the most accessible accessory in terms of price, and one that was exempt from the problem of sizing. Some handbags—for example, the Kelly bag by Hermès or the Chanel quilted bag—evolved into symbols of the great luxury houses. The latter spawned a

huge number of quilted bags, such as the Lady Dior Cannage bag, inspired by the canework of Napoleon III chairs, and Marc Jacobs bags. From the Louis Vuitton monogram and Bottega Veneta's woven leather to Coach's turnlock hardware and the Gucci horse bit, handbag details have come to define their brands.

By the 1990s, the artistic directors of luxury firms had begun to design new bags with a view to their creations attaining the status of emblems of their brand. Fendi launched the oblong Baguette bag; and on his arrival at Dior, John Galliano debuted the Saddle bag, created in a new edition for each season. In their attempts to exploit what is currently the most profitable sector of the luxury market, the big labels now vie to create the "It" bag of the season, which has reached a fetishistic status heretofore reserved for shoes or jewels. It also triggered a booming industry of fakes and knockoffs, and by the time a style filters down to the street, the fashion cognoscente have moved on to the next big bag.

Above:
An advertising campaign for Dior's Lady Di bag from 1999. Photograph by Laziz Hamani.

Who was Norman Norell?

Designers

• BEGINNING IN THE 1970S

JEAN-CHARLES DE CASTELBAJAC, ISSEY MIYAKE, SONIA RYKIEL, KENZO, JEAN PAUL GAULTIER, THIERRY MUGLER, CLAUDE MONTANA, ANNE-MARIE BERETTA, CHANTAL THOMASS, AZZEDINE ALAÏ

!

A former assistant to couturiere Hattie Carnegie (1886–1956), Norman Norell (1900–72) founded his house in 1943, partnering with Anthony Traina. He became the darling of New York high society and was known for creations such as evening pants, which mingled sophistication with comfort.

Today's fashion designers owe much to two men who, in 1973, founded the Fédération Française de la Couture, du Prêt-à-Porter des Couturiers et des Créateurs de Mode, the French fashion industry's governing body. Pierre Bergé and Jacques Mouclier's brainchild added two new Paris Fashion Weeks (in March and October) to the traditional fashion-show schedule in January and July. The new shows featured ready-to-wear collections by both couturiers and designers—the *créateurs* of Bergé and Mouclier's federation. Widespread confusion arose among the public concerning the roles of couturier and designer—a confusion that deepened further as designers began to replace couturiers as arbiters of style.

The first group in this new breed of designers had started out by working for ready-to-wear manufacturers. They then launched their own labels, using the design and communications tools of haute couture and adapting them to ready-to-wear. Because ready-to-wear could not rival haute couture in quality, it was essential that the styles exhibit originality and media appeal; thus the fashion show became a key component of these new designers' images. The clothes were often cut from ordinary fabrics, but the mise-en-scène was dazzling enough to impress the world's fashion press.

During the 1980s, designers became the rock stars of the fashion world, with instantly recognizable media profiles: Azzedine Alaïa sported distinctive Chinese suits; Jean Paul Gaultier, a sailor's T-shirt; and Emmanuelle Khanh, outsize glasses. Karl Lagerfeld's image was cemented with his ponytail and fan, and Sonia Rykiel's with her mane of red hair. The fashion worlds that they created were tailored to their personalities. Claude Montana evoked Hollywood style; Jean-Charles de Castelbajac mixed materials; Gaultier exhibited enfant terrible flamboyance; Kenzo lived in florals; and Issey Miyake brought the East to meet the West.

This generation introduced seismic changes to the fashion world. Around 1979, Anne-Marie Beretta, Montana, and Thierry Mugler brought back a structured silhouette with padded shoulders that banished the hippie legacy of the 1960s and '70s. Alaïa put the female body on display in his skintight dresses. With her flirtatious plays on underwear as outerwear,

This dress from Claude Montana's fall-winter 1985–6 collection displays all the sophistication and originality that characterizes the design phenomenon.

Chantal Thomass lent a new sophistication to lingerie. Jean-Rémy Daumas, Popy Moreni, and Kansai Yamamoto, meanwhile, imbued fashion with their love of color, the circus, and the theater. Generations of students were inspired by the images of the superstar designers of the 1980s. But in the fierce competition for publicity and press attention, a note of pretension crept in. By the 1990s, talented newcomers risked being overlooked amid the noise, even if their collections proved inspirational for established labels. Young designers would benefit from a flurry of interest late in the decade, when big luxury groups hunted for artistic directors from among their ranks. Once again, the fashion press attended shows by unknown designers. Many fashion students graduating today gravitate toward the established couture houses, rather than taking their chances as independent designers.

Handbags of the stars

Which celebrity lent her name to which bag?

Answer

1. JANE BIRKIN, Hermès Birkin handbag. **2. GRACE KELLY**, Hermès Kelly bag. **3. LADY DIANA**, Lady Dior handbag by Dior. **4. SOFIA COPPOLA**, Sophia bag by Marc Jacobs. **5. JACQUELINE KENNEDY ONASSIS**, Jackie O. bag by Gucci. **6. CHARLOTTE GAINSBOURG**, Charlotte bag by Gérard Darel.

1

2

JACQUELINE KENNEDY ONASSIS

•

GRACE KELLY

•

JANE BIRKIN

•

SOFIA COPPOLA

•

CHARLOTTE GAINSBOURG

•

LADY DIANA

3

4

5

6

Fashion Icons

From 1980 to the present

Inès de la Fressange captured by the photographer André Rau.

Below:
Top models, the uncontested stars of the 1980s: (from left) Naomi Campbell, Linda Evangelista, Tatjana Patitz, Christy Turlington, and Cindy Crawford, photographed by Peter Lindbergh.

For many years, models had mere walk-on parts (quite literally) in the fashion world. With a few exceptions, such as Nathalie Paley, Lisa Fonssagrives, Jean Shrimpton, and Twiggy, models were largely unknown to the public until the explosive growth of fashion magazines gradually transformed them into mirrors of femininity.
The phenomenon of supermodels

emerged in the 1980s. At a time when cinema and the arts offered few icons who were truly modern in image, Inès de la Fressange was the first model to walk the runway in a natural manner, expressing her personality and her individual Latina beauty. In her wake, Linda Evangelista, Claudia Schiffer, Christy Turlington, Cindy Crawford, Eva Herzigova, Naomi Campbell, Elle Macpherson, Gisèle Bündchen, and Carla Bruni represented the new superwoman. Supermodels were now the standard measure of female beauty, rivaled by television stars such as Sarah Jessica Parker and Jennifer Aniston. Today, Hollywood provides a formidable galaxy of popular icons, including

Kate Moss, photographed by Solve Sundsbo.

Kirsten Dunst, Lindsay Lohan, Jennifer Lopez, Gwyneth Paltrow, Sofia Coppola, Cameron Diaz, Chloë Sevigny, and Uma Thurman, and the looks adopted by these women are seized upon by fashion magazines. To date, the supermodel who has broken the most records for appearances, magazine covers, and advertisements is Kate Moss—dazzling proof that a contemporary icon must in part reflect real women and not be too perfect.

?

Which top model has nicknamed Azzedine Alaïa "Papa"?

Prada

• HOUSE FOUNDED IN 1913
CONTEMPORARY ART, SPORT-LUXE, CONTEMPORARY MATERIALS, AVANT-GARDE, MINIMALISM...
PRADA EAU DE PARFUM, INFUSION D'IRIS, PRADA POUR HOMME...

A design from the fall-winter 1995–6 collection.

Opposite:
Fall-winter collection, 2004–5.

A skillful cocktail of cutting-edge inspiration, exquisite craftsmanship, clean lines, and haute couture fabrics, cleverly shaken, makes up the Prada style. If the devil does indeed wear Prada, then it is because this is the label that—under the guidance of Miuccia Prada and her husband, Patrizio Bertelli—sums up the very quintessence of fashion.

The young student who in 1978 had been awarded her doctorate in political science had never imagined taking over the family leather-goods firm, Fratelli Prada, founded in 1913 by her grandfather Mario Prada. Instead, Miuccia was studying mime at the Piccolo Teatro in Milan and had imagined a future for herself on the stage, combined with active involvement in Milanese politics as a card-carrying member of the Communist Party. In 1978, nevertheless, she took over the running of the business from her mother and was soon designing bags and accessories. Meeting her future husband would prove to be a turning point, as Bertelli brought with him a flair for business, experience in the Florentine leather industry, and his leather factory near Arezzo. In the 1980s, the pair assured their fame with the launch of an accessory that managed to combine desirability, luxury, and affordability: a nylon-and-leather handbag with the brand's signature metallic logo. The two were ready to expand their offerings, and in 1985 they launched a ready-to-wear line. Though the venture did not take off until the 1990s, when they hired Marc Audibet as a designer, success would soon find the brand in other arenas, including its Red label, its archetypal urban sports shoe, and its technology-ready sportswear. In 1993, Prada

! Naomi Campbell.

launched a less-expensive bridge line called Miu Miu (Miuccia's nickname). It immediately proved popular with younger women and has been a huge success in Japan. As a designer, Miuccia offers unique, expensive looks in her ready-to-wear collections through the use of luxurious fabrics. Though sophisticated, the Prada style, as embodied by the famously makeup-free Miuccia, is concerned less with sex appeal than with enjoyment: "I love fashion, but I think it should stay in its place, not rule your life," she explains. "It's a very nice part of your life, but I think it should be fun." This exuberance is evident in the Prada stores that dot the globe. Miuccia has entrusted the design of her flagship stores to distinguished architects with various visions, and in so doing has deliberately flouted the golden rule of 1990s retailing: the principle of unity of design. The Dutch architect Rem Koolhaas and the Swiss partnership Herzog and de Meuron have built sumptuous and distinct premises, in New York (SoHo) and Tokyo, respectively, that tourists flock to as though they were art galleries.

By the late 1990s, Prada had become a true luxury conglomerate, like the LVMH group, with major shareholdings in such brands as Azzedine Alaïa, Car Shoe, Church's, Fendi, Genny, Helmut Lang, and Jil Sander.

From the advertising campaign produced by Karl Lagerfeld for H & M in November 2004.

The Fast-Fashion Phenomenon

- STARTING AT THE END OF THE 1970S
- NAF NAF, KOOKAÏ, MORGAN, H & M, MANGO, NEW LOOK, TOP SHOP, ZARA, MASSIMO DUTTI, BERSHKA, STRADIVARIUS, OYSHO...

The list of big names in budget fashion, a massive phenomenon now at the heart of the industry, is a long one, including H & M, New Look, Top Shop, Mango, Forever 21, and the immensely powerful Inditex group, which owns Zara, among others. The way was prepared for these mass-distribution giants by the French chain Etam, originally a lingerie company, which moved toward fashion in the 1960s with the opening of its 1.2.3 shops and its Tammy line for teens. Etam was also one of the first to break into the Chinese mass market. Today the competition among fashion retailers is intense, and the leaders, H & M and Zara, have thousands of outlets worldwide.

The strength of newcomers to the field lies in their ability to offer a tremendous range of fashions at bargain prices. Relying on huge networks of designers, style analysts, and researchers, they are able to respond quickly to every new direction in fashion. Whether the trends come from haute couture runways, magazines, or the club scene, they can be reinterpreted in an affordable form. Shop-window displays have become like the editorial pages of fashion magazines, offering guides to the latest looks for customers, who eagerly snatch up the goods.

Until recently, the appearances of these fast-fashion labels in the editorial pages of fashion magazines had been few and far between. Not long after Sharon Stone appeared at the 1996 Oscars ceremony wearing a Valentino skirt, an Armani coat, and a plain black Gap T-shirt, editors warmed to the radical idea of the high-low mix. The rise of budget fashion also created a more hospitable environment for stylists, who see themselves as the interpreters of the many fashion languages, from haute couture to high street, daring to mingle a mass-market tank with a beaded evening skirt, and their famous clients are regularly profiled in gossip rags linking celebrity X with label Y.

The popularity of budget fashion gave its purveyors new clout, and they began to invite major names to design and collaborate. Karl Lagerfeld started this trend when he designed a collection of thirty items—suits, cocktail dresses,

How many people design the H & M collections?

Windows at a Zara store in London.

and lingerie—for H & M. The launch of this collection in November 2004 provoked mob scenes in the stores. The Lagerfeld collection rails were stripped bare by eager hands within seconds, and assistants laden with replacement supplies were left empty-handed before they could even reach the racks. Lagerfeld's example was followed by fashion, film, and music celebrities, such as Roberto Cavalli, Stella McCartney, Viktor & Rolf, Emmanuelle Béart, Madonna, and Kylie Minogue. Mango invited Milla Jovovich to design a collection; Giles Deacon, the young British fashion prodigy, created a collection for New Look; the chain also had the singer Lily Allen sign the Lily Loves collection, based largely on her fondness for 1980s fashions.

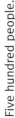

! Five hundred people.

The practice of inviting celebrities to design or represent a mass-market label has proved most potent when the label finds its embodiment in a fashion icon whom customers admire. The arrival of Kate Moss at Top Shop was the apotheosis of this high-media profile for low-cost fashion. When her collection was launched in May 2007, a long line snaked down Oxford Street. In the Top Shop window, a heavy red curtain rose to reveal Moss herself, wearing a red dress and smiling at her fans, only to vanish again a few seconds later. Later that year, Gap sought the imprimatur of actors, musicians, and fashion celebrities—including Selma Blair, Liev Schrieber, Forest Whitaker, Twyla Tharp, and Lucy Liu—dressed in Gap clothes for its "Classics Redefined" ad campaign. These chains have, in a way, become as

The Kate Moss section in the Top Shop on London's Oxford Street, from the launch of her collection in 2007.

visionary as the couture houses by signing lines with designers like Rei Kawakubo of Comme des Garçons—as H & M recently did.

Photographers and muses
Who inspired whom?

Answer

1. Penelope Tree and Richard Avedon.
2. Jean Shrimpton and David Bailey.
3. Laetitia Casta and Dominique Issermann.
4. Lisa Fonssagrives and Irving Penn.
5. Kate Moss and Mario Sorrenti.
6. Nicole de Lamargé and Peter Knapp.
7. Peggy Moffitt and William Claxton.
8. Grace Jones and Jean-Paul Goude.
9. Gisele Bündchen and Mario Testino.
10. Veruschka and Franco Rubartelli.

1

2

3

4

5

6

7

8

9

10

Minimalism & Conceptualism

• SINCE THE 1990S
HELMUT LANG, COSTUME NATIONAL, A.P.C., CALVIN KLEIN, JIL SANDER...

Jil Sander, fall-winter 2005–6 collection.

Opposite:
No jewelry, no coiffure, little makeup:
Ultra sobriety marks the minimalist style, as in this look for the Costume National campaign, fall-winter 1998–9. Photograph by Terry Richardson.

Minimalism is a contemporary art movement that developed in America in the 1960s, based partly on architect Mies van der Rohe's maxim "Less is more." In the early 1980s, the term entered the fashion vocabulary when it was used to describe the style of certain designers, chiefly Helmut Lang, with his shows featuring models in unadorned dresses and little make-up, in spartan settings. Others, such as Costume National, Jil Sander, A.P.C., Adeline André, and, to a degree, Prada, offered less-austere versions of the same style. The absence of decoration and an economy of means spread to include many designers in the 1990s. A notable consequence of the minimalist trend in fashion, however, was the absence of accessories, believed to be responsible for a number of bankruptcies among jewelry designers.

The borrowing of the term "minimalism" from the art world appears only loosely justified. Yet the minimalist movement in fashion shares a number of points in common with that of contemporary art: a reaction to the flashy expressionism of the 1980s; a chilly, detached feel; and a rejection of anything superfluous, from illusion to makeup. For these reasons, many critics accused minimalist

fashion of being cerebral and closely related to another movement, conceptualism. As in the plastic arts, conceptualist fashion places greater emphasis on the process of idea and design than on the finished appearance of a piece. Rei Kawakubo of Comme des Garçons, Martin Margiela, and several other Belgian and Dutch designers were at the forefront of the movement. Even if the resulting garments were unwearable, the experimentation and research on which they were based fueled advances in fashion: Hussein Chalayan showed a filmy silk dress held aloft not by straps but by helium-filled balloons in 1994.

Whereas the market for conceptual design was fairly narrow, minimalist fashion was easy to interpret, and the mass-market labels were quick to exploit it as a source of inspiration. This contributed to the collapse of minimalism around 2000, also brought about by the success of John Galliano's flamboyant excesses for Dior. But minimalism and conceptualism have not disappeared altogether; they still form the basis of the work of student designers, who are encouraged by their teachers to deconstruct every garment, in order to imagine how they might reinvent the fundamentals of fashion.

To which couturier did Wim Wenders dedicate a film?

Hats

From 1945 to the present

JEAN BARTHET, PHILIPPE MODEL, STEPHEN JONES, MARIE MERCIÉ, PHILIP TREACY...
CAPS, FELT MATERIAL, BORSALINOS...

The Bettina allure. Photographed by Arik Nepo in 1951 at Place de la Concorde, in Paris.

After World War II, embellishment gave way to more tailored styles. In the early 1960s, then–first lady Jacqueline Kennedy sparked a craze with her felted-wool pillbox, but the ubiquity of hats had begun to disappear. The new generation's quest for liberty buried the hat for many years. Only special events continued to require the wearing of hats, though African-American women churchgoers carried on the tradition of wearing extravagant and fashionable hats to their Sunday services. In the 1980s, Jacques Le Corre, Marie Mercié, and Philippe Model relaunched haute hats for women, while for men, the baseball caps of the 1970s and '80s led to golf caps, top hats, bowlers, and fifties-inspired straw or felt fedoras in the new millenium. Women gravitated toward the casual insouciance of Eugenia Kim's newsboy caps, a style popularized by Sarah Jessica Parker on *Sex and the City*. On the catwalk, meanwhile, top designers spiced their collections with high-fashion hats: The flamboyance of Stephen Jones's creations matched the dresses of John Galliano. Philip Treacy's hats—as much sculpture as headwear—ratcheted up the level of glamour for various collections and graced the heads of figures as diverse as the fashionably eccentric Isabella Blow and the somewhat more staid Camilla Parker Bowles; the latter wore one of his creations for her marriage to the Prince of Wales. As indisputable king of contemporary headwear, Treacy splices the decadence of the royal court with surrealist humor.

! Yohji Yamamoto. Wenders created a cinematographic portrait with his documentary *Notebook on Cities and Clothes*.

Opposite:
The English-inspired aristocratic eccentricity of a fashion diva: Isabella Blow at the Blow family estate, Hilles, near Gloucestershire, England. She is wearing Philip Treacy's Pheasant hat with gilt pheasant feathers and a jewel-embroidered Christian Lacroix jacket. Photograph by Ellen Von Unwerth.

Logos

Match the brands.

Answer

1. BURBERRY. 2. LOUIS VUITTON. 3. HERMÈS. 4. MADELEINE VIONNET. 5. RALPH LAUREN. 6. VERSACE. 7. CÉLINE. 8. LANVIN.

1

2

3

4

LOUIS VUITTON

VERSACE

MADELEINE VIONNET

LANVIN

RALPH LAUREN

HERMÈS

CÉLINE

BURBERRY

5

6

7

8

Luxury, calm, and voluptuousness: a wall of vintage suitcases in the Louis Vuitton Ginza Namikidori store in Tokyo.

Luxury Brands

• STARTING IN THE 1990S
LVMH, GUCCI GROUP, HERMÈS, RICHEMONT, PRADA, CLARINS, TOD'S, VALENTINO FASHION GROUP, ALLIANCE DESIGNERS...

In the fashion world, luxury labels are generally derived from one of three areas in fashion. Some base their claim to such illustrious status on their origins as haute couture houses and on the legacy of a great founding couturier. Others point to an equally prestigious pedigree in the field of luxury leather goods alone. A final category cannot lay claim to a long heritage but instead boasts the creative, "revolutionary" nature of its prêt-à-porter. Luxury brands with such pedigrees include Chanel, Dior, Giorgio Armani, Comme des Garçons, Jean Paul Gaultier, Gucci, Hermès, Prada, Sonia Rykiel, Yves Saint Laurent, and Louis Vuitton.

Clearly, a diverse range of companies has given rise to the concept of luxury labels. Yet as a group, they have adopted several common traits that mark the luxury category. The development of ready-to-wear departments has given companies specializing in leather goods a higher profile in the press and a more visible place among high-fashion labels. The couture houses, meanwhile, have branched out into perfumes, shoes, and bags—taking a cue from leather-goods companies that can credit these last two categories for their sound economic health. And designers, finally, have diversified their original ready-to-wear lines to include products derived from both leather goods and perfumes.

These changes were accompanied by an upheaval in the financial structure of high-end brands. During the 1990s, the financial world entered the field of luxury goods, and labels were bought out by or expanded into financial groups. Quotation on the world's stock exchanges brought with it a new dynamic—a responsibility to shareholders and an obligation to produce rapid results for investors. Through strong networks of boutiques and sales outlets and a constant advertising presence, luxury brands spread their products all over the world. However, balancing the globalization of a brand's image with the protection of its unique luxury identity threatened to become a perilous enterprise.

And so in the early 1990s, most luxury labels reestablished proprietary rights over their products in order

?

When did the first Hermès scarves appear?

to protect their exclusive nature and to ensure the continued strength of their identity. In this way, they managed to reassure the traditional elite that historically had formed the backbone of their clientele, while also appealing to ordinary consumers. By the end of the decade, however, a number of problems became apparent. Boutiques for any given brand had been designed to reflect an identical image no matter the city or country they happened to be in. But once the initial curiosity aroused by the opening of these "temples of luxury" had died away, their sameness bred a certain ennui. In a new strategy, many companies decided that each luxury outlet within a brand should have its own distinctive character: the Dior boutique on Avenue Montaigne in Paris, for example, was conceived as a warm and welcoming apartment, decorated in a way that could not be replicated. The "guerrilla" stores of Comme des Garçons, meanwhile, were designed as ephemeral boutiques in unique settings, quickly opening and then quickly closing. Luxury labels have also made efforts to stress their individual identities and to minimize the damage caused by the overmarketing of their products, which during the 1990s had become too uniform. To remedy this problem, each label returned to its roots in a quest for its own "DNA," to distinguish it from its rivals.

Another danger, still present, lies in the generalization of the concept of luxury. Many companies are appropriating the word, when in fact they sell only the appearance of luxury and are actually mid-range (such as Gérard Darel, Lancel, Longchamps, Maje, and Paul & Joe) or low-range. Although the latter may not make any explicit claim to luxury, they display its outward signs, constantly improve manufacturing techniques, and possess a capacity to react swiftly to microchanges in fashions during each season with judicious reinterpretations of the creations of star designers.

In response, luxury labels have increased the number of lines they offer, to as many as ten at Chanel and Dior. They ensure that stock of their precollection lines reaches their boutiques early, avoiding the problem of copies being available on the Internet before the originals have even reached the boutiques. These precollection lines do not appear in shows and are not presented to the press: Instead,

!

In 1937. The first ones were called *Jeu des omnibus* and *Dames blanches*, or "The Omnibus Set" and "White Ladies," respectively. These scarves are printed on silk twill, and the rolled hemlines are sewn by hand.

The famous corner window of Hermès at 24 Faubourg Saint-Honoré.

buyers place orders for them a month before the main shows. With their men's collections, precollections, cruise-wear collections (developed in America in the 1920s to supply the needs of passengers on the first Caribbean cruises), and capsule collections, the luxury labels have managed to maintain their customers' curiosity throughout the year and to present something new on a near-monthly basis.

THE FASHION GAZETTE

CURRENT AFFAIRS AND NEWS

• Naomi Campbell collapses in the middle of the runway during a Vivienne Westwood show! The cause of her fall? Giant platform shoes. (1993)

• **Oh shocking!** Vivienne Westwood was not wearing any panties underneath her elegant flowing skirt when she met the Queen of England, who was to bestow upon Westwood the prestigious Order of the British Empire. A pirouette by the designer revealed everything and scandalized everyone.
Can Westwood's punk spirit justify such an affront to the monarchy? (1992)

• **The Gap?** Sharon Stone, nominated for an Oscar for her role in Martin Scorsese's *Casino*, attended the star-studded ceremony wearing a T-shirt with an off-the-rack Valentino skirt and an Armani dress (as a coat). Stone says that she had no intention of playing with provocation and stated that she chose "clothes in which she felt good." (1995)

• **A couturier at the National Assembly** Jack Lang caused a scandal and provoked a certain hilarity at the French National Assembly by appearing at the podium in a Thierry Mugler suit with a Mao collar. (1985)

• **Invisible couture!** Thierry Mugler conducted a new experiment: the first virtual runway show on his brand's Web site. (1998)

• **A couturier at the Academy.** Pierre Cardin is the first couturier to be invited into the French Académie des Beaux-Arts. It took almost two centuries for haute couture to be included among the represented arts. (1991)

• **High fashion in Hollywood.** The list of designers is growing in Hollywood—to the great confusion of producers. *Prestige oblige*, Edward Norton requested an Armani suit for his role of Sheldon Mopes in the film *Death to Smoochy*, produced by Danny DeVito. But he is supposed to be playing a bum! Happily, Norton seems to have found a solution: He asked the designer to create suits especially for him—made of hemp. (2002)

• **The Japanese new wave.** The couturier Hiroaki Ohya presented his spring 2002 collection to the press. Riding the technological wave that has swept his country, he created a blouse in the shape of a computer, with a "screen" across the bosom, a keyboard at the waist, and the distinctive shape of an iMac across the back. (2002)

RUMORS AND SCANDALS

“I won’t get out of bed in the morning for less than $10,000!”

LINDA EVANGELISTA (*Vogue,* 1990)

“We’re happy to pose for the ‘puparazzi’!”

Princess Tamara Borbon and her Yorkshire terrier, Bugsy, aged five, made a much-remarked-upon entrance to the canine fashion show organized by Harrods in December 2003. Bugsy was wearing a Scooby-Doo dog tag made of diamond and platinum (valued at more than $23,000) and a coat by the designer Eric Way, encrusted with crystal. Harrods told us that Bugsy and Princess Tamara, a cousin of King Juan Carlos of Spain, were both happy to pose for the ‘puparazzi.’ (2003)

• **2005.** Dogged by her “youthful error,” the memorable statement about $10,000, Linda Evangelista says that today she gets out of bed for very good reasons, such as raising funds to fight HIV/AIDS worldwide.

“FASHION FREAK”

This is the controversy of the moment! On October 8, 2005, John Galliano paraded unconventional models—the elderly, the obese, dwarves, and transvestites—alongside garden-variety catwalkers in a show of clothing from his own label. American media applauded this paean to diversity; the French press was less sure about it. (2005)

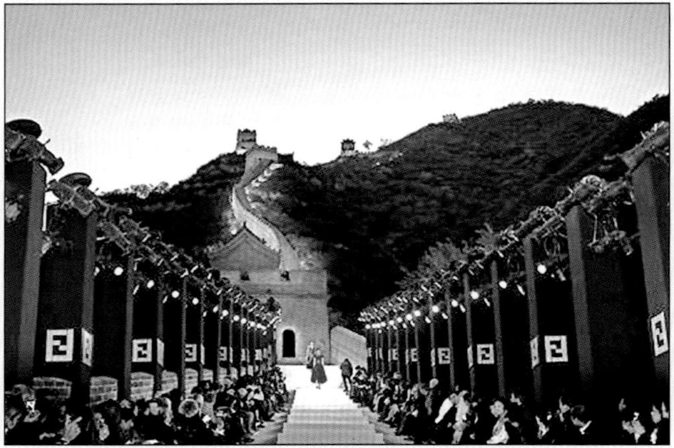

First runway show visible from the moon!

On October 19, 2007, Karl Lagerfeld presented the first runway show visible from the moon for the House of Fendi! By choosing the Great Wall of China as his set, the designer created the most costly fashion show in history and on the longest runway ever used. This show, illuminated by five thousand spotlights, required one year of negotiations with the Chinese authorities and employed three hundred people. It recalled the giant parade at the 1987 International Fashion Festival designed by Olivier Massard and presented by one thousand models on the slopes of the Trocadéro in Paris. (2007)

In the Harajuku district in Tokyo, the Mecca of eccentric Japanese street wear.

Street Fashion

• SINCE WORLD WAR II
BEATNIKS, HIPPIES, ROCKERS, PUNKS, HIP-HOP, GRUNGE...

Street style emerged in the second half of the twentieth century as an alternative approach to fashion—and as a direct challenge to the "official" style of the great couturiers.

Beatniks in America and Left Bank intellectuals in Paris were the first to spurn the dictates of the couture collections. They used this defiance as a symbol of their rejection of the establishment in general, preferring the demimonde of nightclubs, cafés, and the street.

Drawing their inspiration from music, movies, and politics, these style pioneers came to embrace "authentic" Indian and Afghan garments, military uniforms from army-surplus stores, and vintage tops and skirts from secondhand shops and flea markets.

Moving in lockstep with youth culture, street style evolved creatively, with looks that set a new standard for lagging labels. Styles that began as self-conscious rebellion became badges of a "tribal" identity among young people: safety-pin earrings and studded bracelets and belts for punks; glitter and neon colors that glowed under black light for club kids.

In the 1990s, the vogue for skateboarding and Rollerblading spawned several skate-focused clothing labels. Typical street wear for boys consisted of oversize sweatshirts and baggy jeans, while girls bared their navels between microtops and loose tracksuit bottoms. Hip-hop culture became a major influence, adding supersize gold and diamond accessories to the mix. In Japan, manga culture produced a dazzling array of gothic, Lolita-like punk. In 2000, the return of rock brought with it a revival of 1980s fashions.

Young dandies inspired by guitar heroes sported skinny jeans and derbies or fedoras, and young women rediscovered leggings and loose tunics. Pete Doherty and Kate Moss became icons for this generation.

The latest revolution in the dissemination of street fashion is taking place on the Internet. Street style–oriented Web sites, showing photos taken on streets of cities all over the world, allow trends to be transmitted on a global scale. Many fashion labels now conduct sophisticated

? What do the letters in the store name H & M stand for?

In 1947, the first store, named Hennes, was created by the Swede Erling Person. In 1968, he changed the name to Hennes & Mauritz, as he had purchased a store from a man named Mauritz Widforss.

research to uncover the latest street trends as they are happening—teenage blogs are scrutinized by style analysts, and young consumers are targeted with online questionnaires about new products.

Though initially conceived as a rebellion, many street styles find their way into couture collections. Vivienne Westwood applied a punk aesthetic to her deconstructed gowns, and Marc Jacobs's early-1990s Grunge collection took its inspiration from cult figures like Nirvana's Kurt Cobain.

Today, as quickly as a street trend is absorbed into high fashion, fast-fashion outlets churn out versions for the mass market.

But there are signs that the pendulum is beginning to swing away from youth culture: The street-wear label School Rag has recruited a former show director from Givenchy.

On a street in Paris. Photograph published in *WAD*, spring 2004.

Opposite:
Street style par excellence: Messengers often have their own sense of style. Photograph by Philippe Bialobos.

The British School

- FROM THE 1950S TO THE PRESENT
- REDFERN, LUCILE (LADY DUFF-GORDON), EDWARD MOLYNEUX, HARDY AMIES, NORMAN HARTNELL, MARY QUANT, ZANDRA RHODES, BRUCE OLDFIELD, JEAN MUIR, OSSIE CLARK, VIVIENNE WESTWOOD, PAUL SMITH, JOHN GALLIANO, ALEXANDER MCQUEEN, HUSSEIN CHALAYAN, STELLA MCCARTNEY, GILLES DEACON, GARETH PUGH, CHRISTOPHER KANE...

The designer Ossie Clark at the Gatwick Airport, in London, in 1971.

Opposite: Zandra Rhodes by Peter Knapp.

Supremacy in the fashion world has been disputed between France and Britain for centuries. Until World War II, they divided the territory between them, with France reigning over women's wear and the U.K. over menswear. But the creative explosion of 1960s London—which spawned such designers as Mary Quant, Foale & Tuffin, and Biba—followed by the rise of punk in the mid-1970s, focused world attention on the British capital. This emergence of alternative fashion paved the way for designers who would achieve international recognition: Manolo Blahnik, Jimmy Choo, Ossie Clark, Patrick Cox, Stephen Jones, Jean Muir, Bruce Oldfield, Rifat Ozbek, Antony Price, Zandra Rhodes, David Shilling, Paul Smith, and Vivienne Westwood.

In the 1990s, seduced by the originality of designers such as Westwood, John Galliano, Alexander McQueen, Hussein Chalayan, Stella McCartney, and Philip Treacy, the international press tended to snub Paris while feting London. The influential Central Saint Martins College of Art and Design in London, furthermore, is widely viewed as the best art school in the world, and each graduation show in the new century has thrust new star designers into the limelight, including Gilles Deacon, Christopher Kane, and Gareth Pugh. Eccentricity is the ineffably British quality that is usually put forward as the explanation for this phenomenon. In her introduction to *The Cutting Edge: Fifty Years of British Fashion 1947–1997*, Amy de la Haye examines the apparent contradiction between flamboyant excess in fashion and the dominant Protestant morality, to which such

ostentatious delight in luxury and extravagance is anathema. Other historians have traced the origins of British eccentricity to different roots: Paradoxically, they suggest, the stability of the British political system is what allows young (and not so young) Brits to be so non-conformist in their appearance. According to this view, originality in dress and self-expression is the only possible form of escape from a rigidly ordered society. This order is represented, moreover, in the strength of "classic" British style, copied throughout the world

Which designer created the concept of mix-and-match separates in the United States?

The British School

and exemplified by the excellence of British tailoring, with its use of cashmere and its hats, shoes, and raincoats of unrivaled reputation. Contemporary exclusive labels such as Ozwald Boateng, Burberry, Joe Casely-Hayford, and John Smedley ride the crest of this tradition of solid quality while reenergizing it with their own innovations. British couturiers whose reputations had been forged in the early twentieth century, including Hardy Amies, John Cavanagh, Norman Hartnell, Edward Molyneux, and John Redfern, also formed part of this new trend. The British school therefore bridged the ground between the opposing poles of eccentricity and classicism, bridging the gulf with a combination of tradition and innovation. But—though the British often view their eccentricity with a fond, if baffled, tolerance—the British school seems to flourish most freely beyond England's shores.

Ozwald Boateng.

Above:
From the "Panoramic" show by Hussein Chalayan, fall-winter 1998–9.

Claire McCardell, who wished to expand the wardrobes of America's young working women without costing them their newfound financial independence.

From the Alexander McQueen show in Paris, fall-winter 2006–7.

Art and fashion
Who made what?

Answer

1. GOTSCHO FOR THE HOUSE OF MARTIN MARGIELA. 2. ANNIE MORRIS FOR BURBERRY. 3. JEFF KOONS FOR STELLA MCCARTNEY. 4. ANH DUONG FOR DOLCE & GABBANA.

1

2

ANH DUONG
(DOLCE & GABBANA)
•
GOTSCHO
(MARTIN MARGIELA)
•
ANNIE MORRIS
(BURBERRY)
•
JEFF KOONS
(STELLA MCCARTNEY)

3

4

The model Daria photographed in a Chanel dress by Karl Lagerfeld for French *Vogue*, 2004.

House of Chanel

• HOUSE FOUNDED IN 1909
GABRIELLE CHANEL (1909), PHILIPPE GUIBOURGÉ (1971), KARL LAGERFELD (1983)
ALLURE, COCO, COCO MADEMOISELLE, ÉGOÏSTE...

Coco Chanel was a woman of ideas, and upon her death, in 1971, the great “Mademoiselle” bequeathed a formidable heritage of house styles, a treasure chest of ideas from which Karl Lagerfeld was able to draw when he relaunched the brand, in 1983. Lagerfeld likened his role at Chanel to that of a composer of music, creating new scores but using the same notes. While the components of the original Chanel look were constant points of reference, Lagerfeld avoided a too-literal interpretation of the past, which enabled him to create collections committed to innovation. Starting in the 1980s, he gave the classic Chanel tweed suit a shorter, tighter treatment, replaced tweed with denim, layered on more gold chains, and showed dresses with biker boots. More recently, Lagerfeld translated the tweed suit into a bathing suit and reinvented Chanel’s “deluxe poor” look with frayed edges and, for fall-winter 2008–9, worn elbows. From a small couture house to an international luxury brand, Chanel is at the forefront of fashion, accessories, jewelry, and perfumes. Lagerfeld has thus succeeded in rejuvenating a couture house whose prominence as an arbiter of fashion is envied by many other luxury brands.

A drawing by Karl Lagerfeld for the Chanel collection, spring-summer 2001.

Couturier Lucien Lelong (1889–1958) helped to introduce what new idea in fashion?

?

Boutiques

Multilabel, single-label, and concept stores

- BEGINNING IN THE 1970S–1980S
- CORSO COMO, HYPER HYPER, ISETAN, CHARIVARI, L'ÉCLAIREUR, MARIA LUISA, BROWNS, COLETTE, DOVER STREET MARKET, BARNEY'S...

! Lucien Lelong created a lower-priced collection alongside his traditional haute couture collection. He thus opened the door to the conept of ready to wear.

TThe 1980s saw a decline in spending. Women began to devote less time to shopping and more time to their careers and to spend less money on clothes and more on leisure and general well-being. And so the concept of recreational shopping was born. Luxury sales were divided between boutiques devoted to a number of designers, those dedicated to a single designer, and concept stores, which aimed to turn shopping into a life experience. Japanese designers pioneered the shopping-as-experience trend with stores such as Comme des Garçons, Shiseido, and the Hanae Mori Foundation. Another early example is Milan's 10 Corso Como, which features fashion, accessories, home furnishings, fine wines, a restaurant, a café, and a bookshop. In Paris, the concept store Colette, which opened in 1997, is now a cult address despite its small size. Among the latest generation of concept stores is Dover Street Market, opened in London in 2004 by Rei Kawakubo, who—taking her inspiration from the mazelike Kensington Market of the 1970s and 1980s—introduced the idea of the "luxury souk." Many visitors from abroad and the provinces include these famous addresses on their tours of the capitals, reflecting yet another trend—the boutique as destination.

During the 1980s, the focus had shifted toward boutiques founded by fashion designers, who took ownership and control of these carefully and comprehensively designed spaces and turned them into standard-bearers for their images. Thus, Martin Margiela's boutiques in Paris and Tokyo invite his clients to enter his personal world. Created by the world's most distinguished architects, these new urban

The Prada boutique in the Aoyama district in Tokyo, inaugurated in July 2003 and designed by the architects Jacques Herzog and Pierre de Meuron.

Opposite:
The Chanel boutique, in the Ginza district of Tokyo, opened on December 4, 2004. The ten-story high building was designed by the American architect Peter Marino.

temples are now rivaling the place of famous museums and churches on travelers' itineraries. Jacques Herzog and Pierre de Meuron have designed a store for Prada in Tokyo; Kazuyo Sejima and Ryue Nishizawa for Dior in Japan; Jun Aoki for Vuitton in New York and Tokyo; and Peter Marino for Armani, Chanel, Dior, Fendi, and Valentino in various cities. Luxury labels such as these took exclusive control over their worldwide distribution and sales networks in the 1990s, while the mass-market labels battled among themselves to open retail outlets on the most desirable sites in every town. At the opposite end of the spectrum from these art-gallery and single-label boutiques are those devoted to several designers—such as Browns in London and L'Éclaireur and Maria Luisa in Paris. These stores give star billing to the clothes. Such shopping destinations have the power to launch the careers of up-and-coming designers like Rick Owens. With spare window exhibits and rails laden with garments chosen as much for their originality as for their wearability, the clientele's wishes—and not the image of the store—are of paramount concern.

John Galliano

• (1960–) - SPAIN
HEROINES OF PAST AND PRESENT, MIX AND MATCH, ECCENTRICITY, CONTEMPORARY ART, POP CULTURE, THE HISTORY OF ART AND STYLE...
ESSENCE OF JOHN GALLIANO (HOME FRAGRANCE BY DIPTYQUE)...

Opposite :
From the John Galliano fall-winter 2004–5 collection.

The House of Dior owes so much of the success of its relaunch in 1997 to John Galliano that in the public mind the two are inextricably linked. But Galliano also has his own label, which benefits from the solid support of the LVMH group. Galliano designs and lives fashion with intense devotion. His dedication became apparent during his early childhood in Gibraltar and his adolescent years in London. As a teenager, he would get dressed to the nines to go to the supermarket with his mother and his sister. As a young man, he learned the secrets of stage artifice when he worked as a theatrical dresser. In the London club scene, and especially at Taboo, he became, in his own words, a "club demon," experimenting with outrageous looks. These experiences fostered his innate love of disguise and of the intense creativity required for such fabulous and flamboyant transformations. According to Colin McDowell, who taught art history to Galliano at the Central Saint Martins College of Art and Design, the designer is "inhabited and impregnated" by his research, until he is taken over by it.
As early as his graduation show of 1984, Galliano's work attracted attention: Browns devoted its shop window on South Molton Street in London to his collection, which Galliano called "Les Incroyables," after the exaggerated styles of the French Revolution. The following year, he confirmed the originality of his talent with a collection that mixed traditional tailoring and Eastern-inspired fabrics. His fashion sensibilities are based on the shock of opposites and on a quixotic eclecticism that combines Hollywood glamour, the world of Japanese manga, street wear, fallen aristocrats and dandies, and unfettered fantasy and eccentricity into one cohesive point of view.
The softness of Galliano's draperies, asymmetrical cuts, structured tailoring, and flowing bias cuts counterbalances and underscores the sensuality of his lines. For a long time, the outrageous shows he produced under his own name pigeonholed him as the wild child of fashion, support-

ed by a handful of admirers and respected by fashion professionals. But his entry into the LVMH group as artistic director of Givenchy, in 1996, defined him as a major player in the industry. Because of his radical originality, the public eagerly awaits each Galliano collection. His menswear shows still manage to amaze even the most blasé members of the fashion press. His models are transfigured into exotic, fantastical creations—sublimated versions of Galliano's individual looks. His final bow on the runway, like that of a torero in the ring, is his apotheosis, every time.

?

What design most shocked in the Comme de Garçons "End of the World" collection?

Marc Jacobs

• (1963–) - UNITED STATES
PARISIANS, NEW YORKERS, MUSIC AND CONTEMPORARY ART, AVANT-GARDE, BOHEMIAN CHIC, POP CULTURE...
MARC JACOBS PERFUME, MARC JACOBS FOR MEN, MARC JACOBS DAISY, MARC JACOBS SPLASH...

Robert Duffy (left) and Marc Jacobs in 2002.

Opposite: From the Marc Jacobs show in New York, fall-winter 2006–7.

A sweater with large holes that appeared to be moth-eaten.

With Marc Jacobs, the close client-couturier relationship traditional to haute couture has been recreated around bonds of friendship: His career is filled with celebrities who over time have formed a veritable family. The first of these, Robert Duffy, was there to applaud the young designer's graduation show at the Parsons School of Design, in 1984, and together they founded Jacobs Duffy Designs. His female friends lent their names to his bags: Sofia was named after the film director Sofia Coppola and Venetia after the stylist Venetia Scott, responsible for his shows and advertising campaigns. Today, the front rows of his shows are studded with celebrities, including Zoe Cassavetes, Kirsten Dunst, Kim Gordon, Sarah Jessica Parker, and Winona Ryder.

Marc Jacobs effortlessly defines youth. Even today, his heritage as a graduate of New York's High School of Art and Design remains clearly in evidence. His muse, Sofia Coppola, perfectly embodies the Marc Jacobs style, and she has lent her dreamy grunge princess look to publicity campaigns shot by Elizabeth Peyton and Jurgen Teller. Theirs is a world in which chic mingles with cool, intimacy with glamour, sophistication with trash, and poetry with rock. A former denizen of the Los Angeles club Area, his shows combine romanticism with an edge of pop culture and punk. Music is central to his inspiration, from Blondie to Serge Gainsbourg to Iggy Pop to Sonic Youth and the White Stripes. He dedicated his winter 1992 collection to the Rolling Stones.

His embrace of both high and low fashion hit a defining point in 1993. That year, his Grunge collection for Perry Ellis was like a slap in the face to the American fashion world. With its expensive price tags and cheap looks, grunge was a commercial aberration in the eyes of America, and Marc Jacobs was forced out of Perry Ellis.

But Jacobs proved to be an incubator of new trends, an insightful observer of street fashion—and the 1990s embraced grunge with abandon. Jacobs takes his inspiration from the 1950s and '60s and scours flea markets the world over for relics of those decades. Chanel and Courrèges, young girls as well as their mothers, uniforms, and Parisian chic are all points of reference in his retro-contemporary approach. He's been said to take a cliché and reinvent it, creating something unique and new that slyly references its point of origin. Yet it was only with the imprimatur of LVMH in 1997 for the launch of Louis Vuitton prêt-à-porter that Marc Jacobs really took off commercially. His ability to capture the zeitgeist perfectly suited Vuitton's entrance into the ephemeral world of fashion. In parallel, LVMH's majority holding in Jacobs Duffy Designs would enable the duo to expand by opening boutiques and launching successful lines of shoes and bags; its first fragrances, for women in 2000 and men in 2002; and Little Marc for children in 2003.

Models
Who's who?

Answer

1. HELENA CHRISTENSEN, for the cover of British *Vogue*, June 1997. **2. STEPHANIE SEYMOUR**, for the cover of *W*. **3. STELLA TENNANT**, for the cover of British *Vogue*, December 1997. **4. TYRA BANKS**, for the cover of Spanish *Elle*.

1

2

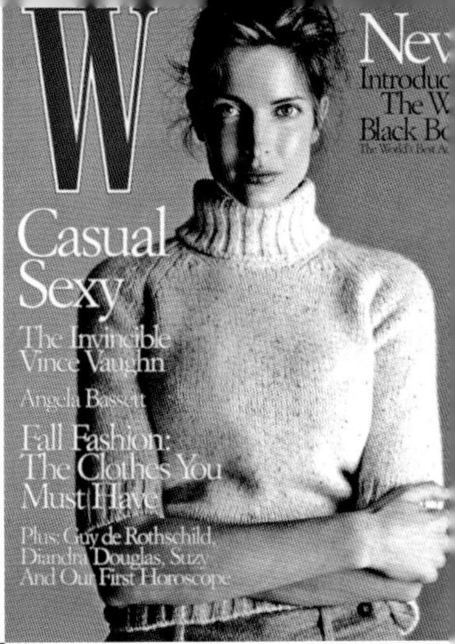

STELLA TENNANT

•

STEPHANIE SEYMOUR

•

HELENA CHRISTENSEN

•

TYRA BANKS

3

4

Hermès

• HOUSE FOUNDED IN 1837 BY THIERRY HERMÈS (1801–78) - GERMANY
THE EQUESTRIAN WORLD, TRAVEL, SAVOIR-FAIRE, TRADITION AND MODERNITY, SPORT-CHIC...
24 FAUBOURG, AMAZONE, CALÈCHE, EAU D'ORANGE VERTE, ÉQUIPAGE, EAU D'HERMÈS, UN JARDIN SUR LE NIL...

From the fall-winter 1998–9 collection by Martin Margiela. Photographed by John Midgley.

Opposite: From the fall-winter 2004–5 collection, photographed by Paolo Roversi.

Several decades after the founding of the House of Hermès, by Thierry Hermès in 1837, the symbol of unrivaled luxury that we know today came into being. Originally, Hermès was a saddlery business in the lively Madeleine area of Paris, before moving in 1878 to 24 Rue du Faubourg Saint-Honoré, where it attracted a wealthy clientele who lived in the neighboring opulent residences. By the late nineteenth century, Hermès had become a supplier to the royal courts of Europe, and it was growing increasingly aware of the threat to its business posed by developments in transportation.

In order to diversify, Emile-Maurice Hermès had the inspired idea of applying the techniques of saddlery to ladies' handbags, small leather goods, and luggage, then a booming industry. In 1922, he opened departments selling couture, gloves, jewelry, and clocks and watches. The first garments to carry the Hermès label were suede golf jackets; these were a great success thanks to the zippers—a new phenomenon to which Emile-Maurice Hermès had bought the exclusive rights from its inventor. Continuing with this policy of innovation, Lola Prusac, recruited in 1926 to coordinate the women's wear and sportswear departments, launched a clothing line combining knitwear and leather. Sonia Delaunay designed the patterns for magnificent silk scarves. A semi-ready-to-wear department was inaugurated in 1949, headed by a succession of notable figures: Jacques Delahaye, Christian Lacroix, Eric Bergère, Claude Brouet, Christiane Bailly, Myrène de Prémonville, Tomas Maier, Tan Giudicelli, Marc Audibet, Michèle and Olivier Chatenet, Martin Margiela, and currently Jean Paul Gaultier.

Which company introduced a horse bit–inspired bracelet made of leather and metal in 1927?

Some Hermès designs have become desirable perennials par excellence, notably the silk square first created in 1937 and printed using traditional woodblocks, and the Kelly bag, descended from traditional saddle carriers and brought to public prominence in 1956, when Princess Grace was pictured with hers on the cover of *Life* magazine.

Hermès was the first fashion house to integrate in-house production and sales departments. Put in place by Jean-Louis Dumas-Hermès at a time when an older system of licensing and franchising predominated, it has since become the business model for all luxury companies. Faithful to its credo, Hermès remains the master of innovation steeped in tradition.

Vuitton

• HOUSE FOUNDED IN 1854
TRAVEL, CONTEMPORARY ART, SAVOIR-FAIRE, SPORT-CHIC, ADVENTURE...

Site of the gala for the 150th anniversary of the House of Louis Vuitton, April 2004 in Hong Kong.

Before becoming a fashion label, the name Vuitton was synonymous with travel. Louis Vuitton's first prestigious client was the Empress Eugénie, when Napoleon III employed him as *layetier* to his wife, responsible for packing up her immense crinolines on their travels. Establishing himself as a trunkmaker, Vuitton introduced technical innovations, replacing the traditional leather covering with lightweight gray canvas and supplanting the rounded top with a flat one, which lent itself to easy stacking on train journeys. In 1875, the workshop at Asnières produced his first wardrobe trunk, with its revolutionary system of compartments.

Twenty-one years later, in 1896, the famous monogrammed canvas appeared, designed initially to deter counterfeiters. Ironically, this instantly recognizable monogram today pads the accounts of untold knockoff suppliers.

Indeed, the monogrammed canvas announced the arrival of Vuitton in the fashion world, heralded by a masterstroke of publicity. To celebrate the centennial of the canvas, in 1996, Azzedine Alaïa, Manolo Blahnik, Romeo Gigli, Helmut Lang, Isaac Mizrahi, Sybilla, and Vivienne Westwood were each invited to design a bag in the famous fabric. The following year, Vuitton invited Marc Jacobs, enfant terrible of the

! Hermès.

American fashion world, to become the company's art director and to preside over the launch of its ready-to-wear line. Under his creative guidance, the Vuitton spirit was unveiled: The Vuitton woman possessed an urbane, cosmopolitan, confident femininity with a strong Parisian accent; she was highly appreciative of haute couture and combined luxury with practicality. Vuitton leather goods formed part of this creative vision, as Jacobs brought in artists such as Stephen Sprouse to create the Graffiti bag in 2001 and Takashi Murakami to reinvent the monogrammed canvas bag in 2005. In 2008, Richard Prince covered Vuitton bags with his texts and spray paint. The opening of the Vuitton flagship store on the Champs-Elysées in 2006 (replacing the store that had opened there in 1914) offered Jacobs the opportunity to enlarge the place of art in the Vuitton empire. Olafur Eliasson installed a gigantic eye in one of the windows; Vanessa Beecroft, meanwhile, placed barely clad living models on the display shelves along with the luggage and extended the inaugural exhibition in the top-floor gallery space.

Dress made of silk duchess satin, black leather open-toed heels, and a white Speedy 30 handbag made of multicolored monogrammed canvas designed by artist Takashi Murakami for spring-summer 2003.

Celebrities' words
Who said what?

Cecil Beaton

Sharon Stone

Sophia Loren

Diana Vreeland

Emily Blunt in *The Devil Wears Prada*

Quentin Crisp

Alicia Siverstone in *Clueless*

Gilda Radner

Katharine Hepburn

Carson Kressley

Karl Lagerfeld

• (1938–) - GERMANY
MODERNITY, PEOPLE AND THE TIMES, BOOKS, THE PAST, THE PRESENT...
KL FEMME, PHOTO, SUN MOON STARS, LAGERFELD, JAKO...

Spring-summer 2001 collection.

Opposite: Karl Lagerfeld, self-portrait.

According to the wisdom of the fashion world, Karl Lagerfeld is the Platonic ideal of what a designer should be: a true chameleon, able to slip into a multitude of fashion histories, the perfect savior of ready-to-wear labels in search of an identity.

It tends to be forgotten that he is also a couturier who, after being awarded the Woolmark prize by the International Wool Secretariat in the coat category in 1955, spent several years in couture houses, first with Pierre Balmain (who had noticed him during the I.W.S. competition) and then with Jean Patou. A highly gifted draughtsman, prolific and rapid in his sketches, Lagerfeld originally wanted to be a cartoonist; his gift for observation would later inspire his impeccable designs.

In the early 1960s, Lagerfeld realized that the haute couture path taken by his friend Yves Saint Laurent did not match his idea of modernity. Instead, he could see the many possibilities of the emerging ready-to-wear business, and so he embarked on a career as a freelance designer. Soon his collaborators included Mario Valentino, Repetto, Monoprix, Timwear, Krizia, Ballantyne, Charles Jourdan, and Cadette. But it was at Chloé, and afterward at Fendi, that his talent was first recognized by the fashion press. His arrival at Chanel, in 1983,

launched the era of all-powerful artistic directors.

Paradoxically, Lagerfeld's own house, Lagerfeld Gallery, established in 1998, has never been as successful as his artistic directorships of other companies. However, fashion is not Lagerfeld's only venture. His publishing house, founded in 2000 and specializing in rare books, and his work as a photographer, have been more enthusiastically received. With his rock-star-dandy glamour, his ability to capture the attention of the press, and his razor-sharp wit, Karl Lagerfeld has attained the status of a legend in his own lifetime.

?

It is rumored that Karl Lagerfeld lost weight so that he could wear which designer's clothing?

Gucci

• HOUSE FOUNDED IN 1921 BY GUCCIO GUCCI (1881–1953) - ITALY
GLAMOUR, SPORTS, MINIMALISM, SENSUALITY, ROCK 'N' ROLL...
GUCCI ENVY, GUCCI FEMME, GUCCI RUSH, GUCCI BY GUCCI...

Opposite:
An audaciously low-cut dress, a symbol of a brand, which under the influence of Tom Ford became synonymous with refined sensuality. Fall-winter 2004–5 collection.

The story of Gucci begins in 1921, when Guccio Gucci opened a small shop in Florence specializing in leather and travel goods. Made by local craftsmen, his wares took their inspiration from the English gentlemen that Guccio had observed while working at the Savoy Hotel in London. In the 1930s, the British gentry would again fire Gucci's imagination. Horse racing was their particular passion, and so Guccio began incorporating horse bits and stirrups into decorative hardware for his leather goods. The Bamboo bag—a large leather bag with bamboo handles—appeared during World War II and became Gucci's first icon, to be joined in the 1950s by a trademark red-and-green striped webbing, inspired by a saddle girth. After Guccio's death, in 1953, he was succeeded by his four sons, who shepherded the brand as its popularity skyrocketed among the well-to-do. In the 1960s, film stars and other prestigious clients brought Gucci into the global media spotlight. Jacqueline Kennedy Onassis lent her name to the Jackie O. shoulder bag; Brigitte Bardot lent hers to the Bardot bag; Elizabeth Taylor adopted the Hobo bag; Grace Kelly wore the Flora foulard; and Gucci moccasins with their horse bit–inspired bar became emblematic of Italian chic. In 1982, the third generation of Gucci took the helm. Maurizio, Guccio's grandson, turned the business into a joint-stock company before finally, in the late 1980s, selling it to Investcorp, which became a 50 percent shareholder.
A victim of its own popularity, in the early '90s the brand found its image tarnished by a flood of copies and interpretations. In a bid to restore Gucci to its former splendor, the American designer Tom Ford was appointed artistic director in 1994. Domenico De Sole, who had served as president of Gucci America since 1984, was named managing director in 1995. Four years later, Gucci joined the French conglomerate Pinault-Printemps-Redoute.
The Tom Ford era can be considered the second part of the Gucci story. He is credited with turning the ailing Gucci brand around, marrying sound business sense with design flair—thus pleasing shareholders while also keeping Gucci products on fashion magazine covers. It was a performance that earned him a worldwide reputation. Straightforward and lack-

! Hedi Slimane.

ing pretension, he declared proudly, "I'm lucky. I have mass-market tastes. When I say I like a shoe, generally, thousands of people will like it." Ford established the new role of artistic director in a fashion house, overseeing quality and consistency throughout the company's activities. To this end, he offered up his luxury lifestyle to the media and launched aggressive advertising campaigns that introduced the concept of "porno chic" to a sometimes-shocked public. Who could forget Mario Testino's photographs for Carine Roitfeld at French *Vogue*, showing couples apparently surprised in flagrante delicto? But beyond the shock value of these images lies a style that wraps the body in sensuality while glorifying a rock 'n' roll glamour.

In 2005, after little more than a decade at Gucci, Ford left the house, as did De Sole. The ascension of Frida Giannini, formerly the artistic director of accessories, marked yet another era in the life of this brand: She became design director for women's ready-to-wear, and in the following year, men's ready-to-wear. Combining an understanding of the Gucci past with her own sense of contemporary femininity, Giannini has presided over the launch of La Pelle Guccissima leather line, created using an original heat-printing technique and intended as a new signature for the brand.

The Basics

• END OF THE 1960S TO THE PRESENT
BENETTON, GAP, ESPRIT, J. CREW, MUJI, UNIQLO...
T-SHIRT, WHITE SHIRT, CARDIGAN, POLO, TRENCH COAT...

The basics are those wardrobe essentials that you can take for granted, secure in the knowledge that they capture the zeitgeist. They include timeless classics that are constantly being reinvented—the cardigan, little black dress, polo shirt, T-shirt, trench coat, jeans. And then there are those items once at the cutting edge of fashion that eventually come into the public domain and are downgraded to the ranks of the basics, such as ballet flats and flip-flops. The American label J. Crew champions the movement to balance the timelessness of traditional classics with the latest trends—an exercise aimed at keeping the client's interest constantly engaged and at drawing his or her attention to items that ride the crest of the fashion wave without ever being subsumed by it. Gap, another champion of stylish basics, experienced some difficult years, for instance, when it wandered into the wilderness of the frankly démodé. But its new campaign, focusing on "Classics Redefined," has returned the brand to the desirable fold. The Italian label Benetton is another pioneer in this field. Harking back to its beginnings in the 1970s, the company relaunched its basic sweater in a rainbow palette of no fewer than forty-eight different shades. Its photographic campaigns by the Italian photographer Oliviero Toscani, introduced in 1982, made skillful use of unexpected or shocking images to reinforce its profile as a humanitarian company. There are also the catalog and online sales of the numerous basics offered by mail-order companies such as La Redoute, which offers cardigans and polo shirts from its Les Essentiels line. From Japan come Muji and UNIQLO (Unique Clothing Warehouse, a.k.a. the Japanese Gap), which add a design sensibility to their

The Schott Perfecto: The symbol of rebel attitude has become fashionable.

Gap campaign for fall-winter 2007–8.

range of basics. And finally, everyone has a personal list of old favorites: wardrobe staples that last a lifetime or are eventually replaced by virtually identical items. Labels such as the French companies Saint James, with its nautical sweaters, and Old England, with its range of "British" classics, play on this evocative theme. Burlington boasts of its socks, and Anne Fontaine's simple white shirts stand on their own. But even the most avant-garde of designers are not afraid to offer basic items, such as some of Martin Margiela's Ligne 6 designs. A basic or classic item may even offer opportunities for bravura exercises in style, such as Nicolas Ghesquière's duffle coat or his peacoat for Balenciaga.

House of Lanvin

• COUTURE HOUSE FOUNDED IN 1889
JEANNE LANVIN (1889), MARIE-BLANCHE DE POLIGNAC (1946), ANTONIO CANOVAS DEL CASTILLO (1950), JULES-FRANÇOIS CRAHAY (1964), MARYLL LANVIN (1981), ROBERT NELISSEN (1989), CLAUDE MONTANA (1990), DOMINIQUE MORLOTTI (1992), OCIMAR VERSOLATO (1996), CRISTINA ORTIZ (1998), ALBER ELBAZ (2002)
VETYVER LANVIN, OXYGÈNE, ÉCLAT D'ARPÈGE, RUMEUR...

IIn October 2001, the Taiwanese businesswoman Shaw-Lan Wang bought out Lanvin and appointed Alber Elbaz as artistic director. Elbaz, an admirer of the American designer Geoffrey Beene (for whom he worked for seven years), is a master of the art of wearable yet inventive clothing, updating the touchstones of style of the 1950s and '60s with a modern twist and interpreting the designs of current avant-gardists without falling into a trap of art for art's sake. His control of the cut and choice of fabrics and his use of colors of uncommon subtlety have won him the respect of his peers as well as the fashion press, which lost no time in showering praise on his collections.

Elbaz has resurrected the house by achieving a difficult objective: to revive the Lanvin roots while becoming one of the top designers in the fashion world. The House of Lanvin, which for a long time survived on an image of timeless French elegance, has now opened its doors to international luxury. Discreet and talented, Elbaz perpetuates the Lanvin style in the image of its founder.

From the show for the Lanvin spring-summer 2005 collection by Alber Elbaz.

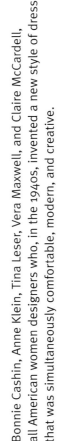

! Bonnie Cashin, Anne Klein, Tina Leser, Vera Maxwell, and Claire McCardell, all American women designers who, in the 1940s, invented a new style of dress that was simultaneously comfortable, modern, and creative.

From the show for the Lanvin spring-summer 2008 collection by Alber Elbaz.

Viktor & Rolf: In celebration of the tenth anniversary of the brand, the duo revisited its basics, which were worn by models “cloned” to look like the designers’ androgynous muse, the actress Tilda Swinton.

The Dutch School

- FROM 1989 TO THE PRESENT
- ALEXANDER VAN SLOBBE, VIKTOR & ROLF, OSCAR SULEYMAN, JOLINE JOLINK, JEROEN TEUNISSEN AND MÉLANIE ROZEMA, MADA VAN GAANS, JAN TAMINIAU, MICHIEL KEUPER AND FRANCISCO VAN BENTHEM, MONIQUE VAN HEIST, DUTCH TOUCH, MANOUK, PAUW, MARIANNE VANDERWILT...

The Dutch school in fashion emerged during the 1990s, borne along by the movement to open the Paris fashion scene to new countries and in pursuit of the group shows that had proved so advantageous to the Belgian school in its infancy. However, the success enjoyed by the Belgian designers meant that their Dutch counterparts did not receive the recognition they deserved for the innovations they brought to international fashion. Rather than enriching their own fashion industry, the originality of the Dutch designers' shows and collections served more often to stimulate the creativity of their foreign rivals—even though old hands at the prestigious Festival International des Arts de la Mode at Hyères, in the South of France, were well aware that many of the prizewinners were Dutch. Alexander van Slobbe is considered to be the brilliant pioneer of the Dutch school, which came to be known as Dutch Modernism. In 1989, he and Nannet van der Kleijn launched the Orson + Bodil label, a trailblazing venture based on a purity of line and innovative fabrics. Van Slobbe's menswear label, SO, followed in 1993, adhering to the same principles and displaying many connections to the worlds of art, literature, and architecture. Van Slobbe thus encouraged the emergence of an entire generation of young Dutch designers; he was aided in this effort by the Dutch Fashion Foundation and the Fashion Institute Arnhem, both directed by Angelique Westerhof. These organizations stage events, exhibitions, and shows promoting Dutch fashion on the international scene, and both attract lively interest from the avant-garde fashion and arts press. But many critics find the Dutch approach too conceptual and bemoan its lack of commercialism. Indeed many Dutch designers do take a conceptual approach, concentrating on the space between garment and skin. The first Dutch fashion designers tended to be the products of art colleges and had little understanding of the economic realities of the fashion industry. To address this concern, the Arnhem institute has rethought its approach. As Westerhof explained in *Le Figaro*, the institute has set up links with professional designers who have "a sense of humor and their feet on the ground."

Who designed the white halter dress that Marilyn Monroe wore in *The Seven Year Itch?*

Joline Jolink, fall-winter 2008–9 collection.

! It was bought off the rack at a department store.

The first Arnhem graduates to find success abroad were Mélanie Rozema and Jeroen Teunissen, under the joint label Rozema Teunissen; Michiel Keuper and Francisco van Benthem, working as KEUPR/van BENTM from 1996 to 2001; and Oscar Raaijmakers and Suleyman Demir, with their brand, Oscar Suleyman, sold in exclusive boutiques and upscale department stores. Other names have since found recognition abroad, including Mada van Gaans, for her colorful graphics; Joline Jolink, former assistant to the duo Viktor & Rolf; and Monique van Heist, for her fresh and sexy creations. Similarly, the Jan Taminiau label has been sold at Colette in Paris and in department stores and offers a sophisticated take on high-heeled femininity. Other labels followed, including Dutch Touch, Manouk, Pauw, and Marianne Vanderwilt. However, two labels have stood out from the pack and enjoyed widespread public success: G-Star made its name in the world of denim, and Viktor & Rolf conquered the world of designer fashion and its press corps. Viktor Horsting and Rolf Snoeren marked their debut by winning first prize at the 1993 Festival International des Arts de la Mode before going on to wow the press with their conceptual shows, in which they featured themselves as the primary models. In 2005, they launched their first perfume, Flowerbomb, with L'Oréal, thereby establishing a secure position from which to develop their brand. A collection for H & M in 2006 affirmed their elevation to the ranks of stars of the international fashion scene.

From the Rozema Teunissen "Transient" collection, spring-summer 2000.

Famous editors
Who's who?

Answer

Illustrations by Gladys Perint Palmer:

1. **ANNA WINTOUR**, editor in chief of American *Vogue*.
2. **SUZY MENKES**, fashion editor of the *International Herald Tribune*.
3. **CARINE ROITFELD**, editor in chief of French *Vogue*.
4. **FRANCA SOZZANI**, editor in chief of Italian *Vogue*; with her sister, Carla, another fashion personality—she is the creator of the celebrated Corso Como 10 boutiques in Milan.

1

2

SUZY MENKES

•

CARINE ROITFELD

•

FRANCA SOZZANI

•

ANNA WINTOUR

3

4

Beyoncé Knowles in an Armani gown, on the red carpet
at the 79th Annual Academy Awards celebration in Hollywood
on February 25, 2007.

The Red Carpet

• BEGINNING IN THE EARLY 1990S
ARMANI, VALENTINO, DIOR...

Since the early 1990s, photographs of celebrities parading in front of the press at film premieres and award ceremonies have given rise to the "red carpet" phenomenon. One no longer simply dons a beautiful gown and lovely jewels and smiles for the camera. These appearances are now meticulously stage-managed down to the smallest detail.

Although long-running society columns such as *Vogue*'s Celebrity Gallery doubtless opened the door, it was the American magazine *In Style* that, in the 1990s, introduced the concept of fashion photos that centered on celebrities. Countless other magazines have since followed suit, joined by television shows and Web sites.

Luxury firms jumped at the opportunity to reach a wider public and to show their creations as clothing worn by "real" women who would then be identified with their brands. In addition, many women found it easier to relate to celebrities than to runway models. Hence couture houses and luxury-goods firms began increasingly wooing eligible stars—sending a choice of gowns and often paying the famous recipients to wear them.

Specialized departments at fashion houses now devote their efforts exclusively to red-carpet appearances, and designers frequently create gowns to fit the stars who generate the most exposure.

Many actresses have discovered the advantages of this system. Prior to the red-carpet trend, a celebrity might only receive press coverage when promoting her latest film, but now any red-carpet appearance can guarantee massive publicity. The photographs are generally accompanied by reflections on a star's looks and tastes, which in turn raises her public profile.

But while an unknown starlet might make a modest tabloid splash with a spectacular gown, for an unknown designer, dressing the right star at the right time can catapult a brand from obscure label to household name.

Today the expanding red-carpet industry embraces all types of media personalities, from political figures such as Senator Hillary Clinton, Ségolène Royal, Cécilia Sarkozy, and Carla Bruni-Sarkozy to television stars like Oprah Winfrey and Sarah Jessica Parker. Trapped in this world of appearances (in both senses of the word), celebrities such as Paris Hilton, who are famous for being famous, are now often feted solely for their latest outfit.

?

For whom did Andy Warhol draw shoes?

Shoes

The outer limits of creativity

- FROM THE 1970S TO THE PRESENT
- MANOLO BLAHNIK, ROBERT CLERGERIE, STÉPHANE KÉLIAN, MAUD FRIZON, CHRISTIAN LOUBOUTIN, RODOLPHE MENUDIER, PIERRE HARDY...
- PRADA-SPORT SHOES...

Beginning in the 1980s, shoes abandoned their supporting role to take center stage in the fashion world. No longer merely accessories, shoes now played an active part in the presentation of catwalk shows, and young designers began to specialize in this area.

In the up-and-coming neighborhood of Place des Victoires in Paris, fashionistas fought over the eccentric designs of Tokio Kumagai and raced one another to Andrea Pfister's boutique on Rue Cambon. After studying art history at the University of Florence and shoe design at the Ars Sutoria in Milan, Pfister became known for his gifts as a colorist, his witty shapes, and his subtle heels. Meanwhile Manolo Blahnik, born in the Canary Islands and a graduate of the University of Geneva and the École du Louvre, was embarking on his meteoric career as a legendary shoe designer to couturiers and the stars. In 1970, he moved to London, and, after designing shoes for Ossie Clark, launched his own label in 1973. By the 1980s, Blahnik was well known for the elegance and dizzying height of his heels, for his talent for creating harmonious combinations of materials, and for his ability to move effortlessly from the purest classicism to the most outré strokes of boldness.

Other individuals also shaped shoe design around this time. Stéphane

! The I. Miller shoe company; his drawings were published as magazine advertisements.

Kélian and Robert Clergerie both transformed family businesses into fashionable names. In London, the shoe shopper's smartest address on King's Road was Johnny Moke, while Emma Hope created designs for Nicole Farhi, Betty Jackson, and Jean Muir, specializing in luxurious handmade materials and slender shapes which recalled Elizabethan and medieval styles.

The 1990s saw the triumph of Italian leather: Prada had launched its shoe line in 1985, and Gucci moccasins had been coveted since the 1960s. But toward the end of the decade, as minimalism caught on, Italian design lost its creative edge. Fortunately, Benoît Méléard, a former designer for Charles Jourdan, was about to shake up the world of shoe design with "happenings" featuring shoes that pushed the limits of possibility—true contemporary works of art. This fleeting initiative soon inspired a new generation of designers who were passionate about shoes and who, around 2005, cast off the conventions of a field in which creativity had always been limited by the morphology of the foot. Karine Arabian, Patrick Cox, Bruno Frisoni, Pierre Hardy, Rodolphe Menudier, Karena Scheussler, Alain Tondowski, and Michel Vivien rivaled one another in sheer inventiveness, whether under their own names or for luxury labels. This explosion of innovation in shoe design energized the profession and encouraged the emergence of new names such as Maloles and Estelle Yomeda, and today women seek out stylish shoes that epitomize the latest fashions.

Opposite:
Top:
Sergio Rossi pumps, Veronica design in patent leather, with various colors and materials, spring-summer 2007 collection.
Bottom:
Christian Louboutin shoe, fall-winter 2007–8 collection.

Below:
Drawing of a Manolo Blahnik shoe.

Appendixes

Fashion Schools

⇢ AUSTRALIA

• **ROYAL MELBOURNE INSTITUTE OF TECHNOLOGY**
www.rmit.edu.au
• **UNIVERSITY OF TECHNOLOGY SYDNEY**
www.uts.edu.au
• **QUEENSLAND UNIVERSITY OF TECHNOLOGY**
www.qut.edu.au

⇢ AUSTRIA

• **MODESCHULE DER STADT WIEN**
www.modeschulewien.at
• **UNIVERSITY OF APPLIED ARTS VIENNA**
www.modeklasse.at

⇢ BELGIUM

• **ACADÉMIE DE GAND / HOGESCHOOL GENT**
www.hogent.be
• **ACADÉMIE ROYALE DES BEAUX ARTS D'ANVERS**
www.antwerp-fashion.be
• **ATELIER DE STYLISME ET CRÉATION DE MODE DE LA CAMBRE**
www.lacambre.be

⇢ CANADA

• **COLLÈGE LASALLE**
www.clasalle.com
• **ÉCOLE SUPÉRIEURE DE MODE**
www.esmm.uqam.ca
• **RYERSON UNIVERSITY**
School of Fashion
www.ryerson.ca/fashion

⇢ CHINA

• **DONG HUA UNIVERSITY**
www.dhu.edu.cn
• **SHANGHAI UNIVERSITY / MOD'ART INTERNATIONAL Institute of Fashion and Arts**
www.modart-sha.com

⇢ CROATIA

• **SVEUCILISTA U ZAGREBU / TEKSTILNO-TEHNOLOSKI FAKULTET**
www.ttf.hr

⇢ CZECH REPUBLIC

• **VYSOKÁ SKOLA UMÊLECKO-PRUMYSLOVÁ V PRAZE**
www.vsup.cz

⇢ DENMARK

• **DESIGNKOLEN KOLDING**
www.designskolenkolding.dk
• **DANMARKS DESIGNSKOLE**
www.dkds.dk
• **HELLERUP TEKSTIL AKADEMI**
www.bec-design.dk

⇢ ESTONIA

• **EESTI KUNSTIAKADEEMIA**
www.artun.ee

⇢ FINLAND

• **LAHDEN AMMATTIKORKEAKOULU**
www.lamk.fi
• **EVTEK-AMMATTIKORKEAKOULU**
www.evtek.fi
• **TAIDETEOLLINEN KORKEAKOULU**
www.uiah.fi
• **HÄMEEN AMMATTIKORKEAKOULU**
www.hamk.fi

⇢ FRANCE

• **ATELIER CHARDON SAVARD**
www.acs-paris.com
• **ÉCOLE DE LA CHAMBRE SYNDICALE DE LA COUTURE PARISIENNE**
www.modeaparis.com/vf/ecoles
• **ÉCOLE SUPÉRIEURE D'ART ET DESIGN DE SAINT-ETIENNE**
www.artschool-st-etienne.com
• **ÉCOLE NATIONALE SUPÉRIEURE D'ARTS DE PARIS-CERGY**
www.ensapc.fr
• **ÉCOLE NATIONALE SUPÉRIEURE DES ARTS DECORATIFS**
www.ensad.fr
• **ÉCOLE SUPÉRIEURE DES ARTS APPLIQUÉS DUPERRÉ**
http://duperre.org
• **ENSAAMA OLIVIER DE SERRES**
www.ensaama.net
• **ESAAT**
www.esaat-roubaix.com
• **ESMOD**
www.esmod.com
• **INSTITUT SUPÉRIEUR DES ARTS APPLIQUÉS (LISAA)**
www.lisaa.com
• **MOD'ART INTERNATIONAL**
www.mod-art.org
• **PARSONS PARIS SCHOOL OF ART AND DESIGN**
www.parsons-paris.com
• **STUDIO BERÇOT**
www.studio-bercot.com
• **UNIVERSITÉ DE LA MODE LYON II**
www.universite-mode.org

···> GERMANY
• **DEUTSCHE MEISTERSCHULE FÜR MODE**
www.designschule-muenchen.de
• **ESMOD BERLIN**
www.esmod.de
• **UNIVERSITÄT DER KÜNSTE BERLIN**
www.udk-berlin.de
• **FACHHOSCHULE FÜR TECHNIK UND WIRTSCHAFT BERLIN**
www.fhtw-berlin.de
• **HOCHSCHULE FÜR ANGEWANDTE WISSENSCHAFTEN HAMBURG**
www.haw-hamburg.de
• **MODESCHULE DÜSSELDORF**
www.fashion-design-institut.de

···> HONG KONG
• **THE HONG KONG POLYTECHNIC UNIVERSITY**
Institute of Textiles and Clothing
www.polyu.edu.hk

···> HUNGARY
• **MOHOLY-NAGY MÜVÉSZETI EGYETEM**
www.mif.hu
• **RKK TANULMÁNYI OSZTÁLY**
www.kmf.hu

···> INDIA
• **NATIONAL INSTITUTE OF DESIGN**
www.nid.edu
• **NATIONAL INSTITUTE OF FASHION TECHNOLOGY**
www.niftindia.com
• **PEARL ACADEMY OF FASHION**
www.pearlacademy.com

···> IRELAND
• **NATIONAL COLLEGE OF ART AND DESIGN**
www.ncad.ie

···> ISRAEL
• **THE SHENKAR COLLEGE OF TEXTILE TECHNOLOGY**
www.shenkar.ac.il

···> ITALY
• **NUOVA ACCADEMIA DI BELLE ARTI MILANO**
www.naba.it
• **DOMUS ACADEMY**
www.domusacademy.com
• **ISTITUTO EUROPEO DI DESIGN**
www.ied.it
• **ISTITUTO MARANGONI**
www.istitutomarangoni.com
• **KOEFIA**
www.koefia.com
• **POLIMODA**
www.polimoda.com

···> JAPAN
• **BUNKA FASHION COLLEGE**
www.bunka-fc.ac.jp
• **BUNKA Women's UNIVERSITY**
www.bunka.ac.jp
• **MODE GAKUEN**
www.mode.ac.jp

···> LEBANON
• **ESMOD BEYROUTH**
www.esmodbeyrouth.com

···> LITHUANIA
• **VILNIUS ACADEMY OF FINE ARTS**
www.vda.lt

···> THE NETHERLANDS
• **ACADEMIE BEELDENDE KUNSTEN MAASTRICHT**
www.abkmaastricht.nl
• **FASHION INSTITUTE ARNHEM**
www.fashioninstitute.nl
• **HOGESCHOOL VAN AMSTERDAM**
www.amfi.hva.nl
• **HOGESCHOOL VOOR DE KUNSTEN**
www.hka.nl
• **HOGESCHOOL VOOR DE KUNSTEN UTRECHT**
www.hku.nl
• **KONINKLIJKE ACADEMIE VAN BEELDENDE KUNSTEN DEN HAAG**
www.kabk.nl

···> NEW ZEALAND
• **OTAGO POLYTECHNIC**
www.tekotago.ac.nz

···> NORWAY
• **HØGSKOLEN I OSLO**
www.hio.no

···> POLAND
• **STRZEMINSKI ACADEMY OF FINE ARTS AND DESIGN, LODZ**
www.asp.lodz.pl

···> PORTUGAL
• **CITEX–Centro de Formação Profissional da Indústria Têxtil**
www.citex.pt

···› RUSSIA
- **THE KOSYGIN MOSCOW STATE TEXTILE ACADEMY**
www.msta.ac.ru
- **URAL STATE ACADEMY**
www.usaaa.ru

···› SINGAPORE
- **TEMASEK POLYTECHNIC**
www.tp.edu.sg

···› SPAIN
- **CENTRO SUPERIOR DE DISEÑO DE MODA DE MADRID**
www.csdmm.upm.es
- **ESCOLA D'ART I SUPERIOR DE DISSENY**
www.easdalcoi.com
- **FELICIDAD DUCE–Escuela Superior de Diseño y Moda**
www.fdmoda.com
- **ESCOLA SUPERIOR DE DISSENY, ESDi**
www.esdi.es
- **ISTITUTO EUROPEO DI DESIGN**
www.ied.es

···› SWEDEN
- **BECKMANS DESIGNHÖGSKOLA**
www.beckmans.se
- **HÖGSKOLAN I BORÅS**
www.hb.se

···› SWITZERLAND
- **ÉCOLE D'ARTS APPLIQUÉS**
www.geneve.ch/eaa
- **HOCHSCHULE FÜR GESTALTUNG UND KÜNST**
www.fhnw.ch/hgk
- **SCHULE FÜR GESTALTUNG BASEL**
www.sfgbasel.ch
- **ZÜRCHER HOCHSCHULE DER KÜNST / STYLE AND DESIGN**
www.zhdk.ch, www.styleanddesign.ch

···› TAIWAN
- **FU-JEN CATHOLIC UNIVERSITY**
www.tc.fju.edu.tw

···› TURKEY
- **DOKUZ EYLÜL ÜNIVERSITESI**
www.deu.edu.tr

···› UNITED KINGDOM
- **BIRMINGHAM INSTITUTE OF ART AND DESIGN**
www.biad.uce.ac.uk
- **CENTRAL SAINT MARTINS COLLEGE OF ART AND DESIGN**
www.csm.arts.ac.uk
- **DE MONTFORT UNIVERSITY**
www.dmu.ac.uk
- **UNIVERSITY COLLEGE FOR THE CREATIVE ARTS**
www.kiad.ac.uk
- **KINGSTON UNIVERSITY**
Department of Fashion Design
www.kingston.ac.uk
- **LONDON COLLEGE OF FASHION**
www.fashion.arts.ac.uk
- **MANCHESTER METROPOLITAN UNIVERSITY**
www.mmu.ac.uk
- **MIDDLESEX UNIVERSITY**
www.mdx.ac.uk
- **NORTHUMBRIA UNIVERSITY**
www.northumbria.ac.uk
- **RAVENSBOURNE COLLEGE OF DESIGN AND COMMUNICATION**
www.rave.ac.uk
- **ROYAL COLLEGE OF ART**
www.rca.ac.uk
- **NOTTINGHAM TRENT SCHOOL OF ART AND DESIGN**
www.ntu.ac.uk
- **UWE BRISTOL**
www.uwe.ac.uk
- **WINCHESTER SCHOOL OF ART**
www.wsa.soton.ac.uk

···› UNITED STATES
- **SCHOOL OF THE ART INSTITUTE OF CHICAGO**
www.saic.edu
- **FASHION INSTITUTE OF TECHNOLOGY**
www.fitnyc.edu
- **OTIS SCHOOL OF ART AND DESIGN**
www.otis.edu
- **PARIS FASHION INSTITUTE**
www.parisfashion.org
- **PARSONS THE NEW SCHOOL FOR DESIGN**
www.parsons.newschool.edu
- **PHILADELPHIA UNIVERSITY**
www.philau.edu
- **PRATT INSTITUTE**
www.pratt.edu
- **RHODE ISLAND SCHOOL OF DESIGN**
www.risd.edu
- **ACADEMY OF ARTS UNIVERSITY, SAN FRANCISCO**
www.academyart.edu

Fashion Museums

⋯ AUSTRIA

• MODESAMMLUNG DES WIEN MUSEUMS (FASHION COLLECTION OF THE VIENNA MUSEUMS)
Hetzendorfer Strasse 79
1120 Wien
+43 1 804 04 68
www.wienmuseum.at/start/Modesammlung.htm

⋯ BELGIUM

• MODEMUSEUM PROVINCIE ANTWERPEN—MOMU (MODE MUSEUM PROVINCE OF ANTWERP)
Nationalestraat 28
2000 Antwerp
+32 3 470 27 70
www.momu.be

• MODEMUSEUM HASSELT
Gasthuisstraat 11
3500 Hasselt
+32 1 123 96 21
www.modemuseum.hasselt.be

• MUSÉE DU COSTUME ET DE LA DENTELLE (MUSEUM OF COSTUME AND LACE)
Rue de la Violette 12
1000 Bruxelles
+32 2 213 44 50
www.brucity.be

⋯ CZECH REPUBLIC

• UMELECKOPRUMYSLOVE MUSEUM (MUSEUM OF DECORATIVE ARTS)
Ulice 17, Listopada 2
Staré Mesto
Praha 1
+42 2 2481 1241
www.upm.cz

⋯ FINLAND

• KANSALLISPUKUKESKUS (NATIONAL COSTUME CENTER)
Kauppakatu 25 & Kilpisenkatu 12
40100 Jyväskylä
+35 8 14 624 946
www.kansallispukukeskus.jkl.fi

⋯ FRANCE

• MUSÉE DE LA MODE ET DU TEXTILE (MUSEUM OF FASHION AND TEXTILES)
Les Arts Décoratifs
107 Rue de Rivoli
75001 Paris
+33 1 44 55 57 50
www.lesartsdecoratifs.fr

• MUSÉE DE LA MODE ET COSTUME (MUSEUM OF FASHION AND COSTUME)
Palais Galliera
10 Avenue Pierre 1er de Serbie
75116 Paris
+33 1 56 52 86 00

• MUSÉE DES TISSUS ET DES ARTS DECORATIFS (MUSEUM OF FABRIC AND DECORATIVE ARTS)
34 Rue de la Charité
69002 Lyon
+33 4 78 38 42 00
www.musee-des-tissus.com

⋯ GERMANY

• MODEMUSEUM
Stadtmuseum
St.-Jakobs-Platz 1
80331 München
+49 89 233 22370
http://münchen.museum.de

• DEUTSCHES TEXTILMUSEUM KREFELD (GERMAN TEXTILE MUSEUM KREFELD)
Andreasmarkt 8
47809 Krefeld
+49 2151 9469
www.krefeld.de/textilmuseum

ITALY

• CENTRO STUDI DI STORIA DEL TESSUTO E DEL COSTUME (STUDY CENTER FOR THE HISTORY OF TEXTILES AND COSTUMES)
Santa Croce, 1992
30125 Venezia
+39 41 721 798
www.museiciviciveneziani.it

• MUSEO DEL TESSUTO (MUSEUM OF TEXTILES)
Via Santa Chiara 24
59100 Prato
+39 0574 611503
www.museodeltessuto.it

JAPAN

• THE KYOTO COSTUME INSTITUTE
103, Shichi-jo Goshonouchi Minamimachi
Shimogyo-ku
Kyoto 600-8864
+81 75 321 9221
www.kci.or.jp

PORTUGAL

• MUSEU DO DESIGN E DA MODA (MUSEUM OF DESIGN AND FASHION)
Sala do Risco Lg. de Sto.
António à Sé, 22
1100-449 Lisboa
+351 21 888 61 17
www.mude.pt

THE NETHERLANDS

• AUDAX TEXTIELMUSEUM (AUDAX TEXTILE MUSEUM)
Goirkestraat 96
Tilburg
+31 13 536 7475
www.textielmuseum.nl

SPAIN

• MUSEO DEL TRAJE (COSTUME MUSEUM)
Avenida de Juan de Herrera, 2
28040 Madrid
+34 91 550 47 00
http://museodeltraje.mcu.es

SWITZERLAND

• TEXTILMUSEUM ST. GALLEN (TEXTILE MUSEUM ST. GALLEN)
Vadianstrasse 2
9000 St. Gallen
+41 71 222 17 44
www.textilmuseum.ch

UNITED KINGDOM

• VICTORIA & ALBERT MUSEUM
V&A, South Kensington, Cromwell Road
SW7 2RL London
+44 20 7942 2000
www.vam.ac.uk

• FASHION MUSEUM
Assembly Rooms, Bennett Street
BA1 2QH Bath
+44 1225 477173
www.fashionmuseum.co.uk

• GALLERY OF ENGLISH COSTUME
Platt Hall & Park, Platt Fields
Wilmslow Road, Rusholme
M14 5LL Manchester
+44 1612 245217
www.manchestergalleries.org/html/costume

• SHAMBELLIE HOUSE MUSEUM OF COSTUME
Shambellie House
New Abbey
Dumfriesshire DG2 8HQ
+44 1387 850375
www.nms.ac.uk/museumofcostumehomepage.aspx

··· UNITED STATES

• THE TEXAS FASHION COLLECTION

University of North Texas
College of Visual Arts and Design
1143 Union Circle
Scoular Hall, Room 124
Denton, Texas 76203-5100
+ 1 940 565 2732
www.art.unt.edu/tfc

• COSTUME INSTITUTE

Metropolitan Museum of Art
1000 Fifth Avenue
New York, New York 10028-0198
+1 212 535 7710
www.metmuseum.org/Works_of_Art/
department.asp

Fashion Weeks

···> JANUARY
- **MILAN (Italy)**
Men's
- **HONG KONG (China)**
Men's and Women's
- **SÃO PAULO (Brazil)**
Men's and Women's
- **PARIS (France)**
Men's
- **PARIS (France)**
Couture and Haute Couture
Spring-Summer
- **BERLIN (Germany)**
Men's and Women's

···> FEBRUARY
- **NEW YORK (United States)**
Men's and Women's
- **COPENHAGEN (Denmark)**
Men's and Women's
- **LONDON (United Kingdom)**
Women's
- **MILAN (Italy)**
Women's

···> MARCH
- **PARIS (France)**
Women's
- **BARCELONA (Spain)**
080 Barcelona Fashion
Men's and Women's
- **TOKYO (Japan)**
Men's and Women's
- **NEW DELHI (India)**
Wills Lifestyle India Fashion Week
Men's and Women's
- **ATHENS (Greece)**
Men's and Women's
- **BEIJING (China)**
Men's and Women's
- **LOS ANGELES (United States)**
Men's and Women's
- **MOSCOW (Russia)**
Men's and Women's

···> APRIL
- **SYDNEY (Australia)**
Rosemount Australian
Fashion Week
Men's and Women's

···> JUNE
- **MILAN (Italy)**
Men's
- **PARIS (France)**
Men's
- **PARIS (France)**
Couture and Haute Couture
Fall-Winter

···> JULY
- **HONG KONG (China)**
Men's and Women's
- **SÃO PAULO (Brazil)**
Men's and Women's
- **BERLIN (Germany)**
Men's and Women's

···> AUGUST
- **COPENHAGEN (Denmark)**
Men's and Women's

···> SEPTEMBER
- **TOKYO (Japan)**
Men's and Women's
- **BARCELONA (Spain)**
080 Barcelona Fashion
Men's and Women's
- **NEW YORK (United States)**
Men's and Women's
- **LONDON (United Kingdom)**
Men's and Women's
- **MILAN (Italy)**
Women's
- **PARIS (France)**
Women's

···> OCTOBER
- **LOS ANGELES (United States)**
Men's and Women's
- **MOSCOW (Russia)**
Men's and Women's
- **ATHENS (Greece)**
Hellenic Fashion Week
Men's and Women's
- **NEW DELHI (India)**
Wills Lifestyle India Fashion Week
Men's and Women's

···> NOVEMBER
- **BEIJING (China)**
Men's and Women's

Bibliography

REFERENCE BOOKS

BAUM, Maggy, and BOYELDIEU, Chantal, *Le dictionnaire des textiles,* Editions du Paillie, 2006.

DE CERVAL, Marguerite, *Dictionnaire international de bijou,* Editions du Regard, 1998.

Dictionnaire de la mode au xxe siècle, Editions du Regard, 1999.

Fashion Glossary Japanese Chinese English French Italian, Itochu Fashion System, 2005.

GEORGE, Sophie, *Le vêtement de A à Z, Encyclopédie de la mode et du textile,* Editions Falbalas, 2007.

HIRSCH, Pierre, *Lexique de l'habillement: français-anglais-espagnol-italien-allemand,* Industrie Textile, 1991.

JOIN-DIÉTERLE, Catherine, *Les mots de la mode,* Editions Actes Sud, 1998.

The Dictionary of Costume, Batsford, 1989.

The Encyclopaedia of Fashion from 1840 to the 1980s, Thames & Hudson, 1986.

Young European Fashion Designers, Daab, 2007.

HISTORY OF FASHION AND COSTUME—GENERAL

AGRON, Stephanie, *Précis d'histoire du costume: le costume masculin,* Editions J. Lanore, 1970.

BAUDOT, François, *Mode du siècle,* Assouline, 1999.

BELFANTI, Carlo Marco, *Calze e maglie: moda e innovazione nell'industria italiana della maglieria dal Rinascimento a oggi,* Tre Lune Edizioni, 2005.

BERG, Maxine, and CLIFFORD, Helen, *Consumers and Luxury: Consumer Culture in Europe 1650–1850,* Manchester University Press, 1999.

BOUCHER, François, *Histoire du costume: en occident de l'antiquité à nos jours,* Flammarion, 1996.

CASTARÈDE, Jean, *Histoire du luxe en France: des origines à nos jours,* Eyrolles, 2007.

CHAUMETTE, Xavier, *Tissus pour un siècle de mode : les textiles et les modes féminines en France au xxe siècle,* Editions Michel Lafon, 2002.

CUISENIER, Jean, *Mille ans de costume français,* Editions Gérard Klopp, 1991.

DEJEAN, Joan, *The Essence of Style: How the French Invented High Fashion, Fine Food, Chic Cafés, Style, Sophistication and Glamour,* Free Press, 2005.

DELPIERRE, Madeleine, *Le costume: Consulat–Empire,* Flammarion, 1990.
Se vêtir au xviiie siècle, Editions Adam Biro, 1996.

DESLANDRES, Yvonne, and MÜLLER, Florence, *Histoire de la mode au xxe siècle,* Somogy, 1986.

DESLANDRES, Yvonne, *Le costume, image de l'homme,* Editions IFM/Regard, 2002.

Fashion : les collections du Kyoto Costume Institute: une histoire de la mode du xviiie au xxe siècle, Taschen, 2002.

Fashion. Une histoire de la mode du XVIIe au XXe siècle, vols 1 & 2,
Taschen, 2005.

GOETZ, Adrien,
Marie-Antoinette Style,
Assouline, 2005.

GRAU, François-Marie,
Histoire du costume,
Presses Universitaires de France, 1999.

GREEN, Nancyl, *Du sentier à la 7ème Avenue, la confection et les immigrés Paris-New York 1880–1980,*
Seuil, 1988.

GRUMBACH, Didier,
Histoires de la mode,
Seuil, 1993.

GUILLAUME, Valérie, and VEILLON, Dominique,
La mode: un demi-siècle conquérant,
Gallimard, 2007.

KODA, Harold,
Goddess: The Classical Mode,
Metropolitan Museum of Art, 2003.

La mode et l'enfant 1780...2000, Exposition du 16 mai au 18 novembre 2001,
Musée Galliera, 2001.

LAVER, James,
Histoire de la mode et du costume,
Thames & Hudson, 1990.

MONNEYRON, Frédéric,
La mode et ses enjeux,
Editions Klincksieck, 2005.

MUSEE GALLIERA,
Modes en miroir. La France et la Hollande au temps des lumières,
Paris-Musees, 2005.

PIPONNIER, Francoise, and MANE, Perrine,
Se vêtir au moyen-age,
Editions Adam Biro, 1995.

RACINET, Auguste,
Histoire du costume,
Bookking International, 1989.

ROLAND, André,
Modes et maillots de bain,
Editions Alan Sutton, 2006.

RUPPERT, Jacques,
Le costume: Renaissance–Louis XIII,
Flammarion, 1990.
Le costume: Louis XIV–Louis XV,
Flammarion, 1990.
Le costume: Louis XVI–Directoire,
Flammarion, 1990.
Le costume: Restauration. Louis-Philippe. Second Empire. Belle-Epoque,
Flammarion, 1990.

SAMET, Janie,
Chère haute couture,
Plon, 2006.

SAPORI, Michelle,
Rose Bertin: Ministre des modes de Marie-Antoinette,
Editions IFM, 2003.

SEELING, Charlotte,
La mode au siècle des créateurs, 1900–1999,
Könemann, 2000.

VIDAL-BLANCHARD, Jocelyne,
Les voies de l'élégance,
Editions de la Martinière, 1997.

WORTH, Jean-Philippe,
A Century of Fashion,
Little, Brown and Company, 1928.

HISTORY OF FASHION AND COSTUME—SOCIOLOGY

BIEHN, Michel,
Cruelle coqueterie: ou les artifices de la contrainte,
Editions de La Martinière, 2006.

BOYER, Bruce G.,
Rebel Style,
Assouline, 2006.

BREWARD, Chrisopher,
Fashion,
Oxford University Press, 2003.

CORBIN, Alain, COURTINE, Jean-Jacques, and VIGARELLO, Georges,
Histoire du corps: de la Renaissance aux Lumières,
Seuil, 2005.

Histoire du corps: de la Révolution à la Grande Guerre,
Seuil, 2005.

Histoire du corps: les mutations du regard. Le XXe siècle,
Seuil, 2006.

COURTINE, Jean-Jacques, and HAROCHE, C.,
Histoire du visage: XVIe–début XIXe siècle,
Editions Rivages, 1984.

DELBOURG-DELPHIS, Marylene,
Le chic et le look: histoire de la mode féminine et des moeurs de 1850 à nos jours,
Hachette, 1981.

ECO, Umberto,
On Ugliness,
Rizzoli, 2007.

FRANKLIN, Alfred Louis August,
La vie privée d'autrefois: modes, moeurs, usages des parisiens,
Plon, 1987.

MÜLLER, Florence,
Excentriques,
Editions du Chêne, 2001.

PERROT, Philippe,
Les dessus et les dessous de la bourgeoisie,
Fayard, 1981.

RIBEIRO, Aileen,
Dress and Morality,
Batsford, 1986.

ROCHE, Daniel,
La culture des apparences: une histoire du vêtement XVIIe-XVIIIe siècle,
Ed. Fayard, 1989.

SOMMIER, Eric,
Mode, le monde en mouvement,
Editions Village Mondial, 2000.

TOUSSAINT-SAMAT, Magueulonne,
Histoire technique et morale du vêtement,
Bordas, 1990.

VIGARELLO, Georges,
Le propre et le sale: l'hygiène du corps depuis le moyen âge,
Seuil, 1985.

Histoire de la beauté: le corps et l'art d'embellir de la renaissance à nos jours,
Seuil, 2004.

WALKLEY, Christina,
Dressed to Impress: 1840–1914,
Batsford, 1989.

FASHION AND LITERATURE

ASSOULY, Olivier,
Goûts à vendre: essais sur la captation esthétique,
Editions IFM/Regard, 2007.

BALZAC, Honoré de,
Traité de la vie élégante suivi de la théorie de la démarche,
Bossard, 1922.

BAUDOT, François,
The Allure of Men,
Assouline, 2000.

BOUCHER, François, and REMAURY, Bruno,
Le vêtement chez Balzac: extraits de la Comédie humaine,
Editions IFM/Regard, 2001.

BREWARD, Christopher, and GILBERT, David,
Fashion's World Cities,
Berg, 2006.

CARTER, Michael,
Fashion Classics from Carlyle to Barthes,
Berg, 2003.

CHENOUNE, Farid,
Des modes et des hommes: deux siècles d'élégance masculine,
Flammarion, 1993.

DEBRAY, Régis, and HUGUES, Patrice,
Dictionnaire culturel du tissu,
Babylone/Fayard, 2005.

FORTASSIER, Rose,
Les écrivains français et la mode: de Balzac à nos jours,
Presses Universitaires de France, 1988.

JOHNSON, Kim K. P.; TORNTORE, Susan J.; and EICHER, Joanne B.,
Fashion Foundations: Early Writings on Fashion and Dress,
Berg, 2003.

KAWAMURA, Yuniya,
Fashion-ology: An Introduction to Fashion Studies, Berg, 2005.

KRAATZ, Anne,
Mode et philosophie, ou le néoplatonisme en silhouette 1470–1500,
Les Belles Lettres, 2005.

La Mode: la passion de la création. Courants et contre-courants, 2 vols.
Revue des deux mondes, 2001.

LANG, Abigail S.,
Mode et contre-mode: une anthologie de Montaigne à Pérec,
Editions IFM/Regard, 2001.

LEHMANN, Ulrich,
Tigersprung: Fashion in Modernity,
MIT Press, 2000.

LUBART, Todd,
Psychologie de la créativité,
Armand Colin, 2003.

MONNEYRON, Frédéric,
La sociologie de la mode,
Presses Universitaires de France, 2006.

REMAURY, Bruno,
Il gentil sesso debole. Le immagini del corpo femminile tra cosmetica e salute,
Meltemi, 2006.

ROSELLE, B.,
La mode,
Imprimerie Nationale, 1980.

SOMMIER, Eric,
Essai sur la mode dans les sociétés modernes,
L'Harmattan, 2007.

WAQUET, Dominique, LAPORTE, Marion,
La mode,
Presses Universitaires de France, 1999.

FASHION AND PHOTOGRAPHY

BOUDIN-LESTIENNE, Stéphane,
Hyères 2007: 22ème festival international de mode et de photographie Villa Noailles,
Archibooks, 2007.

BOURDIN, Guy; MEYER, Nicolle; and VERTHIME, Shelly,
Guy Bourdin: A Message For You, Vols 1 & 2,
Steidl/Dangin, 2006.

Chic Clicks: Creativity and Commerce in Contemporary Fashion Photography,
Institute of Contemporary Art, Boston, 2002.

COTTON, Charlotte,
Imperfect Beauty: The Making of Contemporary Fashion Photographs,
V&A, 2000.

EWING, William A., and SCHINZ, Marina,
Blumenfeld: le culte de la beauté,
Editions de La Martinière, 1996.

HARRISON, Marvin,
Appearances: Fashion Photography since 1945,
Schirmer/Mosel, 1991.

KISMARIC, Susan, and RESPINI, Eva,
Fashioning Fiction in Photography since 1990,
Museum of Modern Art, 2004.

LOVATT-SMITH, Lisa, and REMY, Patrick,
Fashion images de mode n°1,
Steidl, 1996.

Fashion images de mode n°2,
Steidl, 1997.

LOVATT-SMITH, Lisa,
Fashion images de mode n°3,
Steidl, 1998.
Fashion images de mode n°4,
Steidl, 1999.

LOVATT-SMITH, Lisa,
Fashion images de mode n°5,
Steidl, 2000.

Fashion images de mode n°6,
Vision On, 2001.

MANEKER, Marion,
Dressing in the Dark: Lessons in Men's Style from the Movies,
Assouline, 2002.

MÜLLER, Florence,
Belles en Vogue. Collection photographique de 1925 à nos jours,
Editions du Collectionneur, 2004.

NEWMAN, Cathy,
Fashion,
National Geographic, 2001.

PENN, Irving, and VREELAND, Diana,
Les belles robes de Paris: 1909–1939,
Henri Veyrier, 1978.

PROVOYER, Pierre, and BAUDOT, François,
Horst, 60 ans de photographie,
Union Des Arts Decoratifs, 1991.

SOLER JIMÉNEZ, Joan,
Moderníssims !!!,
Centre De Documentació i Museu Tèxtil, 2005.

STOMAN, Chantal,
A Woman's Obsession,
Editions de La Martinière, 2006.

FASHION AND DESIGNERS

ABCDE - MAGAZINE VIKTOR&ROLF par VIKTOR et ROLF, première décennie,
Artimo Foundation, 2004.

BALFOUR, Michael,
Alfred Dunhill: One Hundred Years and More,
Weidenfeld & Nicolson, 1992.

BAUDOT, François,
Massaro,
Assouline, 1999.

Salvatore Ferragamo,
Assouline, 2000.

BECKER, Vivienne; LANGES-SWAROVSKI, Markus; and LE GALLAIS, Rosemarie,
Daniel Swarovski,
Thames & Hudson, 2005.

BELLU, Serge,
Louis Vuitton: The Art of the Automobile,
Harry N. Abrams, 2008.

BENAÏM, Laurence,
Jacques Helleu & Chanel,
Harry N. Abrams, 2006.

BLUM, Dilys E.,
Elsa Schiaparelli,
Musée de la Mode Et du Textile, 2004.

BOMAN, Eric,
Blahnik by Boman: Shoes, Photographs, Conversation,
Chronicle Books, 2005.

BONVICINI, Stéphanie,
Louis Vuitton: une saga française,
Fayard, 2004.

BOTT, Danièle,
Chanel,
Thames & Hudson, 2007.

BRUNHAMMER, Yvonne, and SAUTOT, Dany,
René Lalique: Extraordinary Jewelelry 1890–1912,
Skira, 2007.

CHARLES-ROUX, Edmonde,
Chanel and her World,
Vendome, 2005.

CLAIS, Anne-Marie,
Sergio Rossi,
Assouline, 2008.

COLENO, Nadine,
Christian Lacroix. De fil en aiguille,
Editions du Regard, 2002.

Découvre la mode de Karl Lagerfeld,
Editions du Regard, 2004.

Roger Vivier: d'un soulier l'autre,
Editions du Regard, 2005.

CoolBrands: An Insight into Some of Britain's Coolest Brands,
Superbrands Ltd., 2005.

DALLOZ-RAMAUX, Sophie,
Madeleine Vionnet: créatrice de mode,
Editions Cabédita, 2006.

DE CERVAL, Marguerite,
Mauboussin: joaillier de l'émotion 1827–2007,
Mauboussin, 2007.

DE POTTER, Peter,
Raf Simons Redux,
Fondazione Pitti Discovery/Charta, 2005.

DE SÉLYS, Elodie,
Olivier Strelli: passion et métissage,
La Renaissance du Livre, 2006.

DEMORNEX, Jacqueline,
Lucien Lelong: L'intemporel,
Gallimard, 2007.

DESBIOLLES, Maryline,
Le printemps de Guerlain,
Le Cherche Midi, 2006.

DESCHODT, Anne Marie,
Mariano Fortuny 1871–1949: un magicien de Venise,
Editions du Regard, 1979.

EGGIMANN, Ch.,
Les créateurs de la mode,
Ch. Eggimann, 1910.

Emilio Pucci: Looking at Fashion, Biennal di Firenze,
Skira, 1996.

Esprit Staron: Rubans, soieries et haute couture, 1867-1986,
Somogy, 2007.

FIEMEYER, Isabelle,
Coco Chanel: un parfum de mystère,
Payot, 2004.

FLOCH, Jean-Marie,
L'indémodable total-look de Coco Chanel,
IFM/Regard, 2004.

FOLEY, Bridget,
Marc Jacobs,
Assouline, 2004.

Fortuny e Caramba: la moda a teatro, costumi de scena 1906–1936,
Cataloghi Marsilio, 1987.

FRANKEL, Susannah,
Visionaries: Interviews with Fashion Designers,
V&A, 2001.

GAN, Stephen; DEAN, Cecilia; and KALIARDOS, James,
Dreaming in Print: A decade of Visionaire,
Edition 7L, 2002.

GEOFFROY SCHNEITER, Bérénice,
Africa Is In Style,
Assouline, 2005.

GIDEL, Henri,
Coco Chanel,
Flammarion, 2000.

GIORDANI ARAGNO, Bonizza,
La signora dello stile: Mila Schön,
Edizioni Polistampa, 2003.

GOLBIN, Pamela, and BARON, Fabien,
Balenciaga Paris,
Thames & Hudson, 2006.

GOLBIN, Pamela,
Créateurs de mode,
Editions du Chêne, 1999.

GUÉNÉ, Hélène,
Décoration et haute couture: Armand Albert Rateau pour Jeanne Lanvin, un autre art déco,
Les Arts Decoratifs, 2006.

HATA, Kyojiro,
Louis Vuitton Japan: The Building of Luxury,
Assouline, 2004.

HAYEK, Nicolas G.,
Au-delà de la saga Swatch: entretiens d'un authentique entrepreneur avec Friedmann Bartu,
Albin Michel, 2006.

HEALY, Orla,
Coty: La marque d'un visionnaire,
Assouline, 2004.

JARRATT, Phil,
The Mountain and the Wave: The History of Quiksilver,
Quiksilver, 2006.

JOIN-DIÉTERLE, Catherine,
Givenchy: 40 ans de création,
Paris Musées, 1991.

JONES, Terry, and MAIR, Avril,
Fashion Now,
Taschen, 2003.

JONES, Terry, and RUSHTON, Susie,
Fashion Now 2,
Taschen, 2005.

KAMITSIS, Lydia,
Lesage,
Assouline, 1999.
Madeleine Vionnet,
Assouline, 1996.

KAWAMURA, Yuniya,
The Japanese Revolution in Paris Fashion,
Berg, 2004.

KODA, Harold; BOLTON, Andrew, et al,
Chanel,
Metropolitan Museum of Art, 2005.

KRAATZ, Anne,
Solstiss: The Seduction of Lace,
Assouline, 2006.

KRIES, Mateo; MIYAKE, Issey; and FUJIWARA, Dai,
A-POC Making: Issey Miyake and Dai Fujiwara,
Vitra Design Museum, 2001.

LACROIX, Christian,
Qui est là ?,
Mercure De France, 2004.

LACROIX, Christian; MAURIÈS, Patrick; and SAILLARD, Olivier,
Christian Lacroix: On Fashion,
Thames & Hudson, 2008.

LANGLE, Elisabeth,
Pierre Cardin: Fifty years of Fashion and Design,
Thames & Hudson, 2005.

LAUREN, Ralph,
Ralph Lauren,
Rizzoli, 2007.

LORENZ, Sylvana,
Pierre Cardin, son fabuleux destin,
Editions N°1, 2006.

LYON, Todd,
Land's End Business Attire for Men: Mastering the New ABCs of What to Wear to Work,
Clarkson Potter, 2004.

Land's End Business Attire for Women: Mastering the New ABCs of What to Wear to Work,
Clarkson Potter, 2004.

MAILLARD, Arnaud,
Merci Karl !,
Calmann Lévy, 2007.

MANUSARDI, Jean,
Dix ans avec Pierre Cardin,
Fanval, 1986.

Mode à l'extrême,
Cgri-Awex-Dri, 2004.

Modern Master: Lucien Lelong: couturier 1918–1948,
Museum At FIT, 2006.

MONLLOR, Cecília,
Zarapolis: la historia secreta de un imperio de la moda,
Ediciones Del Bronce, 2003.

Bibliography

MORGUE, Tiffy, and GAILLAC, Jean Yves,
Lolita Lempicka: 20 ans de création,
Editions de La Martinière, 2004.

MOWER, Sarah,
20 Years: Dolce & Gabbana,
5 Continents, 2005.
Gucci by Gucci,
Vendome, 2006.

MUSEO SALVATORE FERRAGAMO,
Idee, modelli, invenzioni: ideas, models, inventions,
Sillabe, 2004.

NADELHOFFER, Hans,
Cartier,
Editions du Regard, 2007.

NOISETTE, Philippe,
Les couturiers de la danse,
Editions de La Martinière, 2003.

OMORI, Yoko,
For a Girl,
2004.

PASOLS, Paul-Gérard,
Louis Vuitton: la naissance du luxe moderne,
Editions de La Martinière, 2005.

PETIT, Marc,
Van Cleef & Arpels: reflets d'éternité,
Editions Cercle D'art, 2005.

PIROTTE, Philippe, et al,
Beyond Desire,
Ludion, 2005.

POIRET, Paul,
En habillant l'époque,
Grasset, 1930.

RASCHE, Adelheid,
Coats! Max Mara, 55 years of Italian fashion,
Skira, 2007.

REMAURY, Bruno,
Marques et récits: la marque face à l'imaginaire culturel et contemporain,
IFM/Regard, 2004.

RICHOUX, Sylvie,
Karine Arabian et les arméniens de la mode XVIIe-XXIe siècle: The armenians in fashion from the 17th to the 21st centuries,
Musée de Marseille, Somogy, 2007.

SAILLARD, Olivier,
Jean Paul Gaultier, Régine Chopinot: le défilé,
Les Arts Decoratifs, 2007.

SAVIGNON, Jéromine,
Jean-Louis Scherrer,
Assouline, 2007.

SCHOUMANN, Helene,
Chloé,
Assouline, 2003.

Gottex: Swimwear Haute Couture,
Assouline, 2006.

SHERRILL, Marcia, and KARMEL, Carey Adina,
Stylemakers: Inside Fashion,
Monacelli, 2002.

SISCHY, Ingrid,
Donna Karan,
Assouline, 1998.

SITBON, Martine,
A MAGAZINE #5, curated by Martine Sitbon,
A Publisher, 2007.

SLESIN, Suzanne,
Over the Top: Helena Rubinstein Extraordinary Style in Beauty, Art, Fashion, and Design,
Pointed Leaf Press, 2003.

Stiletto: spécial Chanel 2005,
2005.

TALLEY, Andre Leon,
Diane Von Furstenberg: The Wrap,
Assouline, 2004.

The Fashion Book,
Phaidon, 1998.

TRIBOUILLARD, Daniel, and PRIVAT-SAVIGNY, Maria-Anne,
Léonard, impressions de mode,
Lieux Dits, 2006.

VAN NOTEN, Dries,
DVN 01–50,
Van Noten, 2004.

VERNUS, Pierre,
Art, luxe & Industrie: Bianchini Férier, un siècle de soieries lyonnaises 1888–1992,
Presses Universitaires de Grenoble, 2006.

Vivienne Westwood talks about her extraordinary life in fashion, V&A magazine,
V&A Publications, 2004.

WATT, Judith,
Ossie Clark 1965–74,
V&A, 2003.

WEISSMAN, Elisabeth,
Coco Chanel,
Maren Sell Editeurs, 2007.

WHITE, Palmer,
Elsa Schiaparelli: Empress of Paris Fashion,
Aurum, 1996.

WILCOX, Claire,
Radical Fashion,
V&A, 2001.
Vivienne Westwood,
V&A, 2004.

WINTOUR, Anna; CARTER, Graydon; and FOLEY, Bridget,
Tom Ford,
Rizzoli, 2002.

YAMAMOTO, Yohji,
A MAGAZINE #2, curated by Yohji Yamamoto,
A Publisher, 2005.

Yves Saint Laurent dialogue avec l'art: catalogue d'exposition, Fondation Pierre Bergé-Yves Saint Laurent du 10 mars au 18 juillet 2004, 5 avenue Marceau 75116 Paris,
Fondation Pierre Bergé Yves Saint Laurent, 2004.

ART AND FASHION

BAUDOT, François,
Fashion and Surrealism,
Assouline, 2002.

COCTEAU, Jean,
Cocteau et la mode, in "Cahiers Jean Cocteau," nouvelle série n°3,
Passage du Marais, 2004.

DE GIVRY, Valerie,
Art et mode: L'inspiration artistique des créateurs de mode,
Editions du Regard, 1998.

DOONAN, Simon,
Andy Warhol Fashion,
Chronicle Books, 2004.

GASPARINA, Jill,
I love Fashion: l'art contemporain et la mode,
Editions Cercle D'art, 2006.

MALOCHET, Annette, and BIANCI, Matteo,
Sonia Delaunay: atelier simultané 1923–1934,
Skira, 2006.

MÜLLER, Florence,
Art and Fashion,
Assouline, 2000.

SOZZANI, Franca,
Black Book: Art and Fashion,
Assouline, 1998.

STERN, Radu,
Against Fashion: Clothing as Art, 1850–1930,
MIT Press, 2004.

Index

A

B

D

E

F

G

H

I

J

K

L

M

N

O

P

Q

R

S

W

Y

Z

Photo Credits

p. 12: © Jacques Boyer/Roger-Viollet; p. 13: © BNF; p. 14: © DR; p. 15: © Photo CNAC/MNAM, Dist. RMN/DR, © Adagp, Paris 2008; p. 16 left : © Leonard de Selva/Corbis, right : © Studio Lipnitzki/Roger-Viollet ; p. 17 : © Studio Lipnitzki/Roger-Viollet ; p. 18 : © Quentin Bertoux ; p. 19 : © DR ; p. 21 : 1. © DR, 2. © Sevenarts Ltd/Adagp, Paris 2008, 3. © Adagp, Paris 2008, 4. © Condé Nast Archive/Corbis, © Adagp, Paris 2008; p. 22: © Bettmann/Corbis; p. 24: © Joseph Sohm/Visions of America/Corbis; p. 25: © Richard T. Nowitz/Corbis; p. 27: © DR; p. 28-29: © Patrimoine Lanvin/DR; p. 30: © Cecil Beaton/Sotheby's Londres; p. 31: © Photo Bellini/Archives Christian Dior; p. 33: © Dries Van Noten; p. 35: © DR; p. 36: © Roger-Viollet; p. 37: © Condé Nast Archive/Corbis; p. 38: © Condé Nast/DR; p. 39: © John Rawlings/Condé Nast Archive/Corbis; p. 41: © DR; p. 42: © Ryersson & Yaccarino/The Casati Archives; p. 43: © BNF; p. 44: © DR; p. 45 top: © DR, bottom: © Schiaparelli; p. 47: 1. © Succession Marcel Duchamp/Adagp, Paris 2008, Photo © Man Ray Trust/Adagp, Paris 2008, 2. © Man Ray Trust/Adagp, Paris 2008, 3. © Adagp, Paris, 2008, Photo © Man Ray Trust/Adagp, Paris 2008, 4. © Succession Miro/Adagp, Paris, 2008, Photo © Man Ray Trust/Adagp, Paris 2008; p. 48 left: © John Springer Collection/ Corbis, right: © Bettmann/Corbis; p. 49: © John Springer Collection/ Corbis; p. 51: © The Kobal Collection; p. 53: 1. © John French/Picture Post/IPC Magazines/Getty Images, 2. © Time Inc./Time Life Pictures/Getty Images, 3. © Gleb Derujinksy, 4. © Sharland/*Life* Magazine/Time Inc./Time Life Pictures/Getty Images; p. 54: © Dior Joaillerie; p. 55: © Gilles Bensimon; p. 56: © DR; p. 57 top: © Jean-Louis Benoît/Archives Roger Vivier/DR, bottom: © DR; p. 58-59: © DR; p. 60: © Assouline; p. 61: © DR; p. 62: © Chanel/Courtesy *Vogue* Paris; p. 63: © René Gruau, www.renegru-au.com; p. 65: © Gilles Trillard; p. 66: © Hachette Filipacchi Photos–Photo: Kammermann; p. 67: © Condé Nast/ *Vogue* France–Photo: Sante Forlano; p. 68-69: © DR; p. 71: © DR; p. 72: © Genevieve Naylor/Corbis; p. 73: © Roger Prigent/Sygma/Corbis; p. 74: © Brigitte Lacombe/*Time* Magazine/Time & Life Pictures/Getty Images; p. 75: © Archives Diane von Furstenberg/DR; p. 77: 1. © Pace Gregory/Corbis Sygma, © Richard Melloul/ Sygma/Corbis, 2. © DR, © Bettmann/Corbis, 3. © DR, © Pierre Vauthey/Corbis Sygma, 4. © DR, © Studio Lipnitzki/Roger-Viollet, 5. © Steve Azzara/Corbis, © Stephane Cardinale/Corbis Sygma, 6. © Bettmann/Corbis, © DR, 7. © Julio Donoso/Corbis Sygma, 8. © Pierre Vauthey/Corbis Sygma, 9. © Julio Donoso/Corbis Sygma, © Corbis Sygma, 10. © DR, © Fondation Pierre Bergé-Yves Saint Laurent; p. 78: © Laziz Hamani; p. 79: © DR; p. 80: © Peter Lindbergh; p. 81: © Laziz Hamani; p. 83: © Laziz Hamani; p. 84-85: © DR; p. 86: © Corbis; p. 87: © Condé Nast Archive/Corbis; p. 88: © Bettmann/Corbis; p. 89: © Ramon Manent/Corbis; p. 90: © Martine Archambault/ EPA/Corbis; p. 91: © WWD/Condé Nast/Corbis, model: Sasha Pivovarova/IMG; p. 93: © Victoria Pearson; p. 94 top: © Julien Claessens/Nina Ricci, bottom: © Nina Ricci; p. 95: © Julien Claessens/Nina Ricci; p. 96: © Franco Rubartelli/Archives Emilio Pucci; p. 97: © Archives Emilio Pucci; p. 98: © Archives Missoni; p. 99: © Carlo Orsi; p. 100: © DR; p. 101: © AFP; p. 106: © Archives Givenchy; p. 107: © DR; p. 108: © Orban Thierry/Corbis Sygma; p. 109: © Guy Marineau/Starface, model: Hana Soukupova/Viva Models; p. 110: © DR, © Hulton-Deutsch Collection/Corbis; p. 111: Courtesy Lord & Taylor Archives; p. 112 : © DR; p. 113: © PG/Magnum Photos; p. 114 left: © DR, right © Fondation Pierre Bergé-Yves Saint Laurent; p. 115: © Fondation Pierre Bergé-Yves Saint Laurent; p. 116: © Condé Nast Archive/Corbis; p. 117: © Stephan C. Archetti/Keystone Features/Getty Images; p. 119: © Rankin/www.jitrois.com; p. 121: © Alexandre Guirkinger; p. 122: © CinemaPhoto/Corbis; p. 123: © Burberry; p. 124 left: © DR, right: © Assouline; p. 125: © Gilles Bensimon; p. 126: © Archives Paco Rabanne; p. 128-129: © Peter Knapp; p. 130-131: Archives Pierre Cardin; p. 132: © Jean-Louis Benoît/Archives Roger Vivier/DR; p. 133: © Estate of Guy Bourdin/Art+Commerce; p. 135: © DR; p. 136: © Bettmann/Corbis; p. 137: © Hulton-Deutsch Collection/Corbis; p. 138: © Hulton-Deutsch Collection/Corbis; p. 139: © Roger-Viollet; p. 140: © Patrice Stable/ Archives Emanuel Ungaro; p. 141: © Marc Hispard; p. 142: © Janos Grapow; p. 143: © Arthur Elgort; p. 145: © Dries Van Noten; p. 147: © Jean-Marie Périer/Photo12.com; p. 148: © Nike; p. 149: © Adidas ; p. 150: © Archives Lee Cooper; p. 151: © Jacques Gavard; p. 153: © Collection Musée Air France/DR; p. 154: © Arthur Elgort/Carolina Herrera; p. 156: © David Ash/Corbis; p. 157: © Condé Nast Archive/Corbis; p. 158 left: © The Kobal Collection/Orion, right: © Keystone/Getty Images; p. 159: © Studio Lipnitzki/Roger Viollet; p. 160-161: © Archives Oscar de la Renta; p. 162: © IFM; p. 163: © Parsons The New School for Design; p. 164: Concept and Styling © Esmeralda Patisso, Photo © Diego Piaz; p. 165: © Nial McInerney/Central Saint Martins College of Art & Design; p. 167: 1. © Peter Knapp/*Elle*, 2, 3 and 4. © DR; p. 168-169: © Céline; p. 170: © Archives Vivienne Westwood; p. 171: © Solve Sundsbo/ Art+Commerce; p. 172-173: © DR; p. 174: © Hans Feurer/Kenzo; p. 175: © Patrice Stable/Kenzo; p. 176: © Archives

Jean-Charles de Castelbajac; p. 177: © Frédérique Dumoulin; p. 178: © Peter Knapp; p. 179: © Archives Sonia Rykiel; p. 180-181: © Issey Miyake; p. 183: 1. Courtesy Galerie Bartsch & Chariau, Munich, © Estate of Antonio Lopez & Juan Ramos, 2. © Thierry Perez/DR, 3. © DR, 4. © Ruben Toledo; p. 185: © Ellen von Unwerth; p. 186-187: © Archives Vivienne Westwood; p. 189: © Roger Prigent/Archives Diane von Furstenberg; p. 190: © DR; p. 191: © PETA; p. 193: © Thierry Mugler; p. 194: © Keiichi Tahara; p. 195: © Assouline; p. 196: © Keiichi Tahara; p. 197: © Quentin Bertoux; p. 198: © Hulton-Deutsch Collection/Corbis; p. 199: © Julio Donoso/Corbis Sygma; p. 200-201: © Archives Jean Paul Gaultier; p. 203: 1. © Columbia/Tri-Star/The Kobal Collection, 2. © Paramount/The Kobal Collection, 3. © Terra/Tamara/Cormoran/The Kobal Collection, 4. © BCA/Rue des Archives; p. 204: © Fwd-Gruber/Retnaus/Starface; p. 205: © AFP; p. 207: © Kishin Shinoyama; p. 208: © Koichi Inakoshi/Archives Yohji Yamamoto; p. 209: © Archives Yohji Yamamoto; p. 210: © Peter Knapp; p. 211: © Guy Marineau/Starface, model: Vlada Roslyakova/Women Management; p. 212: © Charles Platiau/Reuters; p. 214: © Richard Burbridge/Art+Commerce; p. 215: © Nathaniel Goldbergh/Art+Commerce; p. 217: © DR; p. 219: © Ronald Stoops/Archives Martin Margiela; p. 221: © Guy Marineau/Starface, model: Mini Anden/IMG; p. 226: © DR; p. 227: © *Harper's Bazaar*; p. 229: © Michel Comte; p. 230: © Giorgio Armani; p. 231: © Paramount/The Kobal Collection; p. 233: © DR; p. 235: 1. © Time Inc./Time Life Pictures/Getty Images, 2. © Duffy/Elle, 3. © DR, 4. © Time Inc./Time Life Pictures/Getty Images; p. 236-237: © Keiichi Tahara; p. 238-239: © Assouline, model: Helena Christensen/Marilyn Agency; p. 240: © Peter Lindbergh; p. 241: © Peter Lindbergh, model: Beri Smither/MFO and Elite Paris; p. 243: © Thierry Bouët; p. 245: 1. © Christian Lacroix, 2. © Archives Christian Dior, 3. © Croquis Yohji Yamamoto, 4. © Valentino; p. 246: © Guy Marineau/Starface, model: Michelle Alves/IMG; p. 247: © Julio Donoso/Corbis Sygma; p. 248: © Guy Marineau/Starface; p. 249: © Badi-Ftw-Sam/Starface; p. 250: © Dries Van Noten; p. 251: © Willy Vanderperre/Archives Ann Demeulemeester; p. 252: © Dries Van Noten; p. 253: © Willy Vanderperre/Archives Ann Demeulemeester; p. 255: © Dries Van Noten; p. 257: © Schiaparelli; p. 258 top: © DR, bottom: © Louis Vuitton; p. 259: © Laziz Hamani; p. 261: © Archives Claude Montana; p. 263: 1. © Studio des Fleurs/Hermès, 2. © Quentin Bertoux/Hermès, 3, 4 and 5. © DR, 6. © Gérard Darel; p. 264 left: © Peter Lindbergh, right: © André Rau/H&K; p. 265: © Solve Sundsbo/Art+Commerce, model: Kate Moss/Marilyn Agency; p. 266: © Prada; p. 267: © Prada, model: Raquel Zimmermann/Viva Models; p. 268: © Karl Lagerfeld; p. 270: © Inditex; p. 271: © Gareth Cattermole/Getty Images/AFP; p. 273: 1. © DR, © Mitchell Gerber/Corbis, 2. © Hulton-Deutsch Collection/Corbis, 3. © Orban Thierry/Corbis Sygma, © Robert Eric/Corbis Sygma, 4. © Genevieve Naylor/Corbis, © Condé Nast Archive/Corbis, 5. © DR, © *WWD*/Condé Nast/Corbis, 6. © DR, 7. © Bettmann/Corbis, © Gene Blevins/Corbis, 8. © Bettmann/Corbis, © Frédéric Huijbregts/Corbis, 9. © Condé Nast Archive/Corbis, © Peter Andrews/Corbis, 10. © Bettmann/Corbis, © Hulton Archive/Getty Images; p. 274: © Jil Sander, model Gemma Ward/IMG; p. 275: © Terry Richardson/Katy Barker Agency; p. 276: © DR; p. 277: © Ellen von Unwerth/Art+Commerce; p. 279: 1. © Burberry, 2. © Louis Vuitton, 3. © Hermès, 4. © DR, 5. © Ralph Lauren, 6. © Versace, 7. © Céline, 8. © Lanvin; p. 280: © Jimmy Cohrssen; p. 283: © Quentin Bertoux/Hermès; p. 284: © Archives Vivienne Westwood; p. 285: © DR; p. 286: © Toru Yamanaka/AFP; p. 288: © Philippe Bialobos; p. 289: © Philippe Gueguen; p. 290: © Hulton-Deutsch Collection/Corbis; p. 291: © Peter Knapp; p. 292 top: © Archives Hussein Chalayan, bottom: © Bespoke Couture Ltd.; p. 293: © Stephane Cardinale/People Avenue/Corbis, model: Marta Berzkalna/City Models; p. 295: © Richard Burbridge/Art+Commerce; p. 296: Karl Lagerfeld/Chanel, model: Daria/IMG; p. 297: © Croquis Karl Lagerfeld/Chanel; p. 298: © Joey Nigh/Corbis; p. 299: © Janet Jarman/Corbis; p. 301: © Patrice Stable/Archives John Galliano, model: Adina Fohlin/Next Models; p. 302: © Pierre Bailly/DR; p. 303: © Graylock/JPI/Starface, model: Snejana Onopka/Viva Models; p. 305: © DR; p. 306: © John Midgley; p. 307: © Paolo Roversi; p. 308: © Antoine Jarrier/Louis Vuitton; p. 309: © Dan Lecca, model: Deanna Miller/Next Models; p. 314: © Lagerfeld Gallery; p. 315: © Karl Lagerfeld; p. 317: © Lafata/Starface, model: Georgina Grenville/IMG; p. 318: © DR; p. 319: © GAP; p. 320: © Emmanuel Fradin/Reuters, model: Lindsay/DNA Models; p. 321: © Gonzalo Fuentes/Reuters, model: Alyona Osmanova/Women Management; p. 322: © Archives Viktor & Rolf; p. 324: © Peter Stigter; p. 325: © Rozema Teunissen; p. 327: © Gladys Perint Palmer; p.328: © DeBoer/Retna US/Starface; p. 330 top: © Sergio Rossi, bottom: © Louboutin; p. 331: © Manolo Blahnik.

Every effort has been made to identify the copyright owners; errors or omissions that are brought to the publisher's attention will be corrected when the next edition is printed.

Acknowledgments

The author eagerly expresses her thanks to Franc' Pairon and Ana Parodi.

The editor also wishes to thank the celebrities, photographers, and models that participated in this work, and particularly Michelle Alves, Mini Anden, Gilles Bensimon, Quentin Bertoux, Marta Berzkalna, Philippe Bialobos, Thierry Bouët, Richard Burbridge, Helena Christensen, Jimmy Cohrssen, Michel Comte, Cindy Crawford, Gleb Derujinksy, Frédérique Dumoulin, Anh Duong, Arthur Elgort, Adina Fohlin, Inès de la Fressange, Jacques Gavard, Nathaniel Goldberg, Janos Grapow, Georgina Grenville, Philippe Gueguen, Laziz Hamani, Marc Hispard, Peter Knapp, Beyoncé Knowles, Corina and Dan Lecca, Peter Lindbergh, Lindsay, John Midgley, Deanna Miller, Kate Moss, Snejana Onopka, Carlo Orsi, Alyona Osmanova, Victoria Pearson, Jean-Marie Périer, Gladys Perint Palmer, PG, Sasha Pivovarova, André Rau, Terry Richardson, Vlada Roslyakova, Paolo Roversi, Franco Rubartelli, Claudia Schiffer, Kishin Shinoyama, Simone, Beri Smither, Hana Soukupova, Solve Sundsbo, Keiichi Tahara, Stella Tennant, Ruben Toledo, Gilles Trillard, Christy Turlington, Ellen von Unwerth, Gemma Ward, and Raquel Zimmermann.

A thank you also to all those who participated in the pictorial realization of this work: Julie Allanet (Sergio Rossi), Anne-Laure (Starface Photos), Alexis Arnault (KCD Paris), Tiffany Atakorah (Ozwald Boateng), Odile Babin (Chanel), Sonia Benmaouia, Silvana Beretta, Virginie Bergeron (Gaspard Yurkievich), Fabrice Bessière (Reuters), Guus Beumer (Orson+Bodil), Laura Bialobos, Wilfried Bodelot and Sylviane Rudier (Kenzo), Nigel Boekee (Michele Filomeno), Marion Boucard (Vivienne Westwood), Héloïse Brion and Armelle Saint-Mleux (Roger Vivier), Anna Bologna (Giorgio Armani), Eva Bodinet (Magnum Photos), Elisabeth Bonnel (Christian Lacroix), Elise Brown (Spring Court), Paul Caranicas, Françoise Carminati and Thierry Freiberg (Corbis), Py Cha, Lola Chardon (ACS Paris), Joëlle Chariau (Galerie Bartsch & Chariau), Cécile Chary (Montana), Gérald Chevalier (John Galliano), Margot Christmann (Courrèges), Clara Clanchet and Lucia Zamarron (Carolina Herrera), Julien Clisson (IMG Models), Cosi Communication, Joëlle Cotonnec (Studio Berçot), Olivia Couperie Eiffel (Dior Joaillerie), Bénédicte Courtinat (Mod'Spe), Marion Daumas-Duport (Pierre Hardy), Constance de La Rochefoucauld (Thierry Mugler), Chantal Delinot (Paco Rabanne), Alexandra Derouin (Jean-Charles de Castelbajac), Wallis Derujinksy, Caitlin DiStefano (Bill Blass), Pascale Duchemin (City Models), Cédric Edon, Isabel Mössinger, Thibault Rivrain et Virginie Trapenard (Karla Otto), Chantal Fagnou (Viva Models), Nina Farnell-Watson (Philip Treacy), Rocio Diaz Fernandez (Inditex), Didier Fernandez (DNA Models), Joe Fountain (Manolo Blahnik), Odile Fraigneau (Patrimoine Lanvin), Renaud François (Jitrois), Nicolas Frontière and Kate Etter (Nina Ricci), Véronique Garrigues (ADAGP), Valerie-Anne Giscard d'Estaing and Colombe de Meurin (Photos 12), Coralie Gauthier (Yohji Yamamoto), Larissa Giers and Stefanie Raman (Costume National), Caroline Gobert (Versace), Lucien Goddet (Céline), Gotscho, Julien Guerrier (Louis Vuitton), Charline Hamonic (Nike), Jean-Pascal Hesse (Pierre Cardin), Daphne Honeybone (The Casati Archives), Marianne Houtenbos, Odile Idkowiak (Paul Smith), Laurence Isabey (Getty Images), Bruno Jamagne (Women Paris), Joline Jolink, Héloïse Jost (Hermès), Elena Kalogeropoulos (Ferragamo), Karin S. Kato (*Harper's Bazaar*), Laurence Kersuzan (RMN), Pauline Klein (Sonia Rykiel), Sabine Killinger (Elite Model Management), Isabelle Konikoff (Emanuel Ungaro), Colette Lacoste (Louboutin), Francesca Laruccia (Missoni), Caroline Lebar and Caroline Fragner (Lagerfeld Gallery), Klervi Le Collen, Melinda Lee (Neiman Marcus), Jenny Logjes (Dutch Fashion Foundation), Mr. Gérard Lognon and his whole team, Didier Ludot, Edith Mandron and Valérie Toranian (*Elle*), Mister Mansart (Givenchy Archives), Sylvie Marot (Marithé+François Girbaud), Anne-Sophie Marquetty (Comme des Garçons), Katherine Marshall and Joanna Ling (Sotheby's), Laurence Marolleau (Schiaparelli), Julien Mayer and Ophélie Lebas (Prada), Tracy Matthews, Katelyn McCormick (The New School), Yuka Minamitani, Michelle Montagne, Marco Muggiano (Istituto Marangoni), Stewart Mungeam (Gallery Stock), Jelka Music (Jean-Paul Gaultier), Jacques Naudin (Musée Air France), Maria Nishio and Willie Walters (Central Saint Martins College of Art & Design), Sylvie Nissen (René Gruau), Michelle No (Oscar de la Renta), Frédérique Nunez (Chantal Thomass), Francine Pairon (IFM), Delphine Patriat (Ralph Lauren), Françoise Pereira (Burberry), Soizic Pfaff and Philippe Le Moult (Christian Dior Archives), Isabelle Picard (Le Bon Marché), Bruno Pouchin (Roger-Viollet), Didier Poupard, Laudomia Pucci, Michelle Reiner, Sonia Ricour-Lambard and Aliénor van Litsenborgh (Katy Barker Agency), Nathalie Roger (NEXT Models), Lauran Rothstein (Jeff Koons), Raphaëlle Rouyere (Galeries Lafayette), Guillaume Salmon (Colette), Amna Sangare (Valentino), Lise Seguin (Picture Desk), Patty Sicular (Ford Models), Olivia Smart (Bruce Oldfield), Starface Photos, Emese Szenasy (Diane von Furstenberg), Hervé Szerman (H&K), Léa Sznajderman (Gérard Darel), Catherine Terk (Rue des Archives), Jeroen Teunissen, Samantha Thompson (Martin Margiela), Jan Vandewiele (Dries van Noten), Monique van Heist, Véronique and Nathalie (Marilyn Agency), Véronique Vasseur (Issey Miyake), Lucia Vietri, Pierre Violet and Robin (Pierre Bergé-Yves Saint Laurent Foundation), Pauline Wattiez (Michel Vivien), Meisha Welch (Art+Commerce), and Jenny Woods (PETA).